The
Cactus
Eaters

The Cactus Eaters

How I Lost My Mind—and Almost Found Myself—on the Pacific Crest Trail

Dan White

HARPER ● PERENNIAL

NEW YORK ● LONDON ● TORONTO ● SYDNEY ● NEW DELHI ● AUCKLAND

HARPER ● PERENNIAL

The names of certain individuals have been changed to protect their privacy.

P.S.™ is a trademark of HarperCollins Publishers.

HarperCollins books may be purchased for educational, business, or sales promotional use. For information please write: Special Markets Department, HarperCollins Publishers, 10 East 53rd Street, New York, NY 10022.

FIRST EDITION

Designed by Phil Mazzone

Library of Congress Cataloging-in-Publication Data

    White, Dan.
    The cactus eaters : how I lost my mind—and almost found myself—on the Pacific Crest Trail / Dan White.
       p.   cm.
    ISBN 978-0-06-137693-1
    1. Hiking—Pacific Crest Trail—Guidebooks. 2. Pacific Crest Trail—Guidebooks. I. Title.
    GV199.42.P3W45 2008
    917.9—dc22   2007048221

08 09 10 11 12   OV/RRD   10 9 8 7 6 5 4 3 2 1

For Amy

Come to the woods, for here is rest. There is no repose like that of the green deep woods. Here grow the wallflower and the violet. The squirrel will come and sit upon your knee, the logcock will wake you in the morning. Sleep in forgetfulness of all ill.

—John Muir, *The Wilderness World of John Muir*

Many lives are so empty of interest that their subject must first perform some feat like sailing alone around the world or climbing a hazardous peak in order to elevate himself above mere existence, and then, having created a life, to write about it.

—William Gass, *The Art of Self: Autobiography in the Age of Narcissism*

Part I

Chapter 1

Hot Teeth

It's 9:00 A.M. in the southern edge of the Sierra Nevada, eighty-five degrees and rising. The water in our bottles is almost gone, but I don't panic. I suck my tongue. I lick my hot teeth.

Allison, my girlfriend, stirs in her sleeping bag. She wakes up slowly, stretching her arms to the tent's nylon roof. From the way she smiles at me, you'd never know we're in crisis mode again. Yesterday, our unbreakable leakproof water bag broke and leaked all over my $385 Gregory Robson backpack. We've been rationing for fourteen hours now. I take a deep breath, try to stay calm, and smile back at her as best I can. Our love is still strong, in spite of the fact that Allison's hair is shagging into her eyes this morning, making her look like a yak, and in spite of the fact that we haven't had sex in God knows how long. I emerge from our tent on my hands and knees and shake my boots for scorpions. There are none this morning. My socks are brown and hard and smell like ham. I put them on anyway. Allison puts on hers. "Cowboy up," she says. She has splotches of dirt all over her body. I'm not looking so great, either. After

178.3 miles and 2 1/2 weeks of this journey to the north, my shirt rots on my back. Pig bristles sprout from my chin.

We dust ourselves off and load our stuff into our backpacks. I walk out into the dry heat with Allison, my back pain, and the little bit of water we've saved. Five miles to go until we reach Yellow Jacket Spring. I am worried that the spring will not exist, or will have uranium or a dead cow in it. This morning I feel the strain of all we've seen and experienced: the heat blisters, the rashes, the dust devils, the coyotes who keep us up at night with their relentless whining. Still, things could be worse. At least we're making progress. This, after all, is our dream, to be here in a real wilderness. I remind myself that we're here by choice. We walk on. Beads of sweat draw paisley patterns through the dirt on my legs.

I watch Allison move through the landscape with confidence. Though she's dirty and tired, and in spite of what's happening to her hair, she is still lovely. She pouts in concentration as she studies the map and compass. Now she's passing me on the trail, edging around me, taking the recon position without consulting me. Is this an unspoken act of rebellion, I wonder? I walk behind her, and though I wish she'd spoken to me about this leadership change—I'm the designated leader for today—at least I've got a nice view of her calves and her trail-hardened bottom as she leans forward to climb the hill, her hands on her shoulder straps. Her solar-reflective Outdoor Research survival hat shades her face. I try to forget my thirst, but I just can't. Every time I swallow, it feels like there's a Nerf ball in my throat.

The word *Sierra* conjures images of mountains, glaciers, rivers, and charming marmots. Scratch those pictures from your mind. Replace them with dust and dirt and sweat, canyon oak, piñon pine, and in the middle distance, blunt-topped crags the shape and color of an old dog's teeth. Every once in a while there's a hint of darker colors: the slate-gray berries on a juniper bush, the black on the back of a turkey vulture below us in a canyon, but for the most part the scenery is pale beige, the color of stucco, the color of gefilte fish. The Pacific Crest Trail is renowned for its beauty, but this patch of trail is plug-ugly, and we haven't seen a human in five days. We walk downhill along an abandoned jeep road to search for the spring. Every once in a while the top of a piñon pine peeks from behind a stack of boulders. A mirage appears in a bend on the road. Pools of quicksilver fade as we approach. After fifteen minutes, the dirt road levels, then turns uphill on a punishing grade. I'm starting to wonder why we haven't found the water. It seems we've gone far enough. I'm starting to worry that the spring has dried up.

To distract myself, I remember how we boasted about the trail to everyone who would listen. Even Patrick, my sword-fish-nosed barber, knows all about it. Allison and I ditched our jobs in Torrington, Connecticut, to walk the Pacific Crest Trail, a 3-to-10-feet-wide, 2,650-mile-long strip of dirt, mud, snow, ice, and gravel running from Mexico to Canada. The trail starts at the Mexico-California border town of Campo, buzzing with border patrol guards in helicopters. It climbs the Laguna, San Jacinto, and San Bernardino ranges, drops to the Joshua trees and hot sands of the western Mojave Desert, and rises close to the base of Mount Whitney, the highest peak in the lower forty-eight states. The trail nears the thermal stench pots, fumaroles, boiling lakes, and gassy geysers of Lassen. Then it pushes through the Columbia River Gorge and into the North Cascades before coming to a stop in Manning Park, British Columbia. The trail spans California, Oregon, and Washington. On the PCT, you pass through state and federal lands, sovereign Native American territory and timber holdings. You see a thousand lakes, and travel through seven national parks. In the northern lands, mountain goats scale hundred-foot walls in seconds flat. Reach out your hand and you can grab a fistful of huckleberries right off the bush. In northern streams, river otters splash in the shallows.

The PCT is America's loveliest long-distance hiking path, but the trail exacts a toll for a glimpse of its pretty places. In some areas, you must find your way amid the firebreaks and game trails that slither off in all directions like the fever dreams of a serial killer. Ticks, in chaparral lowlands, will crawl onto hikers and bite them in the armpits and groin. Walkers whip off their clothes to find forty or fifty of them at once, looking like M&Ms with legs. More than 50 percent of the people who walk the trail give up in despair, often within the first week. The route has existed in various forms for more than forty years, and in that time, roughly a thousand people have hiked it all. That's fewer than the number of people who have stood atop Mount Everest.

The trail ranges from just above sea level to 13,180 feet. It twists through lands where surface temperatures creep past a hundred degrees, and up into terrain that is snowbound for most of the year. Pacific Crest Trail hikers must time their walks perfectly. If they start too early, they find themselves marooned like Ernest Shackleton, hacking at snow walls with their ice axes. If they start too late, the Mojave toasts them in their boots. Even if they make it through the desert, snowstorms will slam them in the Cascades, sometimes in early September. Unfortunately for Allison and me, we couldn't get out of Connecticut until June. Now it's almost July and the landscape is set on broil. It's empty here. Most hikers passed through these lands six weeks ago. Allison walks beside me now, her footsteps faster and more insistent. "Why," she says, "is it so fucking hard to get a drink around here?"

The guidebook claims there's a spring at the top of the next hill, just off the jeep road. But when we get to the top, there's no water at all, only invasive thistles with barbs sprouting from them. Everything here is thorny. All creatures crouch and squint. A collared lizard rests on the trunk of a dead pine tree and stares at a point in the distance. As I glance at the lizard,

I wonder why he looks so comfortable out here. In fact, the lizard is doing push-ups against a rock, practicing calisthenics in the burning sun. I wonder why he seems relaxed, and how someone as smart as I am could run out of water.

Water is so basic. It's elemental. And it's never been in dispute that I'm smart. I have a degree in English with honors from Wesleyan. The *U.S. News and World Report* ranked Wesleyan higher than Middlebury in its most recent listings, and while we got edged out this year by Swarthmore, we beat the shit out of Bucknell again. My genetic inheritance should also count for something. And unlike the lizard, whose life is a series of simple impulses, I'm complex. There has been life on this planet for 3.8 billion years. Homo sapiens, my people, have been around for only the last 200 odd millennia. A lot of trial and error has gone into our development. Our ancestors started out with gills and mud flaps, but we got over it. I am the result of a painstaking process. The lizard and his kind have been trapped in an evolutionary funk hole for millions of years. My brain, if I had to guess, weighs 1,400 grams, which shakes out to something like 3 1/2 pounds, give or take a gram. The lizard's brain weighs a fraction of a gram. The lizard cannot reason. He has no appreciation for symbols and abstractions, nor can he solve the most basic problems. He can't even regulate his body temperature. So why am I so fucking thirsty? And why is the lizard smiling?

This is nothing, I tell myself, nothing at all, as Allison watches me, squinting. "You'll figure this out, you'll find the water," I tell myself. "You're the smartest guy in the room." In fact, I'm the only guy in the room, but there's no room, and I'm starting to wonder why we didn't just go to Bora Bora. I hear it's overdeveloped but nice. You can get a package deal there. The Beachcomber is, supposedly, pretty sweet. At this moment, we could be out on the warm Pacific Ocean, eating wahoo burgers, drinking cold Hinano lagers, having sex on decorative mats in a glass-bottom over-water bungalow with views of sea cucumbers and eels. Instead, we are here by choice, staggering. Pines rise from the gulches, and while I know it's unwise to anthropomorphize lizards, not to mention trees, you'd have a hard time convincing me that those pine trees don't look like rows of upraised middle fingers. The gulches look as if they must be holding water, but when we walk out into the trees and take a closer look, there's nothing but more dirt. I'm starting to lose it now. We've been thirsty for hours, and while I can't gauge the extent of my dehydration, I can feel the temperature climb past ninety degrees. If the spring has dried up, I suppose we could turn around, get back to the trail, and head north to another spring. But the nearest spring is seven miles to the north, and what if it's not there, either?

I'm scanning the scenery wildly, feeling every heartbeat thump in my temples. I recall a factoid from my high school biology class. Mrs. Caterberg said that donkeys and camels can lose a third of their water weight and suffer no ill effects. But if a human being loses a tenth of his body's water weight, he starts acting crazy. If he loses 25 percent, his blood turns to pudding. His muscles seize up. Then he starts hallucinating. Eventually his tongue turns black. So how much water weight have I lost already? How about Allison? Ten percent? Eleven percent?

At last, a stab of light appears through the trees. We waddle through the underbrush and arrive at a patch of brown-red dirt and dry grass with a sad little sinkhole in the middle of it. In the middle of the sinkhole is a puddle three by two feet, a few inches deep. It's our only option. There are leeches in the water. I poke my index finger into the muck. The water is lukewarm and indescribably filthy, but I don't hyperventilate. Allison takes off her pack and removes our water filtration survival bucket—the sawed-off bottom of a gallon-sized Safeway fruit punch container. I scoop up some water and let the dirt particles and slime settle to the bottom. Then I take out our expensive ceramic water filter, which we ordered during a supply stop in Tehachapi on a warranty replacement several weeks ago, after our first water filter exploded at another water hole. I place the floating intake valve into the water and pray.

"There's a good boy," I say, below my breath, to my filter.

Allison is standing over me, watching. I hold the filter in my hands. Cradling it. Cooing. It's crazy to talk to your gear, I know. Gear is inanimate. But if you *must* talk to your gear, for best results, use a respectful tone. Don't shout at your gear or speak in a condescending manner. Don't try to force your will on your gear or your gear will thwart you. Use a normal voice, with the slightest hint of authority.

"All we need is a few good squirts," I say to the filter. "That's all you need to do."

And the filter works beautifully at first. It is nothing short of alchemy, the way it sucks in cloudy water and turns it clear. We filter enough water to drink on the spot. In fact, we drain several quarts in one sitting, but we want more, even though the water is lukewarm and has a strange gravlax stink to it.

"More, more, more," I say to the filter, "Keep going. You're doing great. Two more quarts. Please."

The gadget lets loose with a digestive burble, followed by a crackling sound, which gives way to a sputter, a wheeze, and an emphysemic rasp, as pressure builds in the intake valve. The filter seizes up. The lever won't crank. The outtake pipe won't release any water. The man at the filter company swore this filter would not let us down. He swore that it was a free upgrade, the schmuck. "Work, goddamn it, work," I snarl as I crank the lever as hard as I can. Out bursts a geyser of pressurized filth water. The filter unscrews itself, coming apart. A feeling of horror comes over me—the feeling that all our past water crises are repeating themselves, as if we are stuck in a wormhole in time. I look around at the scattered bits of filter and Allison and the fat sun. For now, at least, we've drunk enough to drown our thirst—for the moment; the thirst will soon return. And now that our thirst has been quenched, we're suddenly hungry. Allison decides to make lunch with the remaining water. But when she rifles through the food pack, there is nothing left but Velveeta and pasta shells. She accepts this without comment.

Calm and silent, she bends over, takes out the camp stove, lights it, puts a bit of water in the pot, covers the pot with foil, lets the water boil, then dumps in the pasta and Velveeta. The water turns the color of Hi-Liter fluid. Our slender patch of shade pulls itself out from under us, exposing our faces to the spotlight sun. Allison and I are looking at each other quizzically, sizing each other up, and I know what she's thinking and she knows what I'm thinking and I know that she's thinking that I'm thinking that she's thinking the same thing. It does not need to be spoken. It hangs in the air in the form of silence:

"What are we doing here?"

Allison keeps stirring. Pasta rises to the surface, like answers rising from the murk inside a Magic 8-Ball. How I wish I had a Magic 8-Ball now to help us decide. Quit or keep going.

"We could have gone to Thailand," Allison says. "Wouldn't that have been so cool?"

"Or we could have done that pilgrimage to Santiago," I say, even though I'm Jewish and such a walk would have been blasphemous.

"Or backpacked through Europe."

"Or just stayed in the fucking car. Driven around America."

There is a pause, and Allison shakes her head, as if a strange realization had just occurred to her. A dark look comes over her as she stares into the Velveeta.

"This is our dream," she says. "But I think it's too hard. I think it might be the wrong dream. But we told everybody about this. Everyone knows. I mean, we must have told a hundred people, and now there's all this expectation. And a lot of those people already think we're gonna fail."

She has a valid point. A couple of people were actually making bets about when we'd quit.

"You know what?" Allison says. "It's almost as if we're *shamed* into not quitting."

We bat the issue around in the sun for a while. I will my brain to come up with a definitive answer, but nothing bubbles to the surface except the pasta, which is now boiling. The disabled filter lies on its side. A black fly stands in repose, his eyes blank and pitiless. No, on second thought, perhaps the fly is a she, for a second fly lands on the first fly and begins to make vigorous love to him or her from behind. It occurs to me that this is silly, that I don't care if we are "shamed into it" or not. We just can't go on. Quitting is the only responsible option. If we keep going, we're going to die. We have no survival training whatsoever. This trail is going to kill us. We *must* give up. "I can't believe I'm gonna say this," I say. "But I really, truly, deeply want to go home. I don't care what we'll do for work. I don't even care where we live."

But Allison is right as usual. How can we quit at a time like this, with nothing to go back to? Besides, every time I tell myself that we should quit, the words *failure* and *wimp* and *lame-o* and *pusillanimous* flash through my mind, and these words are so much worse than the sun, worse than the Velveeta, worse than the horseflies and our petting zoo smell. There is no "home" now. Even our old apartment is gone. Our lives are gone. The future is a blank, an empty page except for the trail. The trail is our only future. All else has been wiped away. When I look around at the scenery to collect my thoughts, I notice another lizard. He's standing there regarding me at eye level from his perch on a boulder, across from the camp stove. Watching me with beady-eyed intent.

Patient as a mountain. Waiting to see what we'll do next.

Smirking.

Chapter 2

Devil's Island

The year I found out about the Pacific Crest Trail, I was twenty-five. I had been working for three years at a fourteen-thousand-circulation daily newspaper in Torrington, on the northwestern edge of Connecticut. My workplace was a bleak turn-of-the-century printing factory with an ominous brick tower over the parking lot. A set of narrow stairs rose steeply to the second floor, where trussed-up newspapers moldered in the corner. Upstairs, a cracked window offered views of abandoned railroad tracks and derelict buses without wheels. The newsroom smelled of sweat and onions, especially in summer. Shoes squeaked on pigeon-colored floors. Editors stared like lemurs at their terminals, moving only when the lunch truck arrived laden with soups and stale rolls. They chewed their food while reading somniferous accounts of dump-board meetings and church-group bake sales. Holes appeared in the ceiling. One January night, snow fell on the desk and computer of our court reporter, who had been there for decades. Every time I whispered to him about leaving the paper someday, he'd lean forward, smile, and say, "This newspaper is Devil's Island. No one escapes." In the printing room, someone had left a pair of leather shoes that stayed under a table for three years, gathering dust.

The paper had a hate/hate relationship with its readers. People in town never said they "subscribed" to the paper. Instead they said they "took" the newspaper, as if it were a pill or a suppository. We were overworked, there were rumors of the paper getting sold, and strange errors showed up in the newspaper all the time. One of the fruits of our efforts was an above-the-fold headline asking people to remember the bombing of PEAR HARBOR. The headline was especially unfortunate, considering the town was jam-packed with World War II veterans. We ran a story about a fire that gutted a house on the edge of town. According to our report, no humans perished, "but two family poets died in the blaze." We referred to a sign-language training program as a course on "palm reading." We printed two consecutive Wednesday issues in the same week, providing further ammunition for the local crazies who already thought the Earth stood still. In a story about a retiring city clerk named Evelyn Ronalter, I spelled her name several ways, including "Eveline Rinaltier." In the text, I mentioned her "horn-rim glasses" and the "gray bun of hair rising off her head," though neither attribute appeared in the photo that ran alongside the piece, the photo I took myself. We tried our best to reverse the losing streak, but some gremlin always crawled into the machinery. Hoping to turn our luck around, the owners launched a "total quality program" to minimize errors and boost pride. The publisher kicked things off with a banquet at Dick's Restaurant in downtown Torrington. To surprise his staff, he handed out souvenir pencils that were supposed to have our brand-new motto printed across them: STRIVING FOR TOTAL QUALITY . . . The pencils all came out saying, SHRIVING FOR TOTAL QUALITY . . .

In northwest Connecticut, if you hated your job and doubted your purpose in life, one surefire pick-me-up was to drive up Route 8 on a summer night and head to the R&B Sportsworld miniature golf course in Winsted. There, the pygmy windmill made you feel like a giant for a while. That's what I did one evening when the mosquitoes were buzzing and my Polo shirt was stuck to my back. The newspaper's young reporters were hanging out on the course. I first saw her near the third hole. She was leaning on a post between a fake drawbridge and a faux fisherman's shack. She stood to the right of a sign reading, LOST BALLS WILL BE REPLACED. . . . Her hair was blond, light at the roots and darkening as it reached her shoulders. She was giggly and flirty, talking to a male reporter, closing her eyes and showing her white teeth as she laughed at his joke. She had a high forehead, fair skin, and an out-of-context Italian-looking nose. The nose was by no means large but there was something assertive about it. It added an ethnic edge. I fixed my eyes on the young woman's neck and the espresso-colored beauty mark at its base. I noticed her bosom, which I later described in my diary as "quite stately." When it was her turn at hole three, she stepped away from the fence and steadied herself in front of the ball. She thwacked the ball hard but with great control, getting a hole in one. As the others swatted and stumbled around the course, she pulled her fingers through her hair, laughing with the boys or at them. I couldn't tell which.

For the last few weeks, I'd heard all about Allison, the saucy new *Register Citizen* reporter who'd graduated from journalism school in New York City and had published an environmental handbook scolding polluters for dumping toxic waste in the Great Lakes. She'd applied for the *Register Citizen* reporting job because she wanted to stay on the same coast as her lanky film-school boyfriend in Manhattan. I heard that she'd aced her interview with the paper. In fact, she so impressed the editors that they passed her clips around the newsroom, including her

"Cookie Story," a feature about a sweet old lady fond of baking cookies in her high-rise apartment. If memory serves, the first paragraph paints a loving portrait of a granny cooking up a storm, the scent of brown sugar wafting through the hall. The second graph is about the same woman being flung out the window by crackheads. I remember reading that and thinking, "Holy shit! I've got to meet the woman who wrote this thing." Besides, she was now available; her film-school beau had just dumped her.

At the golf course that night, she wore a short dress revealing a small waist, strong hips, and long legs. She was shapely and sexy, but there was something different about her. For one thing she was loose-limbed and goofy. She had a pretty face but she could mold it into crazy expressions. When she walked, she did not flounce. Instead she galumphed across the turf like Jackie Gleason in *The Honeymooners*. Her walk was mannish, loping, and purposeful, shoulders tilted, chin up, arms dangling in front of her. It was as if she couldn't decide whether to flirt with the boys or become one of them. While waiting my turn at the mill hole, I walked over and said hello. She giggled at my nervousness and shook my hand a touch too hard. I'm not sure why I felt sheepish. Maybe it was the story I'd heard about the older sports staffer who hit on all new female hires. Apparently he'd chatted her up in the newsroom while wearing a loud sweater. While he was putting on the charms, she burst out laughing and told him, "You aren't man enough to be wearing that sweater." It was just a tossed-off remark, but he slunk away like a neutered dog. Or perhaps it had something to do with the fact that all women, and in particular, attractive women, make me twitch and blink as if I'm channeling "Rain Man." A product of the low self-esteem movement, I didn't have my first kiss until I was almost twenty-two. Allison's sensuality was too much for my sensibilities.

I was frightened to ask her out. But thoughts of her hair, her giggle, her nose, consumed me. We did not work in the same building. Her office was a rented room forty-five minutes from Torrington that served as the newspaper's rural bureau. There, Allison wrote stories about WASP-y towns with manicured village greens and Congregational churches. I figured out her route to work and went jogging along the rural highway, just so she might see me. She never drove by. I kept seeing her at newspaper parties, in bars, and at the Berkshire Café, the pizza joint where reporters hung out. We had little in common. She was neat and particular. I stored lasagnas in my desk at work. She was Protestant. I was Jewish. She loved dancing to funky music. Dancing makes me ill. There was no logical reason that things would click between us.

Besides, she was emotionally unavailable. She told me she had been "crying like a volcano" over her ex-boyfriend. But we became friends, which slightly diminished my fear of her, while adding a new dimension of torture: since she thought we were "pals," she felt comfortable making offhand comments about cute guys, and making me feel like a eunuch. Chance encounters kept happening. One night we both found ourselves at a party at the rented house of a nerdy reporter from a rival newspaper. I'd heard, for a while, that this man had his eye on her. He approached her but seemed to bore her. That night she came wiggling up to me with a Banks Beer in her hand, her bubble ass bouncing to the music. I wore a stupid T-shirt with a smiling Tyrannosaurus rex across the chest. Someone stuck a James Brown cassette in the ghetto blaster. It was "Get on the Good Foot." Allison stood and forced me to dance by the pool while holding a pineapple stalk against my butt and telling me to pretend it was a rooster feather. "Shake it," she commanded. It was a horrible yet strangely liberating experience.

Later we sat by the pool and talked of ghosts, demons, and Bigfoot, the sunset dyeing the water pink. She smiled, and when she listened, she leaned in tight, a sweetly intent expression on her face as I forced myself to hold her gaze a moment too long. The conversation turned. We got to talking, for some reason, about sex and romance. With a coy expression, she told me about a wild fling she'd had in her younger days while traveling overseas. She'd confided the steamy details to her journal. One day, her twit of a boyfriend found out about it by pawing through the diary when she wasn't home. He was so shocked by what he'd read that he chopped off his hair. "I saw him in the library the next day," she said. "It was so weird. I didn't recognize him. He was practically bald." I knew this was my cue to reveal a sordid past, but none existed. What could I say? The skeletons in my closet had all died of boredom. And it filled me with longing to have such erotic adventures with this woman, doing the kind of things that might drive one of her future boyfriends to shave off all of *his* hair.

And yet I was scared to make a pass. Later that night my best friend, Dave, chided me. "Why don't you plant a lip lock on her?" he said. But I couldn't. Unable to seduce her in any direct way, I had no choice but pull her in, bit by bit. Like a farmer trying to woo a guileless bunny, I threw crumbs of bread in front of her and hoped she would follow me down into the dungeon-dark rabbit hutch of love. I gave Allison two "Heartbreak Healing" tape mixes, designed to foster tenderness in impressionable women on the rebound. My mixes included weepy songs by George Jones, Dolly Parton, Buck Owens, and Randy Travis. I drove for an hour to a Strawberries music store in Canton, just to buy K. D. Lang's *Shadowlands* so I could put "I'm Down to My Last Cigarette" on the mix. But Allison was anything but guileless, and my strategy did not pay off. Finally, I couldn't stand it anymore and I just blurted it out. She said that while my feelings were "not entirely one-sided," she couldn't picture herself in a romantic relationship with me. Though I was crushed for weeks, I got over it. Knowing I had no chance, I gave up trying to woo her. Then one night I got a startling phone call. Allison had gone home to the Midwest for a three-day weekend, and had had a dream in which she kissed me. "I've been thinking," she said. "We're pretty much a couple already. We see each other every day and hang out every weekend. If we're doing all this other stuff, we might as well have the fun part, too." I was surprised, confused, put off, thrilled, insulted, flattered, and annoyed. Why the change of heart now? But that didn't stop me from racing to her apartment in my Honda and running a stop sign on the way. We sat on her couch. Our making out started out squirrelly and tentative—a few lame attempts to put our arms around each other. Soon the halfhearted hugs turned into groping. We kept rearranging ourselves, attempting to kiss, which was hard to do, considering that my nose and her nose were plus-sized; our noses jousted, making it hard for our lips to connect unless we tilted our heads at a violent angle. She apologized as I began to undress her.

She worried that her undergarments were "kind of dowdy; I would have worn much nicer lingerie if I'd known."

I was surprised, too, although the jarring quality of making out with a platonic friend added to the excitement. As we fooled around for hours in her room, I regretted the times I'd held myself back and not acted on impulses because I was afraid. I wondered what other experiences I had missed or ruined because of fear and wimpiness. It occurred to me in the dark that I might get what I wanted just by going for the gusto and taking some risks. I vowed not to waste any more of my life second-guessing my decisions. I promised myself an adventure of epic proportions. It would have to be something so unlikely and grand that no one would think me capable of pulling it off.

And whatever it was, Allison was coming with me.

Chapter 3

"Something Golden"

After that first night, we often went away together, inner-tubing down the listless Farmington River, drinking bottomless glasses of Chianti, spending weekends in bed. On Saturday afternoons, we'd drive out to the old Cornwall Bridge to buy sandwiches and fresh tomatoes. We'd throw them in a backpack and walk into a steep-walled forest overlooking fields full of blue moths and neurotic cows, who would see us coming and start lowing their heads off. On every excursion, Allison identified wild plants to impress me, including a fuzzy green one called a lamb's quarter. "Look," she said. "That's miner's lettuce." I was thrilled she was a gardener, and an expert on weeds and shrubs. I'd killed every plant I'd ever owned, including, of all things, a Wandering Jew. Her garden vegetables thrived. They responded to her innate practicality. "Who knows?" I thought to myself. "Maybe her knowledge of flora will one day save my life."

One morning, we hiked out to Lion's Head, a crown-shaped rock, where Allison leaned over and said, "What if we kept walking and never went home? What if we drove to work one day but kept on driving and didn't stop, with our middle fingers in the air?"

It might have been a tossed-off comment, but my new relationship with Allison, and our weekend adventures, underscored the tedium of my work life. One day I was working the Saturday shift at the newspaper. No one else was around, so I was vegetating, playing with a magnetic paper clip holder, drinking Sanka, examining the lake of grease on my plate of chicken and broccoli chow mein. The police scanner bleeped. Through the hiss and foam of static, a dispatcher barked out cop call codes: Number sixty-eight meant intoxicated person; seventeen, attempted suicide; ninety-eight, missing person; eighty-eight, untimely death; thirty-six, hostage situation. It was giving me a headache, all the goddamned numbers, so I shut off the scanner and called my friend James on the WATS line. James was an environmental writer and editor down in North Carolina. He has a vast knowledge of national parks, paths, and recreational opportunities. I told him I wanted to go on an American safari. I'd thought about through-hiking the Appalachian Trail but had heard rumors about a local man whose nephew tried to walk it but quit after straying from the trail in Georgia and getting a warm two-dollar pistol stuck up his nose. James asked me if I'd ever heard of the Pacific Crest Trail, a wondrous path across the American West. James told me it was the western equivalent of the Appalachian Trail, an epic walk so enormous it spanned 16.5 degrees of latitude. In one stretch, backpackers must venture two hundred miles into a forest without crossing a single road, a power line, or even a fence.

I could hardly believe such a thing existed. I'd grown up in California, and no one there had even mentioned it. When James told me about the mystery trail, something clicked. Think of it! A chance to pass through time, to see America as it looked in the days of fur trappers and Miwok Indians. I'd never felt connected to the Golden State. My parents lived outside L.A. in an A-frame house. I knew what it was like to see office towers rise like ships' masts through the photochemical haze on smog days, when the teacher wouldn't let you play in the fields, on mornings when breathing burned the lungs. But this would be the authentic West, the one I'd seen in the backgrounds of William Boyd's *Hopalong Cassidy* movies on late-night TV, a land of revelations. The trail, it seemed, would be beautiful enough to fulfill my longing for escape and tough enough to meet the conditions of a test, an outdoor finishing school for the soul. Soon I could think of little else except the trail and Allison.

I asked Allison if she would hike it with me. Her answer was an immediate yes. Leaving her job didn't concern her in the least. She disliked it anyhow and was sure she would find better things. I was more nervous about leaving the newspaper. It was the first gig I'd had that didn't involve saying "paper or plastic" all day. Allison wanted to be an environmental journalist. She was hoping to take on the polluters and slimy politicians, and make a name for herself. But first she wanted to go out and see a few wild places before they were ruined forever. "When will we ever have this chance again?" she said. She vowed to bring her notebooks, press wildflowers, make field notes, and climb some mountains on the way.

By then we were sold on the idea, but we still wanted more information. Through a friend of a friend at the newspaper, we got hooked up with two veteran PCT hikers living in north-west Connecticut. Eddie was a twenty-two-year-old auto mechanic fresh off the trail. Kirk, a teacher in his forties with a dark tan and a rangy body, had hiked the trail several years before and was full of missionary zeal for the outdoors.

Eddie invited me, Allison, and Kirk to his house one night for a PCT slideshow. He was lanky with a toddler's face, thick glasses, and stringy hair that touched his shoulders. I remember looking at him and Kirk and thinking, "Those bodies have walked across a continent." I envied their repose and power. Eddie killed the lights. The living room wall disappeared, and in its place a forest grew. The room turned into an Alpine realm of Belding's ground squirrels and black bears. Glaciers glowed above a U-shaped valley. Huckleberries plumped in the sun. How I wished I could walk through the wall into the chill of a lake with minarets reflected on its surface.

The slide-show's glare played in Allison's eyes. As more slides shone against the wall, Eddie told us the trail remade him and that it would remake us. "You'll become different people. You'll hitchhike all the time. You'll do things you never imagined. Your feet will get so hard you could hold a lighter to 'em and feel nothing."

Eddie walked across the room to fiddle with the errant projector. As he walked, he belched loudly and unapologetically. Listening to his gaseous eructation, I wondered if the trail made people regress, like in that movie *Altered States,* where William Hurt locks himself in a floatation chamber and comes out a baboon. The idea appealed to me. Eddie hit the lights again and told us the trail would wear out at least two pairs of the sturdiest hiking boots and that we would drink two gallons of water each per day in the hottest sections. "That's sixteen pounds of water every day," he said. In one section we'd hike forty miles without seeing a stream, so we'd have to carry all the missing water on our backs with us.

The two hikers told us the logistics. To complete the trail, we would have to divide it into twenty-five segments ranging in length from 84 to 150 miles. At the beginning and end of each segment, we would leave the forest and resupply ourselves at designated towns close to the trail. We'd have to mail twenty-five box loads of dried nonperishable food to ourselves, marked GENERAL DELIVERY to post offices near the trailheads. Mail clerks would hold the boxes for up to two weeks. "Make sure somebody reliable sends the boxes for you, so you don't starve," Eddie said. He told us it would cost us twenty dollars to send each box: a total of five hundred dollars just for shipping. Considering that the contents of each food box would cost us roughly forty dollars, our food bill alone for the whole trip would be more than a thousand dollars. Kirk and Eddie also gave us a comprehensive list of "trail angels" who lived in the supply towns. These good Samaritans let hikers sleep in their homes for free, offered rides, and even cached water into the desert for trekkers. Eddie told us how to use a cheap ski pole as a hiking stick and to shake bushes to ward off venomous snakes. He urged us to cram as many calories as we could each day in the High Sierra because the uphills were brutal. "Eat Stovetop Stuffing with margarine dumped in there," he said. "I knew some guy who ate nothing but freeze-dried Mountain House dinners every day. Ended up looking like a Somalian."

"How long will this take?" Allison said. Eddie told us that if we threw down sixteen-mile days we could make it to Canada in six months. If we could manage twenty-mile days, we might do it in five, even if we included some layover days in towns. All this advice led up to the big message, a speech that would rattle in my head like loose change long after the night was over:

"There will be highs and lows," Kirk said in a low voice. "In the North Cascades, it rained on me for eight days. It was enough to make a person quit, but I didn't. In a hike like this, the most important preparation has nothing to do with logistics or gear or any of that. It's all mental. You have to get out there expecting the worst: rain, injuries, boredom. We get these internal clocks in our heads—they're left over from our childhoods—telling us we should be back in school in September. You get antsy when the weather changes, when the days get shorter and you start asking yourself, What am I doing here? Just realize there are gonna be bad times out there. Expect them. Remember, there's something you both want to get out of all this. Those hardships—the rain, all the rest of it—will make you a better person in the end."

Kirk and Eddie must have used the word *hardship* a dozen times that night. I heard it, but it didn't sink in. All of their warnings sounded like abstractions when I was sitting in a living room, on a sofa, watching images of meadows and happy elk.

"Listen," Kirk said as Allison and I were getting up to leave, "if you ever get the urge to quit, I want you to think about this first: Never quit on a down moment. Never make your resolution to quit in a town. Never decide to quit during an eight-day stretch of hard rain. If you must quit, make the decision during four straight sunny days. Make the decision when you're feeling great. Don't decide to quit when you have blisters. Wait til they heal. Maybe you have a legitimate reason to quit, but it's easy to be biased, so easy to let a bad moment influence your decision to give up. Most people will regret quitting for a long time. You may decide it's not for you, but don't quit because you hate rain; don't quit because you hate blisters. I love the outdoors. I love adventure, but not everybody does. It's one thing to read about adventure. It's quite another to experience it, to have it happening all around you." Kirk cleared his throat and a strange look came across his face, something that looked like regret. "Everything's simple out there," he said. "You can get your life, your house, your right and wrong in order out there. And if your house is not in order and you don't know it, you'll sure as hell find that out. You can get straight on a trip like this. Hopefully there's something really truly golden that comes out of it."

Something golden. That's all I needed to hear, in spite of the fact that Eddie and Kirk never really explained what that something golden was. In the early stage of my infatuation with this epic western journey, it never occurred to me that I might be falling in love not with a trail but with a vision of it, with all dangers and hardships erased from the picture. Sometimes ignorance is more than bliss. Sometimes ignorance is the catalyst you need to change your life.

Chapter 4

Blue Crabs, Green Woman

The night before Allison and I took off for the Pacific Crest Trail, my workmates threw a farewell party for us, with beer, card games, and food. It was odd, though. Everyone seemed nervous, including a couple who told me they were concerned that Allison and I were going to die. I was bothered by the fact that our friends called this celebration the Dan-and-Allison Donner Party. I knew a bit about the snowbound cannibals trapped in the northern Sierra Nevada in 1846. I was aware of the fact that they roasted and ate each other less than five miles from where Allison and I would be walking in a few months' time. Most of the Donner Party's exploits, including the preparation of human jerky, and the use of brains to make a rich broth, took place near what is now I-80, the highway Allison and I would use to travel from the East Coast to California. I was wary of bad signs. If Allison and I wound up snowbound up in the mountains, and if I died but she lived, and if rescue workers found her huddled in a shanty near a lake with my butt cheeks roasting on an open fire, some enterprising newspaper reporter was going to find out about the Donner-themed going-away party and have a field day with the "devastating irony."

In spite of this misgiving, I felt for the most part terrific as we rolled out of town. As the church steeples and apartment buildings of Torrington receded in my rearview, I wanted to scream with happiness. We were getting out. The court reporter was wrong. You *can* escape from Devil's Island after all. And so we whipped across the country, getting three speeding tickets along the way. Some people might find it fatuous to drive 3,200 miles across America for the sake of crossing America on foot in an entirely different direction. But for me, speeding through the hills of Iowa and rolling through Wyoming gave Allison and me something in common with the pioneers, beat poets, and Easy Riders who had traveled before us. We were rebels now. The economy was flabby. The country was receding, compromising its values and ambitions, except for us. People were holding on to jobs they hated for fear of never finding anything else. Except for us. For once in my life, I was sticking it to The Man. Good-bye to jobs. Good-bye to corporations, bathing, and respectable living. Now I was going to grow a beard and live in the dirt with my woman for six months. Perhaps the Real World would be waiting when the trail was over. But who knows? Maybe we would never go home. Maybe we would stay in the woods forever.

It took us a week to reach my parents' home outside of Los Angeles, where we planned to rest for a while before driving two hours into the mountains to meet the Pacific Crest Trail. At my childhood house, a 3,200-square-foot A-frame about a mile from the Santa Monica Bay, Allison and I stayed a few days, going over our itinerary and taking trips to Trader Joe's in Redondo Beach to buy cashews and fruit gummies. Everything was going smoothly until the morning we were supposed to leave. All of a sudden, Allison doubled over, sick. Puzzled and concerned, I assumed it was something she'd eaten. Allison did not have a nervous stomach. I wondered out loud if it was the blue crabs we'd scarfed down twenty-four hours before at a grimy seafood shack on the Redondo Beach Pier, where you walk up to the tank, select a twitching crustacean, and wait on a bench while a slob in a bib steams the creature to death. Then you smash it with a mallet and dip it in vinegar sauce. This seafood is enjoyable if you try not to think about the fact that crabs live their lives in total darkness, in filth, dining on excrement. But if the crabs made Allison ill, why did I feel fine? Then I remembered that we hadn't shared our crabs that day. We'd bought separate ones. Maybe Allison had eaten a poisoned crab. I voiced this theory out loud.

"Maybe there was some sickness in your crab," I said. "Fish diseases can make you really sick."

"Ew, Dan, that's disgusting," Allison said. Later, she ducked into one of the downstairs bathrooms. "Please! Please don't mention fish diseases again." She vomited (she would vomit twice that day), washed her mouth, gargled with toothpaste, drank cold water, and lay down. I feared the worst, but Allison seemed to recover quickly. After a while, it seemed the nausea had passed. We decided to stick to the schedule, leave my parents' house and drive to the trail that day anyhow. We threw our packs in the car and sped toward Wrightwood, six thousand feet above sea level, in the San Gabriel Mountains, eighty miles northeast of my parents' house. When we reached the San Gabriels, the landscape was piney, the air dry and cool. The car whipped past cabins with satellite dishes on the roof. I glanced at Allison, sitting to my right looking stoic, her mouth clenched, her white legs showing beneath her polypropylene shorts. She had given me quite a scare at my parents' house, but now she looked hardier. She was stone-faced, but it did not concern me. Maybe she just needed coffee.

But there was no time for Starbucks. We were in a mad rush.

Because of the trail's enormous length, most hikers start the journey in late April, to stay ahead of storms that slam the Pacific Northwest in September or October, depending on the year. It had taken us forever to get out of Connecticut that summer. The reason was Allison's ambitions. In her spare time she'd compiled and edited a book in which eighteen doctors shared stories about their first years of practice. Allison was, justifiably, proud of the anthology, but finishing the project, while holding down her day job, took several months longer than she'd expected. I resented the delays, in part because I wanted to start the trail so badly and in part because I was jealous. She was moving ahead in her life, while my job experience, aside from my stint as a cub reporter, consisted of flipping burgers at a seaside amusement park, bagging groceries, scrubbing toilets, and operating a manual forklift. Now it was mid-June—almost two months after most PCT hikers began their journeys at the Mexico-California border.

For that reason, we had fiddled with our itinerary to give ourselves the best possible chance of finishing the trail. Instead of starting at Mexico, we would begin 360 miles north of the Mexican border. From there we would walk 2,300 miles to Canada, then take a bus back to our starting point in late fall. PCT hikers call this sort of schedule a "Flip-Flop." By mid-October, the foothills of Southern California would be mild and pleasant. We would make up the missing piece by heading south to Mexico. The plan was elegant, original, and even more important, fail-safe.

I glanced over at Allison to see how she was doing. She was slouching, closing her eyes. I supposed she was just pensive, thinking about the journey. I couldn't blame her. This was our big moment. We were about to break free from our old lives at last. I loved the fact that Allison and I were in charge of every aspect of our journey, doing it on our own terms. I was just about to prove wrong all the people who thought we'd never make it out here.

My mom and dad were among the doubters. They thought our dream of hiking the Pacific Crest Trail was inexplicable, and maybe even asinine. They wanted to know if our six-month nature walk was a substitute for genuine achievement, a stand-in for a law degree, grad school, or buying a house. They wanted to know if we'd even discussed who would be leader and follower or how to delegate decisions. My parents found it peculiar that Allison and I, who had never lived together in an apartment with showers and a fridge, were now setting out to do the same thing in a four-by-six tent in a place where vultures outnumbered people. This especially rattled my father, who said he didn't see the point of our putting ourselves in danger on purpose. He worried that we wouldn't be carrying cell phones, radios, or walkie-talkies. And though my father didn't say this out loud, I believe he had a problem with the idea of our spending thousands of dollars to create what he considered to be a false hardship. My father grew up poor on the Lower East Side of Manhattan. His father, Abram, was a tailor, his mother, Yetta, a dress maker. Abram got a tooth infection. There were no antibiotics, and he died. Yetta died nine years later in a mental hospital on Ward's Island. My father was a ward of the state until he was sixteen. He got pawned off on a foster family who didn't love him. And I'm sure he wanted to know who in his right mind would want to go out and try to make things hard for himself on purpose?

While I loved and respected my father, he did not understand what I was trying to do out there. His circumstances were too different. My dad had had a chance to triumph over adversity. He fought his way out of his ghetto hell, joined the army, and bought a house with help from the GI Bill. My father became the president of a successful high-tech security company in Southern California. He moved our family to a seaside suburb where monster homes crouched in the foothills and feral peacocks shrieked from the treetops. I admired his rise from poverty, but my dad did not realize that his success had turned me into a capitulating blob. I was untested and pale, born on the plateau that he had sweated to reach. As a result, I felt unmotivated. I had never been given the opportunity to have a loveless, miserable childhood like he had.

To transform myself from man–boy to man, I had to retreat into the wild, undergo a grand transformation in the outdoors, with Allison to keep me company, serve as my sidekick and helpmate, and attest to my grand achievements. If I walked all six million steps of the Pacific Crest Trail, I would be a hero. Though I'd always been competitive, in my twenty-six years I'd never done anything noteworthy. Though I wanted to wow and inspire people with my physical prowess, I was awful at sports. Still am. My baseball teammates once cornered me in the dugout, threatened to box my ears and rip my hair out in clumps because I blew the big game for them. They didn't make good on their threats, but elementary school never felt safe again. I was so tired of feeling weak. I wanted to start my life over by tracking bears through the Cascades and washing my face in a stream spilling off a thousand-year-old glacier. Some people say you must find beauty and meaning in ordinary life: parking meters, traffic lights, envelopes, or wedges of barbecued chicken stuck between someone's teeth. I never shared this appreciation for the mundane. I needed deserts and mountains to remake me.

Still, even rugged adventurers like us must make certain small concessions. I must confess that Allison and I were not entirely alone in the car. In fact, my father was driving while my mother sat in the front by his side, with a pile of road maps in her lap. Waiting around for a hitchhike or a bus ride would have wasted precious time. Besides, there is nothing shameful about accepting small favors from your parents.

"Danny, sweetheart?" said Mom, a petite woman in her sixties who wore dark sunglasses and Gordian knots of sterling silver in her earlobes. Mom wore snappy outfits, even when driving through wastelands. There was not a speck of dust on her tennis whites. "Danny?" she said. "Darling? Earth to Daniel? Would you like some grapes?"

"They're cold, young Daniel," my dad said. My parents' grape offer, though tender and heartfelt, jolted me out of my reverie. But this was nothing compared to the shock I got when I turned to Allison and noticed that her face was pale, with an ominous blue tint. There was no way she was sick again. The Los Angeles Basin smog had spilled into the foothills that morning. Maybe the light refraction from all that pollution had imparted the zombie color to her cheeks and neck. But the inversion layer had nothing to do with it. She looked terrible, and now she was moaning. I asked her if she was okay, but didn't ask if she wanted to go back home, nor did I insist that my parents turn the car around. I didn't want them to think of us as unprepared. Stopping the journey at that point would have proved right their suspicions that our trip was ridiculous.

My mom and dad couldn't hear Allison's whimpers. They had popped a CD into the deck and were now playing, at deafening volume, the soundtrack of *Carnival*, an old Broadway musical. "Love Makes the World Go Round" was blasting so loud, the rearview mirror trembled. Because of the blaring music, my parents had to holler at each other to be heard. My father was lost, driving in circles, getting more agitated. My mother was scrambling through the road maps.

The ride seemed endless. Buttock-shaped rock formations mooned us as we drove toward Wrightwood. Getting lost had thrown my parents behind schedule, and now they were going to be late for a matinee of a play they had been looking forward to seeing all year. As we hurtled down the highway, my father kept checking his watch every few seconds. Like me, my mother and father plotted out most aspects of their lives several months in advance, and worried constantly about being on time. This fixation blocked certain realities out of our minds, such as a woman in the backseat threatening to spray her guts all over the new upholstery.

"Oh no," Allison said. "I'm gonna throw up again! Make them stop the car now. Please, Dan, please make them stop the car."

They still couldn't hear her, but fortunately we had arrived at our destination. My dad pulled up to the Wrightwood ranger station, eased his six-foot-three frame from the car, and lumbered off to get directions. My mom and I followed. Allison told me she needed to be alone. She bolted from the Mercury, slipping on gravel, holding her stomach.

"What's going on with her?" my father said, looking back at her. "What's she doing in the bushes? What's she pulling back there?"

"She's not pulling anything, Dad. She just isn't feeling so well right now."

"What do you mean she's not feeling well? What's going on?"

"I don't know," I said.

My father looked worried now, and yet he did not suggest we abort the mission. Neither did Allison. Neither did my mom. Neither did I. Any one of us *could* have taken decisive action at that moment but chose not to do so, which was, in itself, a decision.

Allison insisted on staying outside while my parents and I walked into the ranger station, where we approached a woman with a face like a loggerhead tortoise. She had matted hair, a Smokey Bear hat, and a frown. My parents and I stood together by a 3D topography map and a postcard rack. I was so worried about Allison—and, at the same time, convinced that my dream hike was about to be ruined—that my stomach gurgled. To ease my nerves I studied the map, tracing the mountain crest with my index finger. Dad stepped up close to the ranger woman. "My son and his girlfriend are hiking the Pacific Crest Trail," he said, sounding proud and exasperated at the same time. "They're hiking all the way from Mexico to Canada."

The ranger yawned and showed her yellow teeth. "Is that right?" she said in the tone people use on telemarketers. "The Pacific Crest Trail? We see an awful lot of those." She blithely added that the trail near the ranger station was "totally snowed over and impassible. No way you'll make it without snowshoes and ice axes. Do you have snow gear on you?"

"No," I said.

"Well, if I were you I'd start farther north a ways, in the lower elevations, somewhere near Agua Dulce. That's fifty-five miles north of here, near the Antelope Valley."

I was vaguely familiar with the place she was talking about. It was in a parched area of Los Angeles County, forty-four miles north of downtown L.A.

"But . . ." I said. "Isn't that kind of in the desert?"

"Yeah," the ranger said. "But at least there isn't snow."

"Then we'll need directions to Agua Dulce," Dad said.

But the ranger wasn't looking at my mom and dad anymore, and her bored expression had melted away, replaced by a look of restrained horror, for there, outside the window, my girlfriend was on her hands and knees vomiting with abandon all over the landscaping.

Agua Dulce was not what I had in mind. For one thing, it was 454 miles north of the Mexican border. If we hiked to Canada from Agua Dulce, we'd have to come back at some point and make up all those missing miles. In the car, I was having a hard time processing all the new developments. I swore under my breath and kicked my boots together until Allison, still slumped over, with her hair hanging down, scolded me. "Stop freaking out, Dan," she said. "*I'm* the one who's not feeling well."

To reach Agua Dulce, we sped past gated condo towns. Pale

mountains rose. While Wrightwood was cool, the desert sizzled. Waves of heat rose off the blacktop as we entered the parking lot of Vasquez Rocks County Park, Agua Dulce's tourist attraction. Visitors crawled over sandstone shapes that jutted over the Antelope Valley. The rocks, supposedly, would be our starting point on our epic journey. My father stopped the car. Allison got out and sat on a flat-topped rock. She put her face in her hands.

"You sure about this, Daniel?" my mother said.

"I've never been so sure about anything in my life."

"But why are you doing this?" she said.

"Because I want it very, very, very, very badly."

"I know you do," she said. "But wanting something very, very, very, very badly and actually getting it are two different things, Daniel."

Allison was by my side. Even then she could have risen up and said, "Fuck this. Let's go home." Instead she sat in meek silence. I can only guess that she felt subsumed by the desires of others. A whole lot of concerns and neuroses were swirling through the air, and none of them had anything to do with her.

My father got out of the car and started helping me drag the packs from the trunk. "Boy oh boy," he said. "These packs are monsters, young Daniel. Are you sure you need all this?"

"I'm sure," I said. "It's a long way to our next supply town."

My mother gave Allison a brief worried look and whispered to me, "Is she all right, dear? Danny, do you want us to *do* something?"

I greeted the query with silence. I got a quick hug from Mom. Dad—who looked stricken—did not shake my hand. They sped out of the parking lot and were gone.

This was supposed to be a heroic moment. Even now, some part of me still thought we might start hiking that day. But where would we walk? And from what energy source? What the hell had I done? Now I wished my parents would return to rescue us, but we had no cell phone, and neither did they. Allison and I lingered for an hour in the Vasquez Rocks parking lot, in a daze, watching jackrabbits leap and hornets chase each other in wild circles.

Now that it was too late, I was ready to take care of Allison. I left her alone and found a ranger office in the county park. The young female clerk let me use their phone for a local call. Allison and I had brought with us a set of "emergency contact numbers" supplied by Kirk and Eddie back in Connecticut, just in case something bad happened to us along the trail. "Just in case" was now. Among the names on the list was Mark, a postman who lived here in Agua Dulce. Eddie had told us that Mark was a PCT enthusiast who did everything he could to help hikers. I called his work number. Mark answered on the first ring. I asked if he might give us a ride to a motel. I told him Allison had vomited recently and was weak. Mark asked us why on earth we'd left for the trail today if Allison was sick. I had no ready answer. He asked if we needed a doctor. I told him what Allison had said—that she felt rotten but probably just needed some rest.

"Sure, I can help you out," he said. "Your girlfriend had better be feeling hardy before you try that desert crossing. This is unusual, though. I've never had anybody need me to help them out before they've even set foot on the trail."

I didn't know how to respond.

True to his word, Mark was there soon, driving his mail truck. There were no hotels, motels, or a campground in Agua Dulce, so he drove us to Santa Clarita, a city of a hundred thousand people, twenty miles south. Mark was an Italian American in his early thirties, with olive skin and a bushy mustache. He told us he lived here to escape the constraints and bullshit of "normal career society." He used to run a feed and seed store, before becoming a mailman. Mark loaded up our packs for us. I could barely talk to him. Woozy, Allison tried to engage him in a conversation about a recent article she'd read about a mentally scrambled postal worker who gunned down all his coworkers. This led to some awkwardness as we squeezed into the truck. Mark drove us out to the Comfort Inn, on the edge of a busy road. "It's a shame you didn't do some hiking before staying at this place," he said as I handed the clerk our credit card. "A week from now in the backcountry, this place would seem like a palace."

In the lobby near the checkout counter, three spiky-haired rock climbers in Lycra outfits lounged in chairs. One gave me a thumbs-up sign. "Those look like serious backpacks," said one of them. "You guys must be hardcore."

We walked right past them without saying a word.

Chapter 5

The Outpile

Mark helped us drag our packs into the elevator and we rode to the second floor. We invited him into the room, where he shoved the gear against a wall. "Man, those packs are heavy," he said. Allison lay on the king-size bed, under a Cubist portrait of what looked like chopped liver. The painting bothered me. I walked over and tried to remove it but someone had nailed it to the wall. Below the balcony of our second-floor room, a burly janitor dragged a net across the pool. Squinting in the sun, he skimmed bees and spiders from water the color of Mountain Dew. This is not how I had imagined our first day in the desert. Mark glanced at me. I could tell he was alarmed by the heaviness of our packs. I could also tell that he was going to give us a stern lecture about them, but I didn't want to hear it. Allison lay back, grimacing, her hands placed gingerly over her stomach.

"Listen, I've just got to ask you something," Mark said, leaning forward. "Does either one of you have any idea what it's like out there?" He pointed, with his thumb, toward the black-ribbed mountains out the window, jagged in the distance. The sinking sun had turned their edges red. For years, Mark had been a friend to Pacific Crest Trail hikers passing through Agua Dulce. He'd offered them free rides to a camping "super store" a half hour away from the trail, and picked their brains about backpacking. He'd already hiked small sections alone or with friends, and something, he said, always went wrong: sprained ankles, tick bites, loneliness, heat exhaustion, and sometimes all of the above. "I know from experience that this is going to be the most incredibly strenuous thing you've ever done," Mark said. "With all this stuff, I'm sorry, but you will never make it. If she hadn't gotten sick now? If you guys had just waltzed right out there? I mean, you could die out there with all this stuff." He zeroed in on me and my backpack. "There's no reason to bring something that large. Then you're just tempted to stuff it full of things you don't need. So let's start getting rid of stuff right now." I stared at Allison and she stared back. "Come on," Mark said. "Let's see everything you're bringing, in a pile, on the floor."

Allison threw me a baleful look. She sat up on the bed, reached over, and flopped two sacks of food and gear on the ground. Mark's brown eyes narrowed when he saw two Swiss Army knives with beer openers, wine openers, magnifying glasses, and every kind of screwdriver head. He sighed when he saw a German lantern that weighed three pounds and needed four D-cell batteries. He whinnied when he saw our money belts, our wash towels torn in half to save weight, extra batteries for the lantern, and four toothbrushes with the handles lopped off to save even more weight. Next were thirty yards of Ace bandages, four unbreakable Lexan bowls, several spools of twine, a John McPhee anthology, four layers of insulated clothing, one large and putrefying sack of home-dehydrated apples the color of snot, and four bags of mock seafood pasta supreme with freeze-dried protein specks. But the item that puzzled

Mark the most was the kite. He turned it around and around in his hands. "Kite?" he said. "Kite? Tell me when, in the course of walking twenty-six hundred miles, over unbelievably steep terrain, would you have time to fly a kite?"

"Look," I said, "Allison bought the kite for me at an Eddie Bauer store in Connecticut for my birthday. And we decided to take it along with us. We thought it would be . . . I don't know, fun." I pointed out the kite's many attractive features, including five tassels, each six feet long, colored yellow, purple, pink, blue, and chartreuse. "See?" I said. "It's made of parafoil, so it really doesn't weigh very much. And . . . it's collapsible."

Mark reached over and threw the kite on the floor. I thought Allison was going to holler, but she was too weak to fight. Instead she leaned back on her puffy pillow and closed her eyes.

"See that kite?" Mark said. "That's the first item in the 'out pile.' And everything that ends up in the outpile is going home to your mom and dad's. Believe me, I'm doing you a favor." He reached in our packs, grabbing item after item, as methodically as a robotic arm. He ripped our 526-page *Pacific Crest Trail, Volume I: California* guidebook into chunks, divided by chapter, and threw the sections into different piles.

"What are you doing?" I said. "That book cost me twenty-five dollars."

"You carry only the guidebook pages you need for any one section. You send the rest of the pages ahead to yourself, at each supply stop. It's a waste of weight and space. You've got to do this smart, guys, or you'll be off the trail in a week."

Soon food, spoons, and other gear formed a three-foot-high cone that leaned, at a perilous angle, against the coffee table. I was dumbstruck. Every pound that Mark took out of our packs filled me with fear. To me, every ounce of pack weight was a tether to civilization.

"Listen," Mark said. "You're going to burn through all your money before you even set foot on the trail. Why don't I come and get you tomorrow morning, and you can stay over at my grandma's place out in Agua Dulce. Stay there with me as long as you like. Meanwhile, I'll store all the camping stuff you don't need, and later on you can mail it back to your parents."

We said we'd take him up on his kind offer. Even so, I hoped, against reason, that he would have no more advice for us. I couldn't bear to hear any more.

Later, we watched from the balcony as Mark, crouching beneath two big Hefty bags stuffed with our loot, said good-bye. Allison watched Mark shove the mess into his truck and drive off. She sat on the bed and stared at the spot on the floor where our gear used to be. Then she turned and whispered in my ear, "I can't believe our kite is gone."

Chapter 6

Reign of the Jardi-Nazis

Mark honked his horn outside the motel the next day. He was at the wheel of a pickup truck with a sticker on the bumper reading, SAVE A HORSE, RIDE A COWBOY! We shouldered our packs, piled in, and drove to Mark's grandma's bungalow in a canyon full of chaparral, snakes, and silver sage. Allison was feeling better—she was taking in solid food and hadn't puked since the motel, but she wasn't strong enough to hike. I sat there, fidgety, on the carpet of Mark's grandma's living room feeling trapped, watching the big red sun rise over a neighbor's cactus garden. That morning I felt stuck, longing for some outside force to kick-start our stalled adventure. I wanted some deus ex machina to sweep in and rescue us. It was at that moment I first saw The Book.

Ray Jardine's *PCT Hiker's Handbook* had a cover the color of peach yoghurt. Typeset in an awkward font, the book had the thrown-together quality of a smuggled document, a back-country samizdat, something the authorities didn't want you to see. Ray Jardine was a mountaineer, kayaker, long-distance hiker, and inventor of The Friend, a spring-action camming device that had changed the face of rock climbing. Now he was starting a light-packing revolution on the Pacific Crest Trail. Jardine believed people could walk faster and be happier if they carried less than ten pounds of gear on their backs, including the weight of the pack. He urged his readers to hike in running shoes, or go barefoot for a spell, because "the nerves in the soles of our feet provide our brains with a wealth of tactile information." Hikers should shun boots, because they can damage our feet. Eat gooey corn pasta in camp, Jardine said, because it is "rocket fuel" for your legs, and when you're done with the meal, consider guzzling the cookwater to glean a few more carbohydrate calories. These strategies sounded wacky, but the results were indisputable. Most people take five to six months to hike the Pacific Crest Trail, but Jardine, in middle age, had knocked it off with Jenny, his sprightly wife, in less than three and a half months. That's 2,650 miles in 100 days, in heat and snow and rain.

Mark walked in to the living room and caught me reading The Book. He must have noticed my vacant expression, my tongue pushed to the side of my mouth, my eyes bulging as I stared at the pages.

"I see you've found The Book," he said. "Ray Jardine has some great ideas, but I'm not sure how much it will help you to read that now. It's like a textbook. You can't just sit down and absorb all that knowledge in one day."

Mark explained that the book had inspired a lifestyle. In fact, some of the hardest-core followers of "The Ray Way" called themselves Jardi-Nazis. Apparently, the term had started out as a put-down aimed at Jardine's most ardent fans. Essentially, it was a synonym for "joyless speed-walking freak." In response, the Jardi-Nazis appropriated the term for themselves. Mark said these hikers had a few things in common: sculpted legs and buttocks and twiggy arms, because upper-

body muscles tend to atrophy on long-distance walks. To a
Jardi-Nazi, every smidgen of pack weight mattered. Jardi-
Nazis figured it was six million steps from Mexico to Canada,
so if you brought along even one pound of useless crap, that
would be six million pounds of useless crap, enough to kill
a man.

Some Jardi-Nazis considered tents, sleeping bags, and stoves
to be "useless crap." Instead, they slept under lightweight tarps
tied to tree branches. They trained for months before setting
foot on the PCT. To a Jardi-Nazi, taking shortcuts or alternative routes was treasonous. Real Jardi-Nazis would rather choke
on a bungee cord than road-walk even a quarter mile off the
trail or take a ride to the next junction. Jardi-Nazis had ways of
figuring out if other hikers lied about their accomplishments.
One method was to look at rain-proof trail journals posted
alongside the PCT; trail walkers were careful to sign in at every
journal to authenticate their hikes. Skip a journal, and people
might call you a cheater. One young man who had avoided a
snowbound section of the High Sierra by taking a Greyhound
was known forever as Mister Bus Man.*

Mark seemed anxious to share more details about the
Jardi-Nazis but he had something else on his mind. "Look,"
he said, "we'll resume this conversation when I get back. I'm
heading out to pick up Todd. He's another hiker who just
came in off the PCT. He's gonna crash here. Is it okay with
you guys?"

"No problem," I said, startled that there was a Pacific Crest
hiker who had only just now reached Agua Dulce. "But that's

---

*   Jardine himself has disclaimed the notion that he is judgmental about
      other people's backpacking techniques. He once remarked that he wrote
      the handbook simply "to stimulate other people's thinking, where appli-
      cable," and that he saw no "right or wrong" way of hiking and backpack-
      ing. "Anyone who enjoys the wilderness on foot . . . is doing it right."

kind of weird. I thought we were the very last ones in the season."

Mark noticed my downcast expression. "Look," he said, "you don't have to read that book to hike the trail. Plenty of people hiked the PCT before Ray Jardine's book came out."

Mark left me sitting cross-legged on his grandmother's carpet, looking at the book and wondering why no one had told me about it beforehand. Why hadn't anyone told me that there was such a thing as "backpacking technique"? Why hadn't someone told me there was only one "right way" to do the trail?

Somehow I pulled myself out of my trance. I had to be realistic. Reading the handbook now would only lead to impulsive, stupid mistakes. I put the book down and tried to stop thinking about it. Still, it was painful to think I'd be going out there without all the information I needed. I hoped, against reason, that this new guy, Todd, was not one of those goddamned Jardi-Nazis. In the state of mind I was in, meeting one of those cultists would probably derange me.

The door burst open ten minutes later. It was Mark in the company of Todd, lean and muscular, with a Paul Bunyan beard, a black mustache, and a battered survival hat with a broad brim and a bandanna safety-pinned to the back to block the sun's rays. This stranger was tall, with a leathery tan, sneakers instead of boots, and a trim pack, perfectly symmetrical; no bed rolls or food sacks noodling off of it. He was so full of vigor, taking giant steps across the carpet, that you would never suspect he'd slogged 454 miles from the Mexican border to get here. The man looked like he was returning from a spa weekend.

"Good to meet you," he said, heading toward me and Allison. "My name is Todd, but I call myself The Hydra, or Hydrox, like the cookie. Hydra is my trail name. I drink water all the time." He beamed and shook my hand so painfully hard it was like getting Rolfed. Todd the Hydra looked out the window and smiled at the waves of heat rising off the asphalt road. "Quite warm out there," he said with a chuckle. He was sleek with a buoyant frame and ropey muscles. He seemed to fill the room as he moved through it, casting long shadows on the floor. He took a deep breath and sighed at all the stereo equipment and stacks of country CDs, the fuzzy carpet, the big box of muesli on the counter, and the shaggy houseplants. "This place is a palace," he said.

Todd slid his pack off his shoulders and leaned it against the living room wall. He sat down on the carpet and pulled off his trail-battered sneakers. He got back up on his feet, taking massive strides in his ankle socks. What feet he had. Size-thirteen monsters, so big they reminded me of Bigfoot, feral humanoid of the Pacific Northwest. Allison watched him intently. I envied his strut, his way of loping through a room, making it his own. Then the door opened again and a woman—his girlfriend, I presumed—walked in and made my heart stop. She was carrying some of Todd's gear and a shrink-wrapped platter of cookies. Her dark hair spilled to a crook in her back. She leaned forward to shake my hand. As she did, she arched her shoulders, and I could not help but notice the sun-browned cleavage pushing against her tank top. Shyly I asked for one of the cookies, which turned out, on further inspection, to be peanut-butter-and-chocolate Rice Krispies Treats. Todd handed me the platter. "Knock yourself out," he said. While reaching for a gooey square, I noticed that his girlfriend had left a yellow Post-it message for Todd on top of the cookie pile. "You're special," it said.

"I'm Elaine," the woman said.

"But I call her my Sweet Elaine," Todd said, "because that's what she is. She's so sweet to me."

"I meet him at every trail stop."

"She sure does," he said. "I tell you, she keeps my spirits up."

Sweet Elaine giggled, leaving no doubt that the two of them had Yoga-esque pretzel-contortionist grinder sex at every junction. I loved Allison, and sure, we had just as much sex as most other well-scrubbed suburban New England couples. Still, it was hard not to envy a man whose relationship with his girlfriend seemed to consist solely of baked goods and fornication. Allison asked Todd about the HYDRATE OR DIE sticker on his pack; we were not aware at the time that it was the logo of the CamelBak company, which makes backpacks with built-in water pouches.

"Humans lose so much water out there and don't even know it," Todd said softly, his voice turning grave and low. "We're the only mammals on the planet who can't gauge our level of dehydration." He pointed to the Jardine guidebook, open and dog-eared on the table. "That's why you've got to drink all the time out there, and you should eat all the time, too. I eat three pounds a day on the trail. I eat like a horse." To make room for all the food in his pack, Todd carried scant gear. He didn't have a tent or sleeping bag, just a "bivy sack," short for "bivouac sack," which looked to me like a trash bag. He pulled this sack over himself to sleep at night, to keep out the elements. I wondered out loud if such a thing could work. "Good question," he said, smiling. "It does keep me warm, for the most part, though I almost got hypothermia on Mount Baden Powell." Todd pronounced *hypothermia* with slow satisfaction, as if recalling an especially tender cut of porterhouse.

"So," I blurted out, "are you a Jardi-Nazi?"

There was silence for a moment. Todd raised his eyebrows, then shook his head and laughed. "Jardi-Nazi? Hmm. Would I call myself that? Hell, I don't know. But I will tell you one thing. God bless the Jardi-Nazis. God bless 'em. I follow Ray Jardine's advice to the last letter."

"Can you show me some of your gear?" I said meekly.

"Sure," he said. "I'd be glad to. Come here." He fished out
a white wrinkled garment. "Here, catch," he said, tossing it in
my direction. "That's my white shirt for desert crossings. See
the long sleeves? It keeps the ultraviolet rays out." He reached
in his pack and threw me two wrinkled balls of cotton material that were damp to the touch and smelled vaguely of garlic.
"Those," he said, "are trail socks."

Perhaps I was oversensitive, but there was something about
his thunderous voice, his confidence, his smug assurance, and
his method of tossing his gear at my chest that put me on edge.
But Todd returned to my good graces when he asked if I might
take his picture with Mark, Sweet Elaine, and Allison. I was so
flattered by this request that I tried to cast aside my reservations
about him. They all stood together, smiling widely, getting ready,
but when I pulled out my camera, Todd's smile faded. He'd already shown me his camera, a dinky little point-and-shoot that
weighed only a few ounces. My Pentax K1000, a gift from my
father, weighed three pounds. It had a fabric case, a cross-your-
heart carrying strap, and an Ugly American 30-to-75-millimeter
zoom lens that looked like one of those over-the-shoulder things
they shot at Russian choppers in Afghanistan. Todd scratched his
beard, stared at the camera, and frowned.

"Holy shit," he said. "That's a big camera, my friend. How
far do you guys think you're really gonna get?"

"Uh, far," I said, trying to sound strong.

"What do you guys want?" Todd said with an abruptness,
and a change of tone, that took me by surprise. "Where do you
really want to go?"

I stood there, unable to come up with a snappy comeback.

"Are you at a loss for words?" he said.

Allison and I threw each other pained looks.

During a lull in the conversation, when Todd was distracted
talking to Mark, I took Allison aside and had a powwow with
her outside, on the driveway.

"I think he's making fun of us," I said.

"Even out here," she said, "you just can't escape the macho thing, the whole he-man one-upsmanship thing."

"I don't like his attitude," I said. "I don't like him acting as if he knows everything and we're just a couple of over-packed slobs. Well, we'll show Mr. Fancy Pants. We'll pass his dehydrated keister on the side of a Mojave sandbank."

Allison smiled. "We have a mean streak that will serve us well," she said. "And all he has is an ego as big as his feet."

Allison and I were gunning for Todd now. Outside the house, keeping our voices down, we broke into a little Pacific Crest Trail–style gangsta rap, a hiker's variation on NWA's "Gangsta Gangsta." We substituted the N-word with *hiker*, or more specifically, *hikah*, because it sounded more gangsta-rap authentic.

> *'Cause we're the type of hikahs that's built to last*
> *If you fuck with us we'll put a hiking boot in your ass.*

This exchange of lyrics cheered us up immensely. We were ready to go back inside and deal with Todd. He seemed to be waiting for us.

"When are you guys leaving?"

"The day after tomorrow," Allison said. "Just as soon as I'm feeling better."

"Are you psyched?" Todd said, brightening. "Are you psyched?"

Allison and I looked at each other and decided, tentatively, that maybe we were psyched.

"Aw right," Todd shouted, throwing a fist in the air. "Aw right!"

As the sun turned to a murky sliver in the foothills above the house, Todd made out with Sweet Elaine in the kitchen behind a stack of muesli oat-cranberry cereal boxes. It was getting close to 10:00 P.M. When they emerged at last, messy-haired and flushed, Sweet Elaine was blushing, even in her ears. Todd kissed her again, gently, and said they had better turn in quickly because he was returning to the trail early the next morning.

"Won't the sun be bad then?" Allison said.

"I'm prepared," Todd said crisply, "to hike all day any day under most conditions. I wear the lightest garments possible. My sleeves block the sun. I don't get sunburned."

"Do you have any insect repellent," Allison said in a saucy tone, "or is carrying bug juice over-packing?"

Todd just shook his head. "No bug juice. I don't believe in putting chemicals on my body."

Allison laughed out loud and caught my eye. "You must get sucked dry, then," she said. "If I were you, I'd use the bug juice." She turned to me, throwing me a supportive look. I smiled back. Allison and I were a team. Todd smiled, too. He reached in his pack and pulled out a full-body suit made of mosquito-proof mesh. He'd sewn it himself.

Sweet Elaine was lounging near Todd. She asked us if we'd done any other national scenic trails.

Allison told her we'd done a brief overnight practice hike on the Connecticut section of the Appalachian Trail and that it was a disaster. "We ran out of water. We had to suck on oranges. It was a gnarly situation."

Sweet Elaine looked shocked. "You ran out of water on the AT? There's so much water there. It's like the ocean. The PCT is like a desert!"

I blushed. Todd looked even more annoyed now. "You guys have any experience out there at all?" he said. "How far do you really think you're gonna get?"

"All the way," I said. "All the way!" My words sounded hollow.

"Well, you guys sure picked a weird place to start," Todd

said. He folded his maps and stuffed them in the side pocket of his shorts.

Allison and I went off to sleep in the spare room. Todd and Sweet Elaine were offered the living room but declined. They walked out to the lawn in front of Mark's grandmother's house, draped themselves beneath Todd's trail tarp and slept under the stars.

Chapter 7

In the Beginning

The next morning, Todd left for the trail while Sweet Elaine drove back to Los Angeles. One day later, Allison said she felt a hundred percent better, and that all traces of the stomach bug had vanished. Mark drove us out to a place where the stables, dude ranches, and houses became more spread out, until there was nothing but dirt hills and crackling power lines. He was smiling hard now, and I wasn't sure if he was confident in us all of a sudden or just happy to get us the hell out of his grandma's bungalow.

On either side of the foothills rose blocks of rough sandstone, orange and red in the morning light. In the distance through the blue haze were low mountains, bald on top, pink from the sun. Mark killed the truck's motor near a ranch house with a sign reading, RED DUST RANCH. A steer skull hung from a wire on a wooden arch. Its teeth were broken. Mark stopped on a pullout overlooking a valley. Allison and I stood in our blue neon shorts. No sounds intruded except for the crunch of our Vasque Sundowner boots on gravel and a few crows cawing. Near the gravel pullout, I noticed a three-foot-wide footpath. A marker on the path's edge, attached to a five-foot-tall post, read, PACIFIC CREST TRAIL. There was the PCT's logo: shaggy pines and a snow-frosted mountain, but the land looked nothing like the picture on the marker, no snowcapped peaks, just a snakebitten valley the color of moleskin. The sign promised Eden. The scenery was straight out of Exodus.

My pack was so heavy I rested it on the ground, propped it up against the passenger door of Mark's truck, squatted down in the dirt, lowered my shoulders beneath the support straps, cinched the straps tight against my pouching gut and pushed with my legs until I was standing up. It felt as if I had just done an ass-buster crunch at the gym back in Torrington. It takes six million steps to get to Canada. That's six million ass-buster crunches.

Mark looked at me wistfully. "Maybe I didn't take enough stuff out of that pack," he said. "Are you comfortable?"

"Extremely comfortable," I said. "It's an internal frame pack that distributes the weight so evenly you don't even feel it."

"Really?" he said. "You're leaning to one side."

"No, I'm not," I said.

Allison shouldered her pack. She grabbed hold of her support straps, took out her sun reflector hat and put it on. The hat had a creased brow and floppy top. Allison had an expression of openness and expectation. She smiled at me.

"Now, listen," Mark said. "If something goes horribly wrong in the first hundred miles, try to get to a town somehow. Then call me up and I'll come get you in my truck. My offer still stands after the first hundred miles—but it'd better be something really awful, and you'd better tell me about it in a really friendly voice."

Then he reached around my neck to borrow my camera. Smiling, he cupped his hands to frame the shot. The picture would have shown a fresh-faced couple, clothes pressed, packs clean. We probably wore expressions of fear and expectation as we stood by the sign and waved.

But no one would ever see the picture.

There was no film in the camera.

Mark drove away in his truck, leaving Allison and me standing next to the Pacific Crest Trail marker. Allison's hair was tied in a thick ponytail, which stuck out from beneath her survival hat. Her white T-shirt was spotless, and so was her aquamarine sweatshirt made of synthetic fibers. Behind her, black mountains marched east across the broad valley, with a few foothills straggling just behind them. We would head north and cross the horizon line and the horizon beyond it until there were no horizons left. It was time to begin.

It was 6:15 A.M. on June 17, nearly two months after most hikers start out on the Pacific Crest Trail. To our knowledge, we were the last through-hikers of the season. Ahead of us lay a 108-mile walk along the slopes of Liebre Mountain and down into the Mojave's western edge. Soon the dust Mark's truck kicked up, its diesel smell, and then, even the noise of it, were gone. It was just the two of us and the wind and the crows.

Time to take our first steps. I wondered if Allison would throw up again. Perhaps I would strain my hamstring, or space junk would fall from the clouds and crush us. I made a mental inventory. Ten pounds of chocolate and fruit gummi creatures from Trader Joe's, check. Twelve freeze-dried dinners, check. Artisan-quality salami, check. Velveeta and noodles, check. Allison did a few yoga-style stretches, pivoting and waving her arms. I did a halfhearted knee bend and left it at that. Stretching is for pussies. I looked at Allison. "And so it begins," I said, and we were off like a thundering herd of tortoises.

I took the first step. My boots crunched down on brittle grass. Then I took another step, over pebbles and loose earth. It seemed so cretinously simple. All you do is take one step and then another. "Repeat as often as necessary," as it says on the

Luden's cough drop container. This was going to be a snap. My pack was lashed to my back, a purple sandbag, and I felt the weight of it, in spite of Mark's efforts to trim it down, but I didn't care. I just smiled and thought, "We're gonna show everybody." I took another step until I had taken 10 steps and it was still easy. In short order, I'd taken 25 steps. It pleased me to think there were now only 5,999,975 more steps remaining. In fact, I wondered if I had taken the first steps too quickly, without being mindful enough. I stopped in my tracks and breathed.

"Why aren't you moving?" said Allison, just behind me.

"I'm savoring," I said.

I took another breath as we entered Angeles National Forest, with a trail marker at the boundary. We crossed a horse trail and headed north. The air smelled of sage. The trail rose into steep foothills speckled with juniper. Allison saw a coyote down in the valley and a swaying yucca stalk against the deep blue sky. She marveled at fat, poky ants covered with thick fuzz that weighed them down, making them stumble. Allison called them "rug ants." The landscape looked sandy and broken.

Beyond the hills was the Sierra Pelona range. Allison's fingers clutched her pack straps. In the distance behind us was Vasquez Rocks County Park, platforms of hunched sandstone. The rocks were the reputed hiding place of Tiburcio Vasquez, a bandit who terrorized California in the 1870s. I felt like a desperado myself, a wilderness gangster, with Allison as my moll. I wasn't scared. There was nothing to fear out here, for we had two different kinds of insect spray. Vicious animals? I had a Swiss Army knife with which to stab them through and through. Water-borne illnesses? I had one of the most expensive water filters on the market. Getting lost? I had a thirteen-dollar compass. I had also brought a plastic odometer that clipped to my socks. It made a gratifying clackety-clack sound every time I took a step. This device would let us know how far we'd walked each day, down to one tenth of a mile.

The path passed close to a few outbuildings and small houses scattered across the steep countryside. Everywhere we looked, we saw no people but signs of human intrusion—a drainage culvert and deep scars on the hills left by dirt bikes. Our first section of the trail was not characteristic of the PCT as a whole, since the path would cross paved roads, come close to a reservoir, and on three occasions, pass through remote settlements. But we would be all on our own for day-long stretches, on mountain ridges as high as 4,500 feet above sea level. Golden light slanted through the foxtails, the oak trees dangled heavy branches over our heads, and fat lizards dragged their bellies on the ground. A jackrabbit jumped from bush to bush and ran north on the trail. He stopped for a moment. I saw the black veins in his ears. When the wind shook the limbs of an old pine tree, it sounded like a door opening on its hinges.

Allison and I had a strategy. We planned to walk for six days, rising at 6:00 A.M. and walking until 6:00 P.M., with some half-hour rest breaks thrown in. We would average, I hoped, sixteen miles a day. Most of the traverse would take place along the San Andreas Fault, actually, a thousand-mile-long network of parallel-running faults stretching from the Gulf of California to Cape Mendocino. Since the start of California's recorded history, in the mid-eighteenth century, the fault system has produced more than one hundred big temblors, including the quake that flattened San Francisco in 1906. Even as we walked, seismic activity was displacing the land to the west of the fault line; as wedges of continental crust bump and grind against one another, the landmass is shoved northwestward, in increments of two inches each year. The earth here literally "strains against itself."[*]

The landscape here can cook you as well as knock you over.

---

[*]   Philip L. Fradkin, *The Seven States of California: A Natural and Human History,* New York: Henry Holt and Company, 1995, p. 273.

Chaparral—vast stretches of evergreen bushes, some ten feet tall—grew so aggressively that they hemmed the trail, narrowing the path, forcing us to scrape through spiny leaves. It was hard work, battling plants, taking turns leading the way, bashing through the foliage with our ski-pole walking sticks. As we duked it out with plant life, I felt grateful that we didn't own a house near here. These bushes have a symbiotic relationship with fire that goes back millions of years. Chaparral rises from its ashes; the seeds of certain types of chaparral will not germinate without intense heat, although this has not discouraged thousands of Californians from building homes in areas thick with this plant. Every time you turn on the news and read about another California brush fire that has claimed the lives of firefighters and turned mansions into crisps, you had better believe that chaparral played a role in the conflagration.

By noon, six hours into the journey, I was feeling disoriented from all the exertion. From the top of the highest hill we spied a reservoir in the distance and a dirt road scarred with bike tracks. Allison was sweating now. She joked around with me about Todd the Sasquatch probably getting lost out here somewhere, and how we would catch up with him soon and give his sorry ass a talking-to. She talked about him eating our trail dust. Allison took a long slow gulp of water from a bottle. As we entered the midafternoon, I smiled into the sun and took a look at the odometer to see how far we'd gone. It said that we had gone three miles. Piece of shit. No way we were going that slowly.

To take my mind off this minor annoyance, I asked Allison if she might be interested in a gourmet salami and cheese break. She nodded yes emphatically. "Then let the deliciousness begin," I said, but when I reached in the food bag for the snacks, I hadn't realized how the hot sun might alter the appearance of our victuals. The salami now looked like a mummified dog penis, or at least what I imagined such an object might look

like: black, curly, twisted, tapered, and not very appealing to eat.
As for the cheddar, it was vile. Chalky on the inside, slippery on
the outside, the cheese exuded a pus like substance. Allison and
I decided to bury these deli items in the desert, an act that made
us feel sheepish. We considered ourselves "low-impact" hikers,
to the extent that we'd brought along a Ziploc bag to pack out
our unmentionables, which would include soiled toilet paper,
tampons, and the like. I could tell our minor act of pollution
upset Allison, who was ecologically minded, but I convinced
her that carrying smelly deli items in our backpacks was more
demoralizing than the thought of polluting the Sierra Pelona.

"The coyotes will eat 'em, I guess," she said.

We threw the salami and cheddar in a shallow grave.

I should have known this act would return to haunt me. I
have finely tuned karma. When I do the slightest thing wrong,
the Fates conspire, and gather their forces against me. When
we arrived at our first, crucial water source at Bear Spring, it
was a dirty trough, hidden by chaparral. I put my finger in the
miniature pond. Lukewarm. There were several moths in there.
One was dead. The other two were still alive, and they were
not leaving this world quietly. They kicked and flailed like a
swim aerobics class gone awry. Larvae plumped up like gnocchi in water the temperature of blood. Our filter was designed
to block viruses and fungi smaller than a micron. It did not
know quite what to make of water that had fist-sized islands of
organic mucus floating in the middle of it. The filter winced. It
made a small, discouraging sound.

"Buck up," I said. "Do your fucking job." But no water
came out, no matter how hard I pumped. "Filter, you filter!" I
commanded. "Don't be like the odometer."

Almost immediately the filter seized up and choked so violently on the water that Allison had to stop pumping. Unfazed,
she removed a packet of denture tablets from her pack and
handed them to me. Denture tablets? At first I thought she was

making a tart visual comment about my precocious senility. Then I remembered that denture tablets have a chemical that dissolves the muck that clogs water filters. Allison and I took turns soaking the filter components in a solution of tablets and water. It melted the crap right off, but every time we tried to filter more water, the gadget seized up again.

"Let's just forget the filter for now," Allison said. "We'll drink what we have, and wait for a stream, and put some iodine tablets in our bottles to kill the critters."

"But iodine tastes like rust," I said. "It makes me nauseous."

Allison smiled and pulled out a packet of Hi-C she'd saved just for the occasion. Her competence was starting to grate on me.

The nasty water seemed like enough of a punishment for our small transgression, but the trail wasn't finished with its retribution. As we walked north, the PCT markers became scarce, as if an unseen hand had plucked the signposts from the ground. No doubt about it. Someone or something was fucking with us. We were lost, going around in circles until we finally wound up in a dark colonnade of trees. A seasonal spring seeped from a hill, poured through a clutch of wildflowers, and gathered in a puddle at our feet. Though the spring was too mucky to drink, it yielded a comforting sight: in the mud was a row of deep impressions full of black water. We shouted with relief, for there was no mistaking the size-thirteen footprints of Todd the Sasquatch. It's not that we were eager to see him again, but his print suggested we were going the right way, and were close on his heels. After all that bragging, he was around the corner, going as slowly as we were. We decided to speed up and catch him, just to show him up. Allison took the lead, following the prints to a cottonwood overhang in the shade. But soon the ground went from muddy to bone hard. Todd's prints disappeared, and Todd himself was nowhere to be seen. Side paths went off in every direction. Ahead of us, down in a valley, Bouquet Reservoir lay to the northwest in shadows. Or was it southeast? Our guidebook directions did not correspond with the landscape. "Walk .2 miles uphill to a bend in the road," they read. What bend? What road?

I blamed the compass. It must be broken. Allison doubted that anything was wrong with it. The compass was a well-made piece of gear with a sapphire bearing and notches of declination. I did not know what a point of declination was, or why the bearings were made of sapphires. I'd assumed these were good things because the compass cost so much more than the competition. Besides, a person could not be lost while holding a compass that cost thirteen dollars. And yet the reservoir would not keep still. It lay to the north one moment, then the east, then south. The compass needle bobbed and wobbled like a dowsing stick. Perhaps our compass was cursed. I remembered the narrow little salesman who had sold it to us four months before, back East. He had pouches under his eyes. "The Pacific Crest Trail?" he'd said. "Yeah, I tried to hike that thing in 'eighty-five. Tore a ligament the very first day. Then I drank some bad water. Got the trots so bad my friends had to carry me out of there. That'll be thirteen dollars. Would you like a bag?" As I tried to figure out where we were, I wondered if his soul inhabited our compass, causing the needle to twist every which way but the right direction.

Allison had a determined look as she stood behind me. "Will you show me the map and compass?" she said.

"No," I said.

"Why?"

"I can figure it out."

"I can help."

"I don't need any help."

I now understand that the compass was working just fine. The trouble was I couldn't read the goddamned thing. I had no idea that you were supposed to find north first, and then use north to extrapolate the other directions. Adding to our troubles, the Pacific Crest Trail's route had changed recently, because of right-of-way conflicts, and the guidebook company had printed out a pamphlet of revisions. We were carrying the pamphlet with us on the trail, but for reasons I still can't comprehend, we did not consult these new, improved directions. What if hours passed, days, and we still hadn't found the trail? I imagined a search party of men shouting our names through bullhorns, bloodhounds sniffing the earth, chopper blades thwacking, and Mark the postman's look of pity when the authorities brought us back to his grandmother's house. The local press would turn on us like Dobermans. They would run front-page stories and cutesy alliterative headlines at our expense: DESERT DIMWITS RESCUED TWO MILES FROM TOWN.

"Dan?" Allison said. "Would you please hand me that compass now?"

"I just want to keep walking."

"Where?" she said. "Come on. Show me your map. And your compass."

Her demanding voice took me by surprise. There's no word for it in the English language, this feeling of solipsism, when you believe the world revolves around your incompetence. If I couldn't understand a compass, how the hell could anybody else? Nevertheless, I handed it over to her. At 4:00 P.M. she stood before me in a sweat-wicking vest, face to the sun, bottom lip puffed with authority, arms bent. Though I resented, and was confused by, her bossy insistence, she looked sexy as hell then. She held the map up in front of her face, laid the compass directly on top of it, and pivoted, until the shape and angle of the reservoir on the map lined up with the shape and the angle of the reservoir in front of us. "That's it," she said. "We're too far east. All we do is backtrack ten minutes and we'll hit the trail. We just took some dumb turn."

We found the trail in an instant. I threw my arms around the PCT marker and kissed it. Allison took a celebratory picture of me with the still-filmless camera. On we walked. It was a relief, and a disappointment, to be back on the trail. After all, feeling silly in front of Allison was only marginally better than feeling lost. A few days before, I'd resented her for dragging down our nature walk with all her panicking and vomiting. Now I was the one dragging her down, and I somehow resented her for this, too. "Never mind," I told myself. "One of these days I'll even the score by getting us out of a bad situation." I had more pressing matters to deal with now. We had to find camp and cook our first trail meal.

The sun completed its arc across the cloudless sky. At sunset we stood on a windblown hill covered with waist-high foxtails. We had gone just over six miles, execrable by long-distance hiking standards. As the sky grew dark, we made a rough camp and fell into prescribed gender roles, Allison slaving over the stove pot while I sat on a stump "erecting" the tent. When she fired up the stove, a swirling pillar of flame leapt up and singed the hairs off one of her arms. She did not flinch. The wind blew out the flame. She relit the stove. It took sixteen minutes for our organic bunny-shaped Annie's macaroni noodles to boil, and when they were done, they were so rubbery and tasteless that we nibbled only a few of them and threw the rest at a spiny plant. The desert had numbed our appetites anyhow. The sun fell away, catching us in the dark as we stomped through our strewn pots and camp junk.

After climbing into our tent, Allison lay awake for a while, admitting she was scared of "weirdos" coming after us. But she soon drifted to sleep in her mummy bag, leaving me behind. I'd barely settled in when her snoring began, her wet *kromps* and *sherbert* whinnies blending with the calls of distant coyotes. Allison, even while unconscious, was running with the wolves, upstaging me with her sylvan femininity. Still, I loved watching her that night, feeling protective as I saw the rise and fall of her body within the sleeping bag. I tried not to be too hard on myself. I knew we'd cover more miles the next day. But when I closed my eyes, I saw six million steps to Canada laid out like ties on a railroad track to the moon. The average long-distance walker travels twelve to fourteen miles a day starting out, then builds to sixteen to twenty miles a day. If you're gifted at walking, you might hit twenty-five, thirty, even forty miles a day on the trail. I could not stop the racing thoughts about Todd the Sasquatch somewhere out there, tearing up the foothills while exuding massive amounts of man sweat. Stomping all over the American West with his freakish feet. Mastering the learning curve. Making the big miles.

Chapter 8

Mulholland Falls

Henry Miller once wrote that a land can haunt you even if you don't know the past that lies beneath it. When traveling through Greece, he would find himself "profoundly disturbed, shaken to the roots, and by what? By associations born of my knowledge of ancient events? Scarcely, since I have but the scantiest knowledge of Greek history and even that is thoroughly confused . . . No, as with the sacred places, so with the murderous spots. The record of events is written into the earth." And so it was on our second day, when we made a slow descent down a steep-edged ravine into San Francisquito Canyon, a stomp through green gulches, repeating, repeating, like a desolation screensaver. Allison took the lead position that day. Her bright blue backpack rose up high above her head, and reached so far below her waist that when I viewed her from behind, only her boots were visible. Watching her wobble, I felt guilty that she was carrying such a big load, and worried it would wear her down. She had been having a bit of knee pain on the steeper descents. Every so often, I'd stop, take some of her gear or water, and stuff it into my pack, which was now crammed to the bursting point. Mark had, indeed, done us a favor by taking so much of our stuff from the packs, but they were still very heavy, in spite of his best efforts. Our pack weight, once suicidal, was now merely ridiculous.

Most of the time we were in the blasting sun, but sometimes we found a lovely surprise, a colonnade through the boughs of hanging trees, or a wall of fragrant flowers shaped like trumpets, stars, and baseball gloves. Already I felt the first day's growth of beard, the scratch of it against my fingers. It made me feel steely. We pushed our way down to the canyon and to the highway across the trail. No other hikers there, no cars along the blacktop striped across the ravine. Plumes of smoke rose from distant forests to the north. We walked along the two-lane road awhile, until we arrived at a small and sparsely manned Department of Agriculture fire station. Four firefighters stood by the cooler, their faces smeared. The first humans we'd seen in twenty-four hours had been out extinguishing a minor but difficult-to-reach wildcat blaze in the hills. One of them, a cherubic fellow with grease spots on his dungarees, asked where we'd started.

"Agua Dulce," Allison said, her face full of expectation, as if she sensed an awed response was coming, something along the lines of "Holy shit, you walked all the way from Agua Dulce?"

"Agua Dulce," the firefighter grunted. "So you only just started."

We asked him if he'd seen our "friend" Todd the Sasquatch. The firefighter said Todd had passed there more than two days ago. Allison and I frowned. Todd was practically sprinting.

The firefighters loaded our canteens with sweet water out of the cooler, and let us camp for the night on a patch of grass behind the fire station. That night Allison cooked us freeze-dried couscous. We read in the dark in our sleeping bags with our headlamps. As the sun sank and the ravines faded to black, an absolute quiet came over the yard near the fire station. I felt uneasy for no reason at all.

To borrow a phrase from Henry Miller, the canyon was "a murderous spot," though I didn't know it then. William Mulholland, chief water engineer for the city of Los Angeles through most of the 1920s, had his fall here. Now that I know his story, I feel a certain kinship with him. Both of us came to California to remake ourselves. The circumstances were a bit different; I moved back after a long absence, while Mulholland, born in Ireland, made his way out west to find his fortunes in the goldfields, a scheme that never panned out. I could sympathize with his desire to impose his will on a landscape, to make it conform to his plans. Mulholland, in his prime, had a prizefighter's nose and a scrub brush for a mustache. Arriving in Los Angeles in 1877, he found work pulling weeds, garbage, and branches out of ditches in the hot sun. Some might consider this a demeaning job, but he was proud, even arrogant, in his labors. When a supervisor stopped by and asked him his name, Mulholland told him to mind his own goddamned business and let him do his job. Impressed by his cheekiness, the boss promoted him.

Mulholland was fond of his work and loved his town. Looking back on those days, he wrote, the "world was my oyster and I was just opening it. Los Angeles was a place after my own heart." L.A. had once been a backwater slum, cut off from the gold rush spoils that turned San Francisco into a boomtown in the 1840s. Los Angeles had no port. Until the 1870s, the city didn't even have a rail link to the rest of America. But when Mulholland gazed upon Los Angeles, he saw a great American city in the making. He was sure it could be a contender, if not for one incontrovertible fact: two thirds of the water in California was concentrated in the northern third of the state. Southern California was essentially a desert, and L.A. sat on its edges, with the anemic L.A. River dribbling through town. Meanwhile, all that precious moisture was just sitting up in northern California. Mulholland thought this was a dreadful waste.

Mulholland, after becoming L.A.'s water chief, was a relentless cheerleader for a 250-mile aqueduct, the largest engineering feat since Roman times. The structure—dismissively known as "Mulholland's Ditch"—siphoned water by gravity feed from the Owens River, beneath the High Sierra's eastern edge. Mulholland's project turned Los Angeles green, with circling sprinklers, swimming pools, and jungles sprouting from Hollywood back lots. Six years after the aqueduct's completion in 1913, the population of L.A. doubled, to two hundred thousand. By 1922, the population had surpassed 500,000.

Los Angeles's success happened on the backs of Owens Valley farmers, who now realized that Mulholland and his cronies had misrepresented themselves while coaxing ranchers into selling parcels with the best water rights. Mulholland's project bled the water tables dry. His aqueduct had a striking if unintended consequence: all those gallons of diverted water turned Owens Valley so barren that Hollywood producers started using it to film low-budget oaters starring Buck Jones and Hoot Gibson.

Owens Valley farmers were furious when they found out their lush pastureland was being turned into a nouveau desert. They filed lawsuits and took up arms. Saboteurs staged spectacular attacks on the aqueduct, blowing up sixteen- and forty-foot chunks of it, prompting Mulholland to bring in an army of Tommy gun– and Winchester rifle–slinging "detectives," with shoot-to-kill orders. The attacks hastened plans to build a massive water storage facility far from the tensions of Owens Valley. Mulholland chose a spot close to where Allison and I spent the night, San Francisquito Canyon, where an army of workers took two years to build an arch support dam 180 feet high and 600 feet long. By spring of 1928, St. Francis Dam was filled to capacity.

That night, in our campground near the fire station, I stayed up for a while, leaning from the tent, looking at the violet clouds. Unable to sleep, I wandered the field and stared up at the black rock bowl that surrounded us. Fire ants, perhaps smelling the minty Dr. Bronner's soap I'd used to bathe that night, crawled from their nest and took wet chomps out of my ankles. Each bite burned like a hot needle. At midnight, the clouds cracked open and moonlight spilled across our campsite, a great flood filling the canyon, until the waves of white and yellow washed over our tent.

On March 12, 1928, Mulholland's men noticed a crack in the dam and a brown trickle of water. Mulholland told his men to put some caulking in the crack and go home. He wasn't about to lose sleep over a chink in his fail-safe creation. Three minutes to midnight, the dam exploded. As it roared down the valley, the twelve billion gallons of water carried with it a moving wall of mud, dirt, and concrete blocks piled seventy feet high and rolling at thirty miles an hour. Floodwaters smashed through Piru, Fillmore, Bardsdale, Santa Paula, and Saticoy. The black mass crashed into its victims with such force that it ripped their clothes away. Floodwaters swallowed farms, work camps, and apiaries and cut a two-mile-wide, seventy-mile-long swath from the canyon to the ocean. Chunks of dam washed up on beaches two hundred miles west. Four hundred people drowned that night.

The arch-support dam was reduced to rubble, and so was Mulholland's reputation.

Mulholland tried to blame the dam's failure on saboteurs, but the jury at a coroner's inquest hearing did not believe him. Instead, the jurors blamed "a monolithic chain of command" that gave Mulholland almost total control over the dam's construction. They ruled that the dam had collapsed because of "the failure of the rock formations upon which it was built." Mulholland had overestimated himself and underestimated a shifting landscape. The valley's secret history destroyed him; he had no way of knowing that he'd built his dam against a slow-motion landslide that had been shifting and slipping since ancient times. Mulholland avoided criminal charges, but he resigned in disgrace. Before he came to this canyon, he was one of the most powerful men in California. By the time he left this place, he said that he "envied the dead."

I recall the evening's strangeness, the traces of fire, and the smoke leaking up from the hills. I had a strong sense of being walled into the bottom of a valley, and the land containing me, along with its past and its stories, as I fell into a deep sleep.

As usual, I dreamed of spirits.

Chapter 9

A Bottle of Mace

One morning on the trail, three days after we left Agua Dulce, I woke up and looked at the bruised-orange sky. We were out in the Angeles National Forest, not far from Lake Hughes. The sun and moon were out. It was cold outside, and yet there were patches of warm air. I lurched around camp, half asleep. Fat ants pottered about. I saw traces of scavengers. A night mouse had chewed a hole in my backpack's lumbar-support pad and gnawed through a strap. Thank God I still had a twenty-five-yard spool of duct tape in my fanny pack. In the desert dirt I sat, cursing the night mouse, fixing my pack, shooing the rug ants away. After a while I let them be. They waddled aimlessly, carrying nothing. Their unhurried purpose-lessness soothed me.

Allison emerged from the tent, a leg, a torso, a mop of hair. She smiled at me and yawned. We woke up exhausted and ate our sloppy breakfast of Grape-Nuts, chocolate chips, and almonds floating in iodized stream water mixed with nonfat dehydrated milk powder. It took us two hours to pack up our

camp. Tired and disoriented, the two of us bounced down the
trail into a box canyon. Our heads were full of sleep. No wonder we screwed up again. Around noon, after four hours of
hiking, we took a wrong turn near Maxwell Truck Road, near
Upper Shake Campground, and wound up in a copse of black
oak. We heard the crunch of gravel. There was something in
the bushes.

"You hear that?" said Allison, who was out in front. "I swear
I heard footsteps."

She pointed into the canyon. Footsteps getting louder.
Something slipping and sliding in the sand, heading for us.

This was an unlovely branch of trail. One recent nature-
walk book had described the section as "pig ugly" and "a punishment." There was no reason a pleasure walker would be here
now, in mid-June, unless he were stupid or crazy.

Allison smiled and squinted. "Wouldn't it be funny," she
said, "if it turned out to be that idiot Todd, after all? Going the
wrong way."

We laughed, puffed our chests, and bellowed like Tarzan to
imitate Todd. But when we rounded the corner, it was most
definitely not Todd. For one thing there were two of them,
two men with blank expressions and pencil-thin mustaches.
They seemed to be in their late thirties to early forties, with
greasy remnants of hair. It was noon, the hottest sun of the day,
but they were wearing long-sleeved buttoned-down shirts and
slacks the color of Italian nougat. Their heads looked like sweaty
thumbs. The men were twenty yards apart but heading in opposite directions, fanning out. They were having some trouble
moving forward. Both wore patent leather shoes, pointy in the
fronts. No traction. They skidded on the gravel. The fat one ran
to us while his thinner companion ran up a firebreak, a vertical slash in the hills to keep wildcat blazes from leaping. Then
he stood on the hill, where he bent down and removed a pair
of binoculars from his pants pocket. The fat one came closer,

sweating. His stomach shoved up against his Oxford shirt, as if trying to break free.

"Where'd you park?" he said. "Where's your car?

"No car," I said.

"We walked," Allison said.

"What do you mean you walked?" the man said, stepping into our space, close enough for us to smell his sweat and a whiff of cologne. "What you got in there?" he said, pointing to our swollen packs.

"A stove," I said. "Our maps."

"What else? Where's your car? Where'd you park? What's in the bags?"

"We're telling the truth," I said. "We're Pacific Crest Trail hikers. We took a wrong turn. And we thought you could tell us how to get back to the turnoff."

Could that work? Bring the man to our side by asking directions? Allison looked blank. I had no proof the fat man was a threat, nothing but a gut feeling from his bulging stomach, his attitude, his questions, his clothes, the cologne. And those terrible shoes.

"I asked where you parked," the man said, sharply.

Huh? Was he deaf? "We walked," I said again. "From Agua Dulce."

He shook his head and smiled. "I been all over this valley," he said. "And I never heard of no Agua Dulce."

The man put his fat fingers in his mouth and signaled to his friend with three shrill toots. The second man, now fifty feet away, whirled and ran down the hill toward us. It was time to get the hell out of there. We "ran" as best we could, but our packs weighed us down. We "ran" in a way that reminded me, at the time, of crustaceans. The scrambling for purchase, the wild motions, the lack of any real forward momentum. As we ran, I thought of hobbled lobsters and crabs on Xanax. These were not similes but the actual images I saw in my brain as we headed for the bushes. My heart was pounding. My tongue felt stiff. We ran through a muddy puddle and got gook all over our boots. Allison led the way. She had astonishing lower-body strength, and though she went slowly, she moved with a measured relentlessness. Allison was leader for now, and I was too frightened to care. I backed her up, occasionally turning, stopping to see if I could hear the men pursuing us. I couldn't tell; it was hard to hear anything above the blood thumping in my ears. A chaparral hedge grew high enough for us to do a duck-and-cover. "This is where we'll make our stand," I said.

I reached in my pack and pulled out a canister of pepper spray I'd bought for $15.75 at a pharmacy in Winsted, Connecticut. You're supposed to go to the local community college and take a two-hour evening class, led by a community service officer, on how to use the spray. Then they give you a permit. I hadn't bothered with all that bureaucratic tedium. I thought it would be a no-brainer. Allison looked pale and uncomfortable. She crouched behind me. At that moment I felt unworthy of having any woman crouch behind me, especially Allison. I crouched behind her. It became unclear who was crouching behind whom. All the crouching was making me queasy. "Those men are in cahoots," Allison whispered to me, emphatically, and though I was scared, my brain also noted that this was the first time I'd ever heard anyone use *cahoots* in a conversation. Allison's hands rifled through my pack to find the pepper spray directions, which, for some reason, had been socked away in a separate compartment. She found them in the fanny pack.

"Congratulations," said the directions. "You have purchased a truly unique combination of tear gas and pepper solution. Security and satisfaction are yours." The directions were astonishingly detailed. They had two columns on the bottom, comparing the ingredients of this cheap generic pepper spray and that of actual Mace. *Mace,* as it turns out, is a registered trademark. How interesting, I thought, but found it unfortunate that the directions didn't tell me what part was the trigger and what part was the aperture, where the squirts come out of. The wind blew up through the valley, straight into our faces, and the chances of macing ourselves were becoming very large.

I was afraid then. Aside from the spray, all I had to defend myself was a Swiss Army knife with an awful lot of peanut butter on the blade. I'd bought the knife in Zermatt, Switzerland, on a high school senior-class trip, in a store that specialized in sculptures of gnomes, Matterhorn desk implements, and plush animals with milky, pleading eyes. The knife came with a special holder to protect it from scratches. It also had my name, DANIEL MURRAY WHITE, power-stenciled on the handle. I'd always been so proud of it, and never let anyone touch it, and stashed it away with my Steiff piglets and *Star Wars* figurines, though it now occurred to me that this knife, at that moment, may have been the wimpiest weapon in the world, if not the universe. I pictured us screaming on the ground from spraying ourselves with the generic pepper solution while the men laughed and stole our stuff and killed us ever so slowly, Jif peanut butter blending with our blood as they cut our throats with that sissy knife.

"You hear anyone moving out there?" Allison said.

I listened. The desert had gone silent. Nothing, not even a breeze.

I sat there, holding the generic pepper spray. Twirling it in my hands like an amulet. Barely breathing, we sat together behind the chokecherry bush, the sun in our faces as we waited for the men. We checked our watches. Ten minutes had passed since we made our retreat. Where the hell were they, anyhow, and would they ever show up? I decided to do a recon maneuver, poking my head above the hedge, while waving, in a threatening manner, the Baggie that contained the pepper spray. The idea was they'd see the Baggie, be scared, and go away. Still, nothing happened. Perhaps I'd frightened them off already. We stepped from behind the hedge. Still nothing. In the distance we heard the vroom of an engine. Allison and I looked down from our rock overhang. Below us, on the trucking road, the fat and thin man were crammed into the cab of a pickup truck. Five other men were sitting on the flatbed. They were staring up the hill in our direction. Talking among themselves and glaring. At last they drove down the trucking road and were gone in a cloud of brown dust. After a while of staring at the dust, listening to the truck sounds fading, we decided the threat was over. "Who the hell were those people?" Allison said. We ran through all possibilities, from contract killers to Jehovah's Witnesses. We took a few minutes to let our pulses return to normal. Then, when we were certain the men were gone, we decided to resume our walk to Canada—but first we had to find the intersection where we'd messed up in the first place. Allison said we should split up.

"But they might come back."

"I really don't think they're coming back," she said. "If you hear anything, get the hell out of there. Let's meet back here in ten minutes."

I left my pack in the bushes and walked down the trucking road while Allison climbed through arm-cutting bushes in front of a barbed-wire fence. I ran down the dirt road looking for a trail sign. I was moving along with the sun in my eyes, wearing my torn-up Gregory Backpacks T-shirt, holding a half-empty quart bottle. I ran, my eyes watering, looking for the white marker. In the distance I saw a distinct pole a quarter mile down the road. It seemed to be a Pacific Crest Trail marker. I whooped. But when I arrived, panting, I found it was just a yucca plant swaying, its white diamond-shaped tuft a dead ringer for a three-pointed PCT sign.

I stood there disappointed as the ground began to vibrate, lightly. Then came the rumbling sound, the motor, the crunch of wheels, the returning car, the men coming up the road toward me. I froze as the sound grew louder, sharper. I could make out the sound of a shot transmission, a muffler coughing, voices. Yucca plants and rocks walled me in on either side. I'd left the generic pepper spray in my backpack. All I had, by way of a weapon, was half a twig I'd found on the ground. No time to run. All I could do was stand there, facing forward, and try to look psychotic. Fortunately my appearance was frightening already. I had not showered in three days. Dirt and sweat gummed my hair, making it stand on end as if by electrocution. Smears of Knorr Swiss instant chocolate mousse, from the previous night's dinner, stained my lower lip. Now, in the desert sun, the stains probably looked fecal.

The vehicle kept getting closer, on the other side of a bend. I could not see it yet, but the noise was increasing. It rounded the corner and I started swearing, using every foul word in my arsenal, while standing in the road with my arms waving. I gnashed my teeth and waved the twig. And it occurred to me, only gradually, that I was glaring and snarling and shaking a twig at the startled occupants of a sad and wheezy pickup truck, a late 1970s model with a banged-up bumper hanging on as if by a thread. The driver was a Mexican man, too sun-beaten and wrinkled to be a minute under seventy-nine. I was surprised he had a driver's license anymore. His cowboy hat kept his face and neck in shadow. In back were three boys, two of them teenagers, the other, kindergarten-age. The littlest wore a white T-shirt with the Calypso-singing crab from a Disney cartoon. He was cringing.

"I'm sorry," I said to all of them. "I thought you were somebody else."

"What are you doing out here?" the old man said in halting English.

"I'm a Pacific Crest Trail hiker," I said.

There was a long and ponderous silence. Finally the old man started barking orders at the kids in back. "Give him a *refresca*," he demanded. "Right now." A skinny arm reached out and handed me a Coke. I grabbed for the can, brushing the kid's hand by accident, and he yanked back the hand so fast, as if by electric shock, that he dropped the unopened Coke in the dirt on the ground. The can rolled as the car lurched past me. The wheels crunched up the hill, just as Allison came stumbling out from between two yucca plants. "Are you okay?" she said, kicking up dirt as she moved toward me. "What the hell happened? I heard a noise. I thought those guys came back and got you. What did you say to them?"

Her voice trailed off when she saw the can of Coke. She fixed me with that gaze of hers, the one that never missed anything.

I handed her the Coke. She opened it. It made a sound just like a gunshot.

Chapter 10

Mojave Crossing

The Pacific Crest Trail guidebook warned us all about it on page 157. "That part of the Mojave traversed by the PCT is now tamed by crisscrossing roads and dotted with homes and ranches, eliminating dangers of dying like French Legionnaires with parched throats and watery dreams. Still the Mojave Desert stretch of the PCT can broil your mind, blister your feet, and turn your mouth to dust."

On mile 62, about a week after we set out from Agua Dulce, we came to the shimmering grid. Ahead of us was a flat outback with dirt roads running through it and no one driving on them. One of those dirt roads was the Pacific Crest Trail. On either side of the road, creosote plants grew in evenly spaced clumps. Their sweet smell hung in the air. Creosote had an eerie symmetry, an evenly spaced emptiness between each clump of leaves and branches. Their tap roots secreted poisons. Rain washed the toxins into hard soil, killing every other plant that tried to get a toehold. Something about the grid, the spaces between plants, the barbed wire and broken fence posts, made us lose perspective. We walked on, arriving at ghost streets with names like "270th Street," heading in an unwavering direction toward limbo. Behind us, nothing receded. In front of us, nothing got bigger. Foothills would not budge. Mountains held fast to their position. Traffic lights were red and green votives in the distance. Allison limped. Her shadow dragged like a black anchor.

In the Mojave, moving things, like us, were reduced to stillness, while inanimate objects ran loose and wild. Tumbleweeds moved of their own volition, blocking the path, chasing us down. They leapt over fences and piled on top of us. They were as full of mischief as vegetable matter could ever be. Allison drop-kicked one and it shattered in the wind. Her blood was up that day. She was in a fighting mood. The landscape was teasing us here. Goading us. Fast-moving water, bound for Los Angeles, flowed tightrope straight beside the road. Here was the Los Angeles Reservoir, its water out of reach beneath a concrete slope behind barbed wire and warning signs: NO TRESPASSING—DANGER—DO NOT ENTER. After a while, we couldn't see the water anymore; it was locked in a pipe across the desert, and then the pipe itself slipped underground, a sandworm returning to its burrow. Millions of gallons of cold Sierra water moved beneath our boots, every gallon sealed away.

In the middle of the road, a dirt hump rose three feet up like an allergic reaction. Allison kicked dirt clods and broke the quiet by naming the tallest peaks with me. "That's Mount Fatso. And that one must be Mount Kilimanjaro," she said. The mountains moved in closer. Their white-sediment tops formed a chalk line in the sky. Allison was full of hyperkinetic energy. She'd often told me the trip would be an escape, a pause from her life of ambitions and journalistic responsibilities. She was here for the ecology, for the chance to squash wildflowers in her journal, but there were no flowers here, no rivers to cross. They called this place Antelope Valley, but we saw no antelopes. She held her ski-pole walking stick like a club as she stomped, her hair blowing beneath her solar-reflective survival hat. Her war march drew me forward. In civilization she kept a tidy apartment, was particular about her appearance, and had lists of every little thing. I liked the entropy that was setting in now. I liked not knowing how far she might devolve. Women rarely realize that their men find displays of primitivism and aggression endlessly alluring, so long as they aren't directed at them.

We walked the road until we saw a geodesic house on the edge of a settlement. A middle-aged man with a stained shirt stood behind a fence. He had a wizard's beard, a dreadlock swinging from his chin. When he smiled, I couldn't tell if it was from sympathy or if he was making fun of us. His dog, the size of a small rhinoceros, stuck his head through a hole in the fence and barked. When I asked if we might make it to Canada, the man smiled and said, "You're last. You're too late." He filled our bottles and drained our hopes, or tried to. "Yes, we were too late," I thought. Too late to stop, too late to go home. A Los Angeles Water and Power truck rolled toward us. The heavyset driver, his collar soaked in sweat, his eyes half closed to the sun, shouted for us to get in.

Allison threw me a pained look, for it was more than 30 miles over steep terrain before we would arrive at the turnoff to Tehachapi, our first supply city, 111 miles from Agua Dulce.

"We're not getting in," she said.

"No rides," I said.

No cheating. No shortcuts. We knew how much that hitchhike would cost. It was a question of merit, of needing to earn and deserve the satisfaction we'd have when we finished this thing. If we missed one bit of the trail, we might miss out on that "something golden" that Kirk and Eddie had promised, whatever the hell it was. We waved the driver away. He made a "you must be crazy" gesture, but we pressed on, beneath a trestle of dripping pipes. Rust-tinted water spilled on piles of garbage. The plastic receiver of a toy phone lay in the dust.

Allison wanted to hear some music to break the quiet. She asked me to scat like Louis Armstrong and grunt like Conway Twitty. She bellowed out a few dance hits. In the lower registers she sounded like a moose or a dying dugong. In the middle range, her voice was mechanical and screechy, metal on metal, car engines dying slow deaths on desert highways. Sometimes on the trail, Allison and I let loose with a little gangsta rap to enliven things. We sang selections from NWA's *Straight Outta Compton*, trading verses. On some occasions, Allison would be Ice Cube and I would be Eazy-E. Other times I'd be Doctor Dre or one of NWA's pathetic second bananas, MC Ren or DJ Yella. If I timed it properly, and picked the right parts of the songs when we alternated verses, I could trick Allison, an ardent feminist, into reciting the most appalling and misogynist lines.

> DAN: *When me and my posse stepped in the house*
> *All the punk-ass hikahs start breaking out!*
> *'Cause you know, they know what's up!*
> ALLISON: *So we started looking for the bitches with*
> *the big butts!*

Then she'd get mad and laugh and try to make it clear that her reaction was ironic in a feminist way. It was amusing for a while, but no amount of singing and scatting could compensate for our utter dislocation. Along the rock-strewn trail, pit bulls ran loops around mobile homes behind concrete and barbed wire. A Confederate flag flapped in the wind. The owners, by living there, had realized their dreams of secession.

It was hard to believe this place was only an hour's drive north from downtown Los Angeles, Hollywood, Universal Studios, and for that matter, Compton. It was late June, and we were seventy miles closer to Canada now, which seemed like progress, until we remembered the Pacific Crest Trail was 2,650 miles long. Each subsection, which hikers refer to as a "leg," is elephantine: Southern California is 648 miles; Central California is 505 miles; northern California, 567; Oregon, 450; Washington, 500. Of all those sections, the Mojave is the most blown-out and haunted-looking. Even the cows seemed possessed, staring at us with bovine menace while drooling from both sides of their mouths. We never saw anyone tend them. The bulls had horns as long as your forearm, and pointy penises, big as Wiffle ball bats, flopping in the cross breeze.

The way was straight and hypnotic. As we trekked, Allison limping, my sunglasses rattling, it made me wonder what some borax prospector's ghost, his skin the color of roast salmon, might think to see us wandering out here with no weapons, one compact kit, twelve king-size Snickers bars, and no definable sense of purpose. Passing through the landscape, I thought about all the other explorers who had come this way. We were about to intersect with the ghostly tracks of John Charles Fremont, whose expeditions and travel writings set off an avalanche of emigration into the West. He made his way to the Antelope Valley in 1844. Fremont claimed he was out west to study geography, wildlife, and plants. Actually, his journey had much more to do with dreams of conquest. One dead giveaway was the fact that most flower-sniffing nature expeditions don't require a Howitzer, four pistols, 33 carbines, forty men, five kegs of gunpowder, and five hundred pounds of ammo.

Two years before President James K. Polk declared war on Mexico, Fremont was doing his part to drum up support for seizing California, calling attention to its fertile soil, hospitable temperatures, and fetching flora. But in spite of all his firepower, Fremont felt edgy in the Mojave. He sugarcoated many of his travelogues, but even he couldn't spin the wasteland before him. He was disgusted and nervous to see horse skeletons picked clean by buzzards, and human bodies in the dirt. The

Mojave was, he declared, "the most sterile and repulsive desert I have ever seen."

His fearful entries about the desert made me wonder about the myth of the self-made conquering hero. Although he cultivated a lone-wolf image, Fremont was dependent on his wife, Jessie Benton Fremont, arguably braver than he was. As a young woman, Jessie shocked her prim Missouri family by butchering her tresses and dressing as an army officer. After marrying Fremont, she grew her hair out again, but she found an outlet for her he-man fantasies by rewriting her husband's memoirs, turning them into swashbuckling adventure stories that would appeal to the masses. Her gambit paid off: Fremont's travelogues were bestsellers.* I could understand Fremont's attraction to Jessie, and his reliance on her. Allison started out as hapless on this trail, vomiting her guts out, threatening to delay our trip indefinitely. Now she was becoming my surrogate backbone, my prosthetic brain. I hated to think about what might happen if Allison up and quit this trail and left me alone out here. I knew it was a ridiculous notion. She was in it for the duration. Still, this place put me on edge, and I couldn't help but wonder how I'd fare out here by myself.

In most sections of the trail, you are days from the nearest town, and all on your own if anything goes wrong. This section was in the middle of nowhere, and yet there were outposts scattered along the desert floor. If we needed help we could have walked into the brush and pounded on the door of someone's aluminum home. But our safety net was about to end. The Pacific Crest Trail route is ever-changing. The guidebook publishers try to compensate for this by sending out annual revision pamphlets, giving backpackers the latest instructions for

---

* This passage is a riff on ideas presented in Rebecca Solnit's *As Eve Said to the Serpent: On Pandscape, Gender, and Art*, Athens, Ga.: University of Georgia Press, 2001, pp. 70–71.

changes and diversions. But Allison and I, for some reason, did
not have the most updated directions through the nearly waterless territory that lay just to the north of us. The Tehachapi
Mountains, row upon row of coffee-stained wisdom teeth in
the distance, were our problem now. Essentially, we would be
walking blind into those foothills.

With no reliable signs to guide us, we took some comfort
in the form of the Joshua trees, which Fremont unfairly ma-
ligned as "stiff and ungraceful . . . The most repulsive tree in the
vegetable kingdom." Each Joshua tree had layer upon layer of
spiked growths peeled back as if unseen hands were trying to
reach something deep inside them. At the end of each branch
were foot-long bayonets in clusters, the spines folded down
the trunk to make armor. Allison and I took snapshots of each
other and tried to find shade beneath the Joshua trees' arms
when the sun cut out through the cloud layers and burst into
flame. The Joshuas enchanted us with their pretzel-logic shapes,
even as they counted our steps, for Joshua trees define the borders of the Mojave. When you no longer see them, you know
you've found your way out of the desert. In fact, I'm surprised
Fremont, "The Pathfinder," wasn't more grateful to Joshua trees
for guiding him out of the wasteland.

But the Joshua trees couldn't tell us whether we were still on
the PCT or not. Trail markers were becoming rare. Some were
shot through with bullet holes or decapitated. Most, it seemed,
had been stolen. For all we knew, we were the last hikers of the
season. We were about to leave this dirt road for a path into the
foothills. No one would find us staggering around up there.

The next reliable water was more than seven miles away, at
Cottonwood Creek, according to my best calculations. Given
our track record for screwing up out here, I knew we would
overshoot that water. If we wound up lost in the Tehachapis, it
could take us days to fight our way to the other side. Why not
turn back this instant? What about the goal was stronger than

fear? I wanted to ask Allison this question but could not bring myself to say the words. Allison looked up at the dry Tehachapis, which were just ahead of us. She pointed at them with her thumb and remarked that we were going "straight up that" with no way of knowing if we were heading the right way, which meant we wouldn't know where to find water or how to reach the highway on the other side. The trail was not even a trail anymore; we followed plastic markers sticking feebly out of the ground.

In the early afternoon we arrived at a wall, the concrete surface covered with graffiti, including a red-and-black helmeted racer, his front wheel pointed to the sky. And just when I thought the Mojave could not throw out any more riddles, I heard crunching footsteps in the bushes. I whirled to see a thin man, six feet tall, dirty and limping, coming straight for us. Dust clouds rose behind him. He moved with speed and determination, though he dragged one leg behind him like a branch.

And he was laughing.

Chapter 11

The
Gingerbread Man

How did he find us here, in the spot where our path vanished in a twist of rabbit brush, a spool of concertina wire to my left, a culvert to my right? He must have been following for some time, hiding in the shadows. He slowed as he advanced. A light-refracting patina of sunburn and crud had turned him orange. In his right hand he carried a ski pole, in the other, a tattered plastic sack. I braced myself for what would happen next. He'd beg for loose change, come at us with a knife he'd whittled from a spoon, or try to drink our stove fuel. I straightened up and looked him dead on in the face. Out here, in the desert, I had to keep my chin high, push my chest out, and never show the slightest fear.

"Dan and Allison!" the hobo roared. I almost wet my pants.

How the hell did he know our names? Evasive action came to mind, but I deliberately muddied my thoughts—when your antagonist might be psychic, you dare not reveal the plan, not even to yourself—but what to do? He was getting closer. "Dan and Allison" he yowled. "I've been waiting seventy miles to say those words."

Jesus Christ, I thought to myself. Seventy miles? So it was true, he'd been following us. I turned to Allison to corroborate my fear, but her facial expression drifted somewhere between amusement and torpor. I took another close look at the stranger, and slowly, gradually, came the realization, like waking from a nightmare. The man was not a beggar, drunk, or hobo. He was a Pacific Crest Trail hiker. Still, he was an odd one, even for my subgroup. He wore a blue bandanna around his head, babushka-style, and wraparound shades, the kind you see on cataract patients at the beach. His pack leaned to one side. He had a filthy foam-rubber sleeping pad and a bunched-up sleeping bag strapped to it. The man had a constant smile, as if delighted at his odor and his entourage of gnats. With no prompting, he announced, "I am the Gingerbread Man."

"And we are lost," Allison said.

"Yeeee-haw!" the Gingerbread Man said, as if our being lost were the funniest joke he'd heard in a while. He had a Texas accent, thick as Karo syrup. "Mark the postman told me all about you."

"Oh no," Allison said. "What did Mark say?"

"Too bad you guys didn't hike the Appalachian Trail first. It passes through towns. Lots of water sources. Great training trail. Very forgiving. They've got piped-in water and shelters. The Pacific Crest Trail's very unforgiving. It doesn't let you make mistakes."

"We only make mistakes," Allison said. "This is way more hardship than we thought."

"Hardship," said the Gingerbread Man, saying the word slowly, savoring it. "Hardship is what it's all about."

He offered to be our guide through the mountains. When I asked if this would inconvenience him, or exhaust him if we ended up hiking until sundown, he let out another deafening yee-haw. "I could hike all day and all night if you want!"

Without waiting for us to announce our decision, the Gingerbread Man began to move at a fast pace up a hill leading into the Tehachapis, with Allison tagging close behind him. I fell behind. A wind picked up. I could see them talking but could not hear them. I felt a surge of surprising jealousy as Allison raced forward to keep up with him, her head cocked close to his as he shared a revelation. She giggled. And yet, as I hurried, I couldn't tell which one of them was making me more jealous: Allison, for her school-girl enthusiasm, or the Gingerbread Man, for sharing some tidbit with her. I was relieved when we stopped to filter water at Cottonwood Creek, a pipe-fed trough. We headed up treeless switchbacks. The tread grew faint as we walked ever higher into the hills above the Mojave, now an expanse of white glare to the east.

The desert dropped out from under us as we rose up a series of crumbled-rock foothills, moving in and out of canyons full of scraggly live-oak bushes, with flies rising off the branches like smoke. The Gingerbread Man followed six-inch survey stakes pounded in the hard ground. A few stray Joshua trees reached with crooked arms. The Gingerbread Man, without even pausing for breath, reached in his pack and pulled out a dairy-free snack. He had wheat-germ Pop Tart knockoffs, corn chips, and a bag filled with some kind of dried fruit or vegetable that looked like small shrunken heads. Many of his food items looked like their expiration date had run out long ago. This turned out to be true. "Some of this stuff I've had in my pack since Mexico," he said. "And that was five hundred miles ago!"

Pumped up with vegan energy, he surged ahead. Allison, taking a breather, motioned me to pass her on a high switchback. Then it was my turn to listen to him, while wondering how a person could walk more than three miles an hour uphill, with a limp and a sack of junk in his arms. Normally Allison and I walked only two miles an hour. The Gingerbread Man planned to walk twenty miles that day. Normally we did fifteen. I had to jog-walk to keep up, sweating. We reached a ravine, and he left me in the dust as he scrambled up the sides to "bag" a lump of sandstone rising twenty feet off the ridge. "Ooooooh-weeeeeee," he screamed. Astride the lump, he shot his arms in the sky in his best Christ pose. With its black gullies, punishing switchbacks, and hills, the land looked like the sort of stark backdrop against which they might shoot a low-rent Bible film. With Allison well behind us now, he climbed down and paused in front of a shaggy plant with a licorice smell. He undid his shorts, yanked them halfway down, and peed, like a riot hose, all over the shrub, while bellowing, "Live again, desert plant. I water thee!" We could hear Allison trying to catch up, mumbling something derogatory about the desert all around us. She was following close behind me, and I was right behind the Gingerbread Man, and then we were all hiking together, as fast as we could go, when the Gingerbread Man suddenly stopped in front of us, and I had to stop in my tracks to avoid a three-way pileup in the desert. He whirled around and started chanting about the desert's wonderful attributes.

"Your clothes dry fast here! You can wear tennis shoes instead of boots! You don't need a big tent! Let's hear it for the desert!"

And right then and there, he started clapping for the wasteland. I clapped, too. I didn't want to be rude.

It was a peculiar display, but I couldn't help myself. I was starting to like him now, against my better judgment. The Gingerbread Man, it seemed, was the Nerd King of the desert, the man who knew how to find all the water, who tried to help his fellow hikers, and had even developed his own technique to immobilize a tick. All you have to do, he later explained, is pinch it in a certain place "to paralyze it temporarily, and feed it

to ant lions, who love to drag them screaming into their lairs."
His bursts of arcane wisdom made me more forgiving when
he strutted around braying Edward Abbey–esque observations
about every juniper bush and crested lizard. Besides, he made
Allison and me feel taken care of for the first time on the trail.
She turned to me at one point and said, "No matter what happens, we're not gonna die in this section."

The Gingerbread Man was a bike messenger who, though
he was thirty-two—six years older than us, impossibly old it
seemed—lived with his mom and dad in Houston. "Amazing,"
Allison whispered in my ear. "Where does the guy get all his energy?" The Gingerbread Man told us he had a crush on a woman and was trying to woo her with letters he composed while
camped on lonely hillsides. Allison asked if the woman liked him
back. He just smiled in a dopey way. We offered to mail the letter for him at Tehachapi, but he wasn't through with it. "I want
to get it right," he said. "I'm an Aries. That means I've got to do
something in a thorough way. I've got to finish what I start."
That, he said, is why he kayaked the Mississippi, where ships
threatened to squash him like a water bug, and biked through
Death Valley in summer. To pay for these excursions, he did odd
jobs, working hard at a parcel service but often finding fault with
the bosses, whom he did not refer to as "sons of bitches," prefer-
ring the gender-nonspecific "sons of bastards," which questioned
their birthrights without impugning their mamas.

A few hours after we started our power walk with him, he
paused at an anonymous hill where the PCT tread disappeared.
"Oh, noooo, an intersection," he howled, and then laughed.
When at last he found the trail, he stooped down and picked
up a few jagged rocks and piled them up, starting with the
widest rock and working up, adding smaller rocks as the tower
rose. "It's a cairn," he said. "That way folks behind us will know
which way to go." Leaving signs was his responsibility, he said,
because the trail was a brotherhood. "I always leave a sign," he

said. "The trail here's so primitive." He squinted into the wind. "You've got to pretend that you're the guys who built the trail. You've got to learn to think like they do."

When Allison got tired and fell far behind again, the Gingerbread Man and I took a break in the shade of Tylerhorse Canyon, lined with stout junipers and pines with cones in fishhook shapes. "Better find ourselves a nice piece of real estate. Gotta wait for the woman," he said. I laughed a little at his seemingly chauvinistic comment. I asked him about his trail nickname. He said it came from a folktale about a cookie boy who outruns all his pursuers. At last he dead-ends at a river, where a fox gives him a ride across and then submerges bit by bit until the cookie boy is forced to stand on the fox's snout. Then the fox devours him. What a lousy ending. You run fast, do your best, then fall for a stupid trick and die. But the Gingerbread Man didn't look as though he took this depressing lesson to heart. For one thing, he seemed insane, not in a threatening way but in the manner of a man whose devotion to something larger than himself had rewired his brain. He had the never-ending smile of someone who'd cashed in his marbles for something more important.

The Gingerbread Man pulled a needle from a pine and stuck it between his teeth, letting it linger. It was a fine, clear day. He bit the needle and fixed his gaze southeast toward the snow-topped pyramids above the desert floor. San Gorgonio Mountain and Mount San Jacinto formed a wall to the south. "Hellacious view," he said. We slouched in the shade, lying with no thoughts of getting up, swatting yellow jackets as the Gingerbread Man launched into a rant against the USDA food pyramid. He believed most Americans had been brainwashed "by bureaucrats trying to make you believe there's a proven human necessity, or for that matter, digestibility, of milk after weaning, especially from other species." He railed about the dairy industry and the federal government in general. "You know," he said, "that's the reason I came here in the first place."

"To get away from milk?" I asked below my breath.

He winced. The Gingerbread Man believed humans had, for far too long, "denied the animal nature of our bodies." He articulated this philosophy in a series of op ed pieces he'd written for his hometown weekly newsletter. After years of conventional living, he'd had enough of a government that, in his view, was forcing the public to eat "wimpy, pre-chewed food" like burgers, fries, and shakes. "Meanwhile, the government tells you that fruits and vegetables are rabbit foods for nerds. This only makes sense when you understand that by America's standards, car-driving, car-dependent couch potatoes have a higher virility status than conscientious walkers."

Allison caught up at last. The sun, fiery a moment ago, was lower in the sky now. She limped. I got up, dusted myself off, and comforted her. "I'll cook dinner for you tonight," I promised, without telling her that dinner would probably be a dismal brick of Big Bill's Beans and Rice, a blob of freeze-dried crud that could cramp the bowels of Satan himself. Allison staggered toward the Gingerbread Man. There were tears in her eyes from the blisters and discomfort. "Just look at you with your pathetic blister walk!" he said when he saw her. Allison recoiled in shock, but then she doubled up, laughing so hard she forgot to start up crying again.

But the laughter died down as the day wore on. Soon we were wheezing and scrambling, forcing ourselves to gulp water and walk at the same time, lest we lose the Gingerbread Man. He took only one five-minute break per hour. By 5:00 P.M., it was all we could do to catch a glimpse of his skinny retreating backside. Mercifully, at 6:00 P.M., he decided we'd all had enough and looked for a place for us to sleep.

"Set your tent down wherever you want," he said as the sun sank below the blades of a wind-energy farm, blades spinning in the breeze, whirring. The sun glinted, like beach glass, on something shiny in the desert far below us. "I bet you guys want your privacy," he said as he watched a distant town fade in the dark. "Set up wherever you like." The Gingerbread Man smiled, sat on a flat-topped rock overlooking the ridge, and crossed his arms over his chest as the sun went away. He reached in his bag and took out miniature versions of the Mexican, U.S., and Canadian flags—a reference to the PCT connecting the borders of three countries—and twirled them in his hands, humming softly to himself and grinning.

Soon it was dinnertime. Cooking dinner was the usual ordeal, with Allison concentrating hard as the water began to warm up. The Gingerbread Man carried no stove. He ate his food cold. After a while, he pulled himself into his tent, little more than a glorified sleeping container with a metal frame to hold it up. He was ready for bed by the time our water was boiling.

I woke up at three in the morning and stepped outside my tent. The Milky Way was frozen foxfire. Satellites blinked. I kept thinking about the Gingerbread Man's peculiar limp. Allison had mumbled something about him telling her the story behind it, about how he had kicked some rock or heavy box in a fit of anger. It surprised me that someone like him, a gentle spirit, would lash out in such a way and hurt himself. It got me thinking, once again, about the reasons for these expeditions, for difficult trips, and wondering if everyone brought along some kind of internal or external injury. Perhaps those wounds are the motivating factors. I'd posed the same question to myself but could not get a straight answer. Was it some unspoken childhood trauma that had brought me here? Or was it the accumulation of those niggling little memories I could never forget, like the one of that goose that went insane and mauled me in that petting zoo in Virginia?

It was during a family vacation. The goose seemed so sweet at first. I fed him a nice big piece of stale bread, and it seemed like we were sharing a moment. Then, out of nowhere, came the goosey fury, the white eyes bulging, the orange beak stabbing as I fled screaming. The goose accelerated—he was fast as hell—and I found myself cornered near the Shetland pony enclosure. No one in my family helped. They just stood there smiling, pointing, snapping so many photos that I could stack the snapshots together now, make a flip-book, and watch the attack unfold in real time fifteen years later. Is that what this trail was all about? Tending to psychic wounds inflicted by poultry?

I had gone back to sleep in the tent, half awake, half dreaming, still processing the petting-zoo memory, when a loud braying noise woke me up. The sky was purple, the sun wasn't up, and yet the Gingerbread Man was ready to walk, with our without us. "Up, time to leave!" he shouted. I emerged from my tent. Allison and I doddered into the cold, taking down our tent as fast as we could, but the Gingerbread Man grew impatient—there were miles to cover—and he left without a word. We ran to catch up, our shirts halfway off, our packs hanging off one shoulder. "No more," I said to myself between gasps. "This just isn't worth it." This was not going to work. I felt as if we'd met someone who might one day be a good friend of ours, and yet sometimes I wanted to stick out my boot and trip him. I appreciated his leadership and guidance, and the way the outdoors seemed benevolent when we were with him, but I longed for self-determination, to hike at my own pace and put the trail in my hands again. Besides, we were hungry, and our packs were full of wrappers, used toilet paper, and other trash that we needed to discard.

We broke up with the Gingerbread Man about ten miles later, or he broke up with us. He had enough provisions so he didn't need to reload in Tehachapi, our destination. The trail was like that sometimes, a turnstile where you never knew who would take the next man's place. "I can never hike with anybody for too long," the Gingerbread Man had said. "After a while we always split up on the trail. There was a guy who hiked with me last week. The most fastidious hiker I've ever met. His trail name's Doctor John. He had to have his bootlaces perfect before he started out every morning. I'm probably the only hiker who could deal with hiking with him for long."

Before leaving us, Gingerbread Man told us it was time we got a proper trail name. "I came up with it last night before I went to sleep," he said as we sat for a while by a stream flowing like a miracle through the bulrushes near the trail, "I'm thinking you should call yourselves the Lois and Clark Expedition, since you're reporters and all. What do you think?"

Allison and I looked at each other, for we knew he'd bestowed upon us a great favor. At that moment, "Dan and Allison" fell to our feet like a molted snakeskin. We were real explorers now. In one instant, the Gingerbread Man had elevated our trip from mere nature walk to full-fledged "expedition." To get a trail name from a respected hiker is like passing an audition. Once you get a name, you become a "trail character," with full membership in the backpackers' cult, a shambling procession of hermits and acolytes making its slow way north toward Monument 78. Besides, we were lucky to get a great trail name. I've known some people who got seriously screwed with their trail monikers. Take, for example, the widely disliked physician who became known as Doctor Dickhead.

That morning, the Gingerbread Man walked us close to the highway shoulder. We didn't know what to say to each other. It's awkward to share a trail with someone, then go around a bend, reach a junction, and know you'll never see him again. He reached in his pack, pulled out a container of translucent goo, and insisted we slosh some on our armpits. "Smells like Ivory," he said. "That way you won't worry about stinking up the car when you hitchhike." We turned to watch him limp into the foothills, his backpack leaning.

In a moment the Gingerbread Man was gone behind a stand of high reeds.

Chapter 12

Doctor John

The vision of the Gingerbread Man lingered long after he left us. He proved by example that people who succeed on the Pacific Crest Trail aren't necessarily strapping or macho like Todd the Sasquatch. Gawky folks with strange sunglasses and chicken legs can do just fine out there, too. The trail doesn't care if you're awkward. The trail doesn't judge you if you're the kind of guy who received more than his share of wedgies, swirlies, and wet willies in middle school. To succeed on the trail, you don't have to be muscular or cute. All you have to do is join the brotherhood and form a secret pact with all the lizards and coyotes. You must accept a certain amount of chaos and confusion as givens, and figure out how to incorporate these things into your life without losing your mind. You must not be uptight or selfish. You've got to leave a cairn of piled stones so the next guy won't get lost. The wilderness is not out to hurt you. The trail isn't out to harm you, either. You just have to become one with the trail, while channeling the collective unconsciousness of those who dwell on this gentle footpath. Or something like that.

In any case, I felt renewed, invigorated, when we left the trail and reached the shoulder of the two-lane Tehachapi Willow Springs Road near a field of dried-out poppies. My only fear was getting from the trailhead to town in one piece. I mean that literally. I'd never hitchhiked in my life. All the newspaper horror stories I'd read about hitchhiking came to mind. They all had an opening paragraph along the lines of "Dan and Allison were a fresh-faced couple. They thought they could thumb their way to Tehachapi." Second paragraph: "But they never made it. Their blowtorch-singed, rat-nibbled remains were found in a Dumpster in Sioux Falls, South Dakota." But Tehachapi was 9.4 miles west of the Pacific Crest Trail. We were starving for burgers, anxious to get supplies, and had no option other than hitchhiking. Car after car whooshed past. Allison hopped up and down, waving a sign reading WEST. She threw in a go-go kick, to no avail. I asked her to "show a little leg," but she pointed out that perverts were the last people we wanted to attract, and besides, she was already wearing shorts. I wagged my thumb all over the place. Drivers just made faces and sped up. At last a white step van with a blue HANDICAPPED card slid to the shoulder and rolled to a stop.

The side door swung open. Behind the wheel sat a sixty-ish woman, heavyset and smelling of cloves. She wore her long ponytail beneath a straw hat. A crested bird with an orange beak stood on the armrest to the right of the driver's seat. "Come in," the woman said. "I'm Samantha and this is Barry. She indicated a white cockatoo sitting in the passenger seat. He's quite a talker." Barry said nothing. We shoved the packs in the back. The woman was a paraplegic. Although the car had a regular steering wheel, the brake and accelerator were mounted below the dashboard; it looked like the controls on an Atari video game. We pulled the door closed. Samantha put the joystick to the floor and the four of us took off like a dustbowl hurricane. After 109 miles and 10 days on the trail, the pitch-forward

sensation of motion thrilled me. Allison opened the window a
crack and the wind ruffled her sweat-stiffened hair.

The Tehachapi Mountains were brawny and tan in the
sun, their folds hiding stables and settlements. On the hills,
electricity-generating windmills spun. We sped past them on
the way to the city, just below the mountain range of the same
name at the southern boundary of the San Joaquin Valley, a
jumping-off point to the southern end of Sierra Nevada, the
430-mile-long granite batholith to the north. Here, forty miles
from Bakersfield, we would reconnect, rest up, and prepare to
take on one more section of pig-dirt desert, frying-pan sunshine, and chaparral foothills before entering John Muir's range
of light. We were heading to a town of many identities, on
the edges of steep terrain where Kawaisu Indians had hunted
game and gathered piñon nuts. You'd be hard-pressed to find
a Kawaisu now—they're lost to time—but they left behind a
name: *Tehachapi,* or *Tihacipia,* or *Tah-ee-chay-Pah,* depending on
your phonetics skills. Historians can't agree on the meaning.
They've interpreted *Tehachapi* to mean "hard-climbing place,"
"sweet water," "windy place," "cold place," and "place of many
acorns."

For us, every meaning was appropriate: hard climbing to be
here, the sweet waters of rest and pent-up sex, the cold wind
against the van and the promise of long-awaited gorging on
burgers and pancakes. Randy Travis's nasal tenor oozed from
the tape deck. We all sang along with the tune, with the bird
screaming, "Grackety grack shit," in the background. Allison
smiled at the wind and the weepy sound of the steel guitar. I
smiled, too, though I felt a twinge of something unexplainable.
The song, the stranger, the sing-along. It was all too perfect, like
that moment inside the Conestoga wagon circle in the purple
midnight of a cowboy movie, where one of the fellas says, "It's
just a little too quiet out there, aint it?" What was the catch?
Where was the trick? The PCT can work that way, make you

think a wrong turn is around the next bend, even when the going is clear. Then I realized I was being silly, thinking too much. It was time to relax.

Samantha let us out in "Old Town Tehachapi," a street of low-slung Western-style buildings near a train depot–themed park with green grass and kids climbing on unused trains standing about like statuary. The street had a dusty look as if the buildings could use a splash of paint or a few words of encouragement, and some of the buildings had flimsy wooden railings, the kind that cowboys are always crashing through in Western-movie fight scenes. It was exciting to us: antiques shops, Laundromats, food, possibility. We checked into a motel. The place was run by an owlish lady who couldn't give one rip about our hike, our room was close to the railroad tracks, the furniture was dingy, and the walls had fist-size holes in them, but who cares? To us, it was the Waldorf Astoria.

"Oh my God, running water," Allison said from the bathroom. The shower was sensational, hot water pulsing, our dirt twirling down the drain like Janet Leigh's blood in *Psycho*.

True, we'd been out in the wilderness for only ten days before coming to town, but desert hiking can warp your perspective, making time stretch out like taffy. We'd allowed the desert to chasten us a bit, and take the edge off our itchy lust for each other. Sun and dust suck the chi force out of man and woman. After a while, you forget you are lovers. There's nothing like a twenty-nine-dollar-a-night motel to make you remember. After two hot showers each, Allison and I could hardly wait to make love in the creaky bed. Allison's wet towel fell to the ground. She was all sunburned neck and blond hair, and with her skin washed clean, she'd never looked more beautiful. Before the trail, both of us lacked muscle tone and color. She now looked longer and taller than usual, as if the bed elongated her as she lay there beneath a poorly rendered oil painting of a chuck wagon charging across a bleak and smeary tundra. The bed bucked and wobbled beneath us, rusty coils squeaking. I felt very much in love then, as if the two of us were celebrating a trial that had made us stronger as a couple, a Mojave litmus test. Afterward, we lay in bed with no thoughts of ever getting up again. The original plan was to spend one night in Tehachapi, then take off early the next morning. But we had so much to do, and were having such a good time, that we decided to prolong our stay.

Next morning the two of us, all showered up and blissed out, took a stroll through town. I was stupidly happy, my arm around my girl, my hand pinching her bottom. Retrieving our first supply of gear and food at the local post office was a joyous experience. It was hard to contain myself when the postal clerk stooped to hoist a twenty-five-pound cardboard box of loot that Allison's parents had mailed to us general delivery from the Midwest. I stabbed it twice in the belly with my Swiss Army knife; out came Snickers, Ziploc bags of espresso-spiked chocolate mousse powder, Farley's Gummi Dinosaurs, dried cherries from Michigan, freeze-dried meals, and DEET spray in plastic bottles. We walked to the other side of town, where we found a wondrous assortment of monolithic, predatory, slave-wage–paying chain stores selling every conceivable kind of lotion, gummi creature, and body wash. One of them had a whole aisle dedicated entirely to scrunchies. There we bought lanolin for our feet, deodorant for our armpits, and moleskin for our blisters.

By then, it was time for brunch. Stout cowboys left a diner, one hand on their guts, the other greeting us with a two-fingered wave, a rural peace sign gesture, in which they propped up their Stetsons with a thumb and forefinger. We waved back. Their satisfied expressions led us to try the diner, which was packed with people, its walls lined with black-and-white photos of a quake that jackhammered the town in 1952. Ravenous, we ducked in and found a booth.

On the trail, it is possible to eat six thousand calories worth of food every day and lose weight. That's why layovers in towns are a sanctioned form of exercise bulimia. In town, hikers can gorge on burgers, shakes, and anything else they please. I had heard stories about a PCT hiker who ate a stick of butter, peeling it like a banana. I felt even hungrier when I saw the people in the diner. They ate like wood chippers. All around were the sounds of smacking mouths. We ordered eggs over hard, biscuits in gravy, and sausages on the side. In towns, you expect to see fellow PCT hikers pigging out. Perhaps that's why I noticed a thin man in the corner of the diner, alone, ignoring his orange juice while an egg congealed on his plate. Why was he not joining in on the gluttony? His joylessness made him stand out like the shy one at an orgy.

There he sat, slouching but meticulous, picking at some unseen annoyance in his beard. A lentil? A bug? His plaid shirt and khaki shorts were beige from washed-out mud and desert dust. His skin was tan, and his pack was covered with dirt. No doubt, he was a Pacific Crest Trail hiker, and yet this realization did not fill me with joy. His woeful countenance made me want to turn away. I wondered why he looked lethargic and depressed as he leaned into his juice and sniffed the rim of the glass. He kept glancing toward us and frowning, but when I'd look back, he'd stare at the table top as if embarrassed. The stranger winced. At last he rose and made his way toward us, a twiggy figure passing rows of fat bodies. "Dan and Allison? Is it you?" he said. He leaned over our biscuits. "Did you meet the Gingerbread Man? We hiked together but we broke up, as hiking partners, I mean. He left me a note, saying you'd gone to town, so I found you. I know it's you. Remember Mark the postman, back in Agua Dulce? He said you were nice but a little unprepared." He gave me his right hand. His fingers were cool and tapered. "I'm Doctor John," he said. "But I'm only a doctor in the Ph.D. sense. Mathematics, actually. I kept looking over at you, trying to get your attention. You kept looking away. It seemed like you were trying to avoid me." His voice was squeaky.

"That isn't true," I said, suddenly vaguely remembering that the Gingerbread Man had warned us of a fussy and difficult hiker coming up behind us. Allison smiled up at him, but I didn't like this intrusion. All I wanted was to be alone with my girlfriend. I wished we were in our motel room again, making the bed rattle and squeak. "Pleased to meet you," Allison said. She rose halfway out of her seat to shake his hand. "How are you doing?"

"Well . . ." he said as he sat down at the table, across from me, next to Allison. "I'm all right, I guess. Actually, it's been very hard. I haven't been doing the trail. The trail has been doing me. I can never quite figure out how much water to bring. Water is so heavy, so I never end up drinking quite enough. Just the other day I was hiking and it was quite warm outside, hot, actually, and my pee, pardon my language, my urine was getting very dark, turning pink, and after a while I could barely urinate at all. I finally came across a bottle of water that someone had left behind, and I thought, well, should I drink it? Should I take this? Suppose someone else needs it more than I do? And then I thought to myself, well, who needs it more than I do? Who? And then I started to cry."

There's nothing as miserable as being thirsty in a desert. I understood this as well as anyone. But why did he have to talk about pee while we were eating? Perhaps I'm oversensitive but I can't bear it when people talk about snot, pee, blood, sweat, mucous, musk, ejaculate, excreta, or the particulars of animal husbandry while I'm enjoying my breakfast.

"And in that dehydrated state of mind," Doctor John said, continuing with his story, "I almost stepped on a rattlesnake. Anyway, there it was, right on the trail, in the middle there, tongue flickering away, and I didn't realize I was about to step on him, not until my boot was hanging in space. In midair I somehow managed to switch my stride to a standing long jump. Up and over the snake I flew."

I sighed, sensing what was coming. This man—seemingly depressive, struggling with every step of the trail—would want to team up with the Lois and Clark Expedition. And I could tell, even after our brief exchange, that this would be disastrous for all three of us. Morale was of the utmost importance at this part of our journey. Allison and I had just gone through a difficult introduction to the PCT. Somehow we had made it through and found happiness in Tehachapi, but our joy was as fragile as the wings of a ghost moth. I had to take care not to let hardship put a damper on our sex life and well-being at this juncture. I did not want a fifth wheel on our expedition, especially one with fatalistic tendencies and a preternatural eagerness to talk about bodily functions.

"I have a poem I made up," Doctor John said. "It helps me forget about my feet, which are in agony all the time. Would you like to hear it?"

"Um . . ." I said.

"It goes like this," Doctor John said. "My feet can not harm me / How can they harm me? / When my feet, my feet, my feet do not exist." He rested a hand on Allison's shoulder and said, "I'll be right back. Save me my place at the table. I might be gone for a while. I'm going to the rest room. In fact, I may be sitting down in there."

I felt a knot in my stomach. Sitting down in there? There was no reason he had to share that detail with me. I stared with dismay at my black and coiled sausages. When Doctor John left us alone, I grabbed Allison's hand. "Sweetheart," I said, "can we go back to the motel?"

"We haven't paid."

"Okay, but when the check comes, can we get out of here?"

She smiled at me. "I'm not done eating."

"Listen," I said. "Nothing against the guy. Nice enough fellow. But we absolutely cannot hike with this guy. Here's what we'll do. We're gonna get out of town early, first thing in the morning, just get out of town the second we get out of bed tomorrow."

"Would you listen to yourself?" Allison said. "Could you please just stop and take a deep breath? I don't want you freaking out on me."

"Listen to me," I said. "All we have is one more section of desert to go and then we're home free. One more section! Then it's mountains, glaciers, gorgeous country, meadows, and wildflowers all the way to Canada. But this next section is going to kick our asses. It's gonna be hard enough as it is. I don't want anybody weighing us down."

"Whatever," she said. "Either way, it's no big deal."

My increasing panic might seem silly or peculiar to those who have never hiked a national scenic trail. But when you're on the PCT, it's impossible to escape from someone if he or she has the same pace as you. The trail is 2,650 miles long, but it's only 3 to 10 feet wide. There are crawl spaces wider than that. The trail can be claustrophobic unless you set boundaries with people, which I've never been able to do.

Allison shook her head and frowned at her biscuit. "He might be a little strange, but you're blowing this out of proportion. If you don't feel comfortable hiking with him, why don't you just tell him?"

"No way," I said. "I couldn't live with myself. Can you imagine how much that's gonna hurt his feelings?"

"Sooner or later, you're going to have to get over your ridiculous fear of confrontation."

"You don't understand. What if it gets back to the Gingerbread Man that we blew off Doctor John? Remember how he said the trail is a brotherhood? After all he did for us. He's gonna think we're a couple of raging assholes."

"Why don't you just relax?" She spied Doctor John emerging from the latrine. "Here he comes. I bet you're making a big deal over nothing at all. I bet you he won't even mention it."

Doctor John sat back down at our table. "Will you hike with me?" he said.

I froze. He waited for our answer, looking annoyed. "It's not a complicated question," he said. Allison and I just stared at each other.

"Listen," I said. "We'd love to hike with you. But we're . . . unfortunately leaving early in the morning."

"Early?" Doctor John said. "When?"

"Maybe too early for you," I said.

"Could you be more specific?"

"Crack of dawn," I said. "When do you get up?"

"Seven," Doctor John said. "I don't like getting up any earlier than that, not normally, or I'm tired for the rest of the day."

"Well, that might not work," I said. "Because we'll probably have to leave at six."

"Oh?" Doctor John said.

"Six?" Allison said.

"That is a little early," Doctor John said. "Though I suppose I could drag myself out of bed this one time if we all wanted to hike together. And it does make sense that we stick together. It's safer that way. Besides, we're all such slow walkers."

"I probably should make myself clearer," I said. "We'll start hiking at six. But that really means we'd have to get up at five. Or four, depending on how much time we give ourselves to hitch a ride and get out to the trailhead."

"Four?" Allison said, giving me a look that could etch glass.

"That's silly," Doctor John said. "I don't see why you'd need to get up *so* early."

The waitress brought the check.

"Where are you staying?" Doctor John said.

Allison, after some hesitation, mumbled the name of our motel.

"I'll follow you there," Doctor John said.

Back in our motel room, we were sitting around, watching television, when we heard a thump at the door. I feared it was Doctor John but when I opened the door, a cowboy stood there. "I'm Dave," he said, "and I'm here to check the electrical wiring in your room." We let him in. Dave looked to be in his early fifties. He had a cowboy hat, big hands, blue jeans, and a pot belly. When he found out we were PCT hikers, he gave us a concerned look. "I used to cowboy all through the foot-hills where you'll be walking tomorrow. You've got some hard miles ahead." He looked at our light switches and squinted at the ceiling light. "Everything looks fine to me. Anyways, I'm sorry to disturb you, and I think you hikers are some of the finest people I've ever met. Always looking out for one other. Tell you what. You need a ride back to the trailhead tomorrow morning, you got it. I'll take you anywhere you want."

"That's fantastic," Allison said.

"How early can you leave?" I said.

Chapter 13

Operation
Water Dump

It was 4:00 A.M. and my head was swimming. I'd barely slept that night, knowing that Doctor John was two doors down at the motel, probably wide awake and dreaming up ways to ruin the Lois and Clark Expedition. Time to get the hell out of Tehachapi. Time to get away from Doctor John and his poetry. Time to flee from his existential anecdotes about sadness, dehydration, loneliness, and his strawberry chiffon–colored urine. Doctor John had told us that he rarely woke before seven. That's why we were leaving at five. But what if he was fibbing, and was waiting for us outside the room right now? I knew Dave wouldn't be late, and he'd blast us back to the trail in no time at all. But Allison was still asleep, in spite of all my fidgeting.

She stayed asleep, even when I flicked on the motel light. In a man's life, there is nothing worse than having to wake up a woman—that awful sinking moment when you shake her shoulder and know that her eyes will open wide, that they will fix on you like motion sensors. Suddenly the beatific expression, the innocence of sleep, melts from her face, and in its place a look of disgust comes over her as she remembers all the annoying things you said and did the previous evening. No, I couldn't bring myself to shake her awake. Instead I lurched about the motel room hoping all my crashing and stumbling would rouse her so it would look like an accident. I tried to find all our stuff, which wasn't easy, for we'd trashed the motel room pretty thoroughly. It looked as if two vaguely hominid creatures from four or five hundred thousand years ago had bedded down for the evening after leaving coal-black footprints on the tiles and filthy garments hanging from the cabinets. Air-dried socks dangled, like drying meat, from the curtain cords. Ski-pole walking sticks tilted like clubs over a copy of Gideon's Bible. Was the trail turning us wild? Is that why I felt so claustrophobic in the motel, so eager to return to the woods? The motel had been a luxury the day before, but now it just seemed weird, with rock-hard curtains against the window, not to mention the stinky little soaps, pink and beige but smelling the same, and the weird paper stripe that housekeeping had stretched over the toilet bowl, as if its inaugural use was an occasion of great pomp and circumstance, a ribbon-cutting ceremony. The time on the clock radio was 4:20. Then it was 4:21. I waited for what seemed like ten minutes, and looked at the clock again. Now it was 4:22.

At last she opened her eyes. She pulled the strands of blond hair out of her face, and I saw the blue eyes that had pulled me in so deeply when we worked in the newsroom together. Allison had a lopsided smile, perhaps left over from a dream she'd had. As I predicted, the smile turned to a wince when she saw me stumble in and out of the bathroom, my hands stuffed with gear, my face grave. She got up, and through the open bathroom door, I could see her make a war face to the mirror as she flossed, working her gum line, massaging each incisor. Allison was thorough and careful. She often talked to me about the importance of rationality and not panicking, and how our expedition was a Democracy of Two, founded on respect and reason, not guesswork and silly craziness. That week, she expressed her desire to have no more fuckups involving water and getting thirsty and walking in circles. All that rational thinking irked me. I believed that real expeditions should be built on improvisation, bravery, and flights of fancy, not caution. All this planning was bringing me down. I wanted to break away from our constant caution. I wanted to be more spontaneous, free, and inventive, like the Gingerbread Man. I wanted to be bold and unconventional, like the Jardi-Nazis. Allison told me that the next reliable water source, Golden Oak Spring, would be a hot twenty-two miles away. She very carefully filled every water bottle, and our fabric canteen.

She had left nothing to chance, and that's what made me edgy. Nature has a way of turning best-laid plans into goulash. I'd seen Allison's emergency contingency plans for the trail. She thought of everything. On four pieces of notepaper, she'd drawn up a list of all possible things that could go awry, from bear attacks to seizures to "if no pulse and is not breathing at all," and the solutions to all these problems. In a spidery scrawl, she'd written, "If lightning should strike, get off the steep peaks. Crouch on an insulator. Keep clear of ski poles. Caves are dangerous. Treatment if struck? Mouth-to-mouth cardiac massage." As a precaution against getting hypothermia, she advised that we should "not get chilled." If we got bitten by a deadly rattlesnake in a remote corner of the backcountry, the solution, she wrote, would be to "go to the hospital." In a pinch, she wrote, you should "sterilize your blade, make two small cuts by either fang mark, avoid major arteries, and use a suction cup." This frightened me. We did not even have a suction cup. If I had a choice between letting poison dribble through my veins or letting my girlfriend slice me open, I wasn't sure what I would do.

She tried to caution me against irrational thinking. She told me that she didn't want to hike with Doctor John, either, but she continued to insist I was making far too big a deal of it. But her moderation was no match for my obsession. What if Doctor John woke up? Every blinking security lamp in the motel, every distant dog bark, seemed to conspire against us then. "Don't make a squeak," I said to Allison as we walked past Doctor John's room, its Venetian blinds half open, the room still dark. I rushed her so hard we left our walking sticks behind.

Dave stood on the sidewalk in the half-light with his ruddy cheeks and kangaroo boots. Between slurps of thermos coffee, he muttered something about it being "real early, even for a cowboy." Allison and I shoved our things in his truck, which roared into the night toward Tehachapi Pass. Safety dots caught the high beams. Something sleek and marble-eyed crossed the highway. Coyote. I glanced back at its receding form, and the lights of Tehachapi. Good-bye, Doctor John, I said. Have a good life. Fare thee well. See you later, but not if I see you first.

I remember the purple-lumped mountains and the sage-brush lining the road, and behind it, the starlight twinkle of trailer-park lights and the gray clouds above us like the insides of a stuffed animal. Dave's tires rasped on the gravel as he spoke, with Allison, about Merle Haggard and Buck Owens and horses while I only pretended to listen. It's a skill I've perfected, nodding like a bobble-head, inserting a "yup" and an "mmm-hmm-mmm" in all the right places so you never suspect I'm not paying attention. But something was getting on my nerves, a hollow slop sound coming from inside our backpacks. Slip, slap, slop, what the hell was it?

Water, that's what it was. Gallons and gallons of Tehachapi tap water, bouncing in our Nalgene containers. Our packs, which were bulging with water, would be unbelievably heavy, at the very time I was trying to flee from Doctor John. I resented having to carry so much of it. I knew full well that water is quite precious, but it was an indisputable fact that water weighs more than 8.3 pounds to the gallon. Eight point three pounds! Because of the hot terrain, and the 22-mile haul until the next water, we'd agreed to carry two and a half gallons of it just to be safe. It now seemed insane to me. That was 20.75 pounds of water weight. The more I thought about this, and Doctor John's droopy countenance and descriptions of bodily functions, the worse I felt. Suddenly a plan rose to the surface of my thoughts. It burst fully formed from my head. And it was pure genius.

True, most of the water in the human body is concentrated in the bloodstream, which means that if we lost even 10 percent of it, we would probably perish. But what would be the harm if I waited for Allison to turn her back for a moment, and I secretly dumped out, let's say, only 40 percent of our water, or maybe even 50 percent? It would not be that big a deal. It would just mean that we'd have to hike a little faster to Golden Oak Spring. But wouldn't it be easier for us to hike much faster, considering we would be carrying less pack weight, which should mean that we'd walk 40 to 50 percent faster than before? Lord, what a brilliant idea. At that moment, I felt wily and free. Now, at last, I'd have my chance to be like Ray Jardine, unencumbered by useless weight, traveling faster than I ever had before, and improving my comfort with pure ingenuity, with Allison racing by my side toward Canada. We'd stay so far ahead of Doctor John that he'd never even glimpse us on the horizon. We'd make love every night, rhapsodize about the desert sunsets, sweat our way into the High Sierras and pass, without incident, through one of the most arduous sections of the trail. And the most beautiful part of all was this: Allison would never even know I was a hero whose improvisation had saved our adventure.

Chapter 14

Golden Oak Spring

The moon was still up and blazing, and there was the barest trace of sun forcing its way up the side of an eroded cliff. Dave's truck bounced along the dirt road. "Lots of chaparral in these parts," he said. "Steep country here. If you like, I'll drive you north a ways, where the hiking is easier, and you can hike from there." Allison and I shook our heads forcefully. If you're going to hike 2,650 miles, there is no point in cutting out four of them and having the missing piece nag you for the rest of your life. "Whatever you say," Dave said, shrugging. He let us off at Oak Creek Canyon, just off the Tehachapi Willow Springs Road. In a short while it was light enough to hike without a flashlight. The air was cool, and the sky was tinged with violet, as I took the lead, with Allison scooting close behind me. I was smiling like mad about what was about to happen.

The water in my pack bore down on me, and the excessive weight made me sweat, but I didn't let it get me down. I'd get rid of all that extra weight soon enough. Sure, we'd struggled with our first section of trail. Sure, we'd been clumsy and made a few silly mistakes we could have avoided if we'd been thinking clearly. But that was then. All we had to do was make it through this one last section. Soon we'd be in the High Sierra, an unbroken mountain range four hundred miles long, full of rivers that poured through the fingers of granite boulders, rocks flecked with light, hard and sparkling like stardust. An impermeable bubble of safety had formed around us in the Tehachapis. The Gingerbread Man had given us his blessing, and a name, and now it protected us like an amulet. There was no need to be scared anymore.

The Pacific Crest Trail ran into a tangle of wicked plants, Italian thistle, pink fleshy stalks with oval heads and needles pointed in all directions. I braced myself, knowing from experience that these weeds could inflict painful pricks, like yellow-jacket stings. But just when we felt trapped, Allison spied a handwritten note from the Gingerbread Man, stuck beneath a rock, urging us to take his "alternate route" around the thistles. Sure enough, we found a trail of stones rising up a ledge above the plants. We made a victory whoop, for it seemed that the Gingerbread Man, though dozens of miles away, was a guardian angel watching over the Lois and Clark Expedition.

It must have taken him hours to make that rock trail. Something about this act of selflessness made me reconsider my water-dump plan for a moment. "Am I being extreme?" I thought. "Why do I want to dump out our water? Is it just because I want to stay ahead of Doctor John? Am I possibly overreacting? What if something goes wrong with my plan? Even worse, what if Allison found out?"

In tall grass near a spreading oak, we took a snack break. The arms of the tree crisscrossed above our heads to block the sun. I took deep breaths and tried to relax. When our short break was over, we walked on, at a leisurely pace, because it was still nice and cool. I felt so happy and clear-headed at that moment. Something snapped me out of my trance. I decided that it was probably a bad idea to dump the water. Why take such a risk? It was time for me to stop ruminating about every little thing and just *walk*. Time for me to stop and appreciate the outdoors and slow down the pace, not think about the goal and stop worrying about Doctor John catching up to us. I kissed Allison. I told her I loved her. It was a wonderful feeling, and it lasted about two and a half seconds.

The trail came to an intersection with a dirt road. In fact, the place looked familiar. Dave had tried to persuade us to get out here so we could shave a few miles off our hike. We were walking along the road when a black Range Rover with tinted windows pulled up beside us. I couldn't see the passenger, but the elderly female driver, through the open window, had that look you see on lizards in terrariums: rueful and grasping, wanting to escape. The passenger door slid open and out stepped Doctor John. I could feel the smile on my face reverse itself, as if unseen hands were pulling down the sides of my lips.

"You're only just getting here now?" Doctor John said. "At eight A.M.? You got a four-hour jump on me, and this is how far you've gone?" He smiled and winked, perhaps to let us know that his ridicule was only part of an unspoken esprit de corps, an assumed intimacy that suggested he was already part of our expedition.

I wanted to scream. At first I was worried that he would join us immediately, giving us no escape opportunity. But like us, Doctor John was a purist who would not skip even a small portion of the trail. The place where he stopped to greet us was six miles north of where Allison and I started out that day, at Oak Creek Canyon Road. But Doctor John stuck to the rules—he was going to have the driver take him all the way down to Oak Creek, but he had a plan to make his day easier. "I'll stash my backpack here behind a bush," he said. "That way, for the first few miles, I'll bring only my water and my camera. I'll take some pictures of windmills. And I'll catch up to you by nightfall!"

Doctor John stuffed his pack behind a sun-beaten snag. He got in the car and waved good-bye. We waved back. I smiled through clenched teeth, grinning and friendly on the outside, caterwauling on the inside.

No turning back now. Operation Water Dump was in full effect. Moments later, Allison turned her back to me, heading behind a tree to pee. The time to act was now. I took out Betty, our trusty black water bag, which held several gallons, and spilled some of her contents on the desert floor. I can't say exactly how much I spilled; all I know is that Betty was quite a bit lighter when I was through. The water made a choking sound, and then an accusing snarl, as it burbled into the cracks of the earth. Allison returned, much more quickly than I'd expected, and caught the tail end of what I was doing.

"What are you doing over there?" she said.

"Uh," I said. "I only got rid of a very small amount of water."

In reality, it was no "small" amount. If I had to guess, I dumped out two or three quarts at least. But I didn't tell her this. Instead, I pointed out, correctly, that we still had about a gallon of water between the two of us for sixteen miles. Allison seemed baffled, but not particularly upset, and my backpack was lighter now. In fact, I was quite comfortable. Allison eyed me warily for a moment but said nothing as we kept walking through the still-mild morning landscape. I had no second thoughts about my admittedly unusual plan. I supposed, on second thought, that I could have just dumped the excess water down my throat instead of on the ground. Aside from this, I had no regrets. And for the next quarter of a mile, the plan worked like a dream. The ground was flat, the rich desert dirt serving as a shock absorber for my knees. Allison led the way.

But just when I was starting to fall into bliss, and wondering whether I should dump out even more water when I got the chance, something happened that gave me pause. The sun got hot, the land got steep, and the sweat started pouring out of me as if through a spigot. A waterfall of perspiration gathered in the brim of my survival hat. Sweat ran down my shirt, and it would not stop, as the trail went from kind and squishy to hard and punishing. We hiked up an expanse of red rocks that slid out from under us as we climbed a mountain above an empty valley with the Mojave sands just beyond it. Edwards Air Force Base, immense squares on a dry lake bed, lay in the middle distance on the desert floor. As I stared across the playa, the flaw in my plan revealed itself. Allison, who had no idea how much water I'd thrown away, did not know that we had to hurry to reach the spring. She saw no reason to quicken the pace. I hiked behind her, making broad flourishes with my arms and hands, trying to make her walk faster through telepathy and voodoo. It didn't work. Instead, she kept borrowing my water bottles, taking hot wet smacks out of them. There was nothing I could do.

"What's wrong?" she asked when she saw my sour face. Scared to be caught in a lie, I kept silent. The land spread out in accordion folds, brown and dusty. Pines hung their heads. Their crisp brown needles lay in piles at our feet. Five hours into our journey, I rounded yet another bend in the trail, and saw nothing but moon rocks and black canyons. It was time to pray. "Please, God, get us out of this. Don't let us die of thirst. Please God. Let me revise what I said. First of all, please don't let Allison find out that this is my fault. Secondly, please don't let us die of thirst."

"I'm getting thirsty," Allison said an hour later.

I pretended, at first, not to hear her request for water. Finally I handed her one of the bottles slowly. She downed a quarter of it on the spot. "Ahhhhh!" she said, and handed the bottle back to me. I was just about to put the bottle back in my pack when she extended her hand again and smiled. "More," she said, and took a second gulp.

I couldn't bear any more of this. I winced. I blinked. I kept leaning back and forth, squashing my face into my left shoulder and grimacing.

"What's wrong?" she said.

"Um. I . . . We don't have as much water as you think."

Hours later, when the sun set, we camped beneath a slowly turning windmill rising over a clearing in the tall trees. We rationed every sip we had left. We even skipped dinner, because it would have taken too much water to boil up our freeze-dried meal. Even then, I did a good job of hiding my treachery. She knew I'd dumped some water, but she still had no idea how much. We ate dinner. Twilight, then cool darkness, covered us. Next morning we decided to gun it as hard as we could for Golden Oak Spring. I revealed to Allison that the state of our water supplies was now truly dire and that I had "gotten rid" of more water than she might have thought. But even then I didn't tell her the extent of what I'd done. I just couldn't bring myself to do it.

For a while we walked without talking. Freight trains moaned their way up Tehachapi Pass in the distance. Nothing grew but the lumpen forms of juniper trees. We passed through a piñon forest for half a mile and dropped to a dirt road that reached to the bottom of a scabby little mountain with no name. Far to the east was Soledad Peak, a pinheaded king in repose, arms outstretched, a road running up its torso. In her hands Allison held a Nalgene bottle with the last sips of our tap water. The drops plinked when she shook the bottle. She would not take a sip. Instead she handed me the bottle.

"Drink," she said. "You're sweating more than I am. You need it more than I do."

Something about the gesture caught me by the throat. I wanted to weep, but my tear ducts were jammed from the dry heat. Allison tried to distract me as we walked into the haze. She wondered if she could find a job as a journalist and I could be a ranger or adjunct professor. But she was trying to flummox me with false joy. She was trying to reassure me with stories of our bright future, but her reassurances had the opposite effect. When you know you've imperiled yourself and your lover, and your lover should be white hot with fury but instead is calm and goofy, you know that things are even worse than you surmised. The desert commented on its own dryness. The wind rushed like water. A mirage washed up against a pile of rocks. To get technical about it, this part of the PCT wasn't true desert, in the strictest sense. The trail passes through only about twenty miles of *real* desert. But the fact that there were some trees out here just made it worse. The trees knew how to find water, but they weren't saying.

My thoughts traveled back to a book I once loved, *The Big Book of Desert Adaptations,* or something like that. The book's undisputed stars were the kangaroo rats, who never drink water in all their lives but manage to survive in the desert, no problem. Kangaroo rats take in moisture by gnawing on seed pods, collecting vapor in their nasal membranes, and—are you listening, Doctor John?—chewing their own turds. Oh to be a spadefoot toad, able to concentrate liquid wastes into 40 percent urea, conserving water while forming a greasy layer that coats the skin like Armor All and seals moisture inside. How I envied the legless lizard, shy and ugly in his burrow. He uses his tongue to grab droplets suspended like jewels between grains of sand.[*] Without the walking stick I'd left behind in the motel, it was hard for me to prop myself up. I tripped into a thorn bush and fell to the ground in the dust as Allison exhorted me to be brave, to stay calm, to cowboy up. She gave me a weak smile.

---

[*]   Details about various desert fauna come from *A Natural History of California,* by Allan A. Schoenherr, Berkeley: University of California Press, 1992.

I smiled back. I knew, in my heart, that my clever girlfriend would find some way out of the misery I had created for us.

My prediction came true a few minutes later. Just off the trail we saw the first fresh, lush thing we had seen in many miles, a prickly pear cactus with fat lobes growing from a thin stalk. Pink flowers caught the sun. The skin was shiny as a Granny Smith apple.

"Did you know," Allison said, in a measured tone, "that you can get water out of a prickly pear cactus?"

I wanted to believe. But when you are as desperate as I was, it's important to play devil's advocate. I looked Allison in the eye and said, "Well, yes. I've heard you can get water from a cactus. But aren't prickly pears . . . poisonous?"

"Prickly pears aren't poisonous," she said.

That was it. I was convinced.

I reached in my shorts and found the Swiss Army knife. I took the blade out and used my bandanna to wipe it clean. I knelt down in front of the prickly pear, my heart beating with excitement. I was about to be a survivalist. Even better, I was about to have a great story to tell my grandchildren, the one about the time when old grandpa was sucking his tongue in a desert, came across a cactus, and got a hell of a good drink out of it. Giddy with thirst, mad with expectation, I hacked off the fattest, juiciest lobe. Good-bye, torment. Farewell, misery. Today I would prove my self-sufficiency to the world. Today I would get the last laugh on nature. It felt so good to be king of the desert, to know for sure that I was doing the right thing, and that all the people who ever doubted me were full of crap. I laughed in triumph as I popped the cactus morsel into my mouth.

If I close my eyes and take deep breaths, the memories return to me—memories separate from each other, yet connected, like flash cards. The first thing I remember was Allison. She was talking to me. No. She was shouting. The second thing I remember was the cactus. Its flavor reminded me of Green Giant green beans with a jicama aftertaste. The next thing I remember is the texture of the prickly pear. I thought it would be luscious, filling my throat with desert nectar, but the cactus had the limp consistency of a cucumber left to wilt overnight in a salad bar. Finally, I remember the pain, as hundreds of needles, known to plant lovers as glochids, plunged themselves like Zulu spears into my mouth, tongue, and gums. The spikes were tiny and translucent, very hard to see when you're sleepy and dehydrated. Some were half buried beneath the cactus's flesh. That's why it surprised me so much when they rose up to penetrate my mouth, slamming into my inner cheeks as if someone had shoveled a small porcupine in my maw. I spat out my spiny food, fell to the ground, and howled. Allison burst into tears. "I guess she isn't all that dehydrated after all," I thought to myself between throbs of pain as the water poured freely from her eyes.

"I'm so sorry!" she said. "I tried to stop you. Didn't you hear me? You're supposed to remove the spines first, Dan! You're supposed to remove the fucking spines!"

At that moment, I felt as if I were watching myself from a crane hanging several dozen feet in the air, and I was a director of a documentary, looking down on the ground and watching a stranger writhe, making sand angels on the desert dirt. I remember Allison's screams, too, and hearing myself scream, our mouths yawping together, until I could no longer separate the screams. It seemed to me that our screams were echoing through the canyon, until it sounded like a chorus of people screaming, a tabernacle choir covered in boiling oil. I did not know, at the time, that the prickly pear comes from the genus Opuntia, which distinguishes itself from its spiny brethren by having not one but two kinds of prickers, "minute bundles of hairlike spines at the base of larger spines."* Often invisible to

---

*   According to the Sierra Club's desert guidebook.

the naked eye, the spines are "almost impossible to remove. The only way to avoid painful encounters is to treat all of them with great respect." I did not know this, nor did I know that southwestern homeowners use prickly pear hedges for security buffers instead of concertina wire, or that you're supposed to handle them only with "metal salad or barbecue tongs with the tips wrapped in duct tape," according to Maureen Gilmer in her article about eating cactuses safely. She also advocates using a blowtorch to sear off the spines. It would also have helped, immensely, to know that you would need a whole acre of these "beverage plants" to get one quart of liquid. Aside from this, the plant has a long history of causing grievous bodily harm to human beings. Take, for example, Aztec priests. As part of a bloodletting ritual, they used the prickly pear's spines to puncture their tongues—and their penises! Ignorant of this secret history, I bit the plant, and it bit me back.

Allison was supposed to be the calm one, but you should have seen her then, tearing into her blue backpack, emptying and throwing things everywhere, trying to find items that might help her injured boyfriend. My lips bled. Pink saliva dripped from my mouth. I could barely speak. "I may require medical attention," I tried to say, but the words came out sounding more like "Moogah boogah boof."

In a blur of motion, Allison, who was still crying, delved into her fanny pack and dug out her plastic compact, a one-inch-by-one-inch beauty mirror with a small powder puff still attached, and then she stumbled toward me like a zombie beautician, reaching for me, eyes glazed. I had no idea what she was planning, and it made me cringe. I became even more afraid when I saw that in her other hand she held my Swiss Army knife. "Listen, Dan," she said. "You're gonna have to stay calm. Please. Stick your tongue out as far as it can go. No, farther." I did as best I could as she reached into the Swiss Army knife, her fingers making their way past the nail file, the saw, the reusable toothpick, the curly wine opener, the scissors, the standard screwdriver, the Phillips head screwdriver.

At last she came to the tweezers, which she removed, with some difficulty, for her hands were shaking. She held my tongue in her hand. She picked at it, poked at it, scraping away at the thorns while I cried out. In spite of her shaking, she worked with precision, until she'd yanked out ten spines, then thirty, but there were many more. Allison had a look of fierce determination. Through sheer will, she stopped crying and became steady and calm. She guided her hand, using the beauty mirror to get a better view of my mouth. In a half hour she must have plucked fifty spines. My mouth felt raw. Talking and swallowing were painful.

"You're gonna be okay," she kept saying. "But we must press on." We had to find the spring. "The longer we stay here, the more we sweat, and the thirstier we get. You can't give up now, Dan. You've got to hold yourself together."

I stood up. We walked, with Allison cooing encouragements all the way. My whole mouth was on fire. We left behind the nibbled cactus blob and walked up a hill through a forest of spindly trees. "You've got to keep going," Allison said.

Her voice trailed off. She stopped, and she gasped. For there, not five minutes away from where I'd been attacked by the cactus, Golden Oak Spring poured freely down the side of a canyon. I should have been grateful, but to my ears at that moment, the sound of the water sounded like the spirits of the desert, the gods of the twigs, the gods of the cacti, the gods of the jackrabbits, the gods of the spadefoot toads.

And they were laughing.

Chapter 15

Golden Oak

The water came through a pipe running into a trough twenty feet up a hill from the Pacific Crest Trail. Though I was almost devoid of energy, I sprinted for the spring. I purified the water, filled my bottles, and drank in goldfish gulps, downing bottlefuls like tequila shots, filling the bottles again, downing them until my stomach inflated, until I felt drunk on water. Allison gulped until her abdomen poofed and she looked pregnant. We sat together in the shade in dried mud, mad with thirst no matter how much we drank, ignoring the bugs that buzzed, the heat that burned. I kept on drinking, even when my stomach wanted to pop. Soon I passed out in the oak shade, drifting away, leaving the ache behind. For a while I floated through an ocean kingdom where I could breathe underwater. Starfish, mussels, and anemones clung to the tidal rocks. The surface of my body was coated in and out with cool bubbles, floating me in and out of consciousness. And I might have gone on snoozing for hours if not for a distinct but familiar voice, like nails screeching down a chalkboard.

"Hello," the voice said. "I can't believe it took so long to catch you, Dan and Allison! You don't look so good. Are you drinking enough water? You *really* need to be drinking more water. I think I'll stop and have a sip myself. I must say, my pee has that reddish sort of tint I warned you about, it's getting thicker, kind of syrupy, and if I don't drink water soon, it's going to turn redder and then I fear I won't be able to pee at all. By the way, where do you think you'll be camping for the night?"

It was 3:45 P.M. in late June in the southern California desert, 568 miles from Mexico and 6 feet from an excrement-obsessed math lecturer. Doctor John stood above me, knees bent, moss beard drooping. Allison lay to the right of me, bare legs on a rock. She leaned on the bottom of her pack and pulled a thread of blond hair from her half-open mouth. Her face was flushed, her cheeks like roasted plums. She stared in my direction but not at me; it was as if she were looking through a Dan-shaped hole in the scenery. I'd been cropped out of the picture and Stalinized from the foothills. Why did she not acknowledge me? Was she mad, dehydrated, or just numb?

Black flies circled. My shirt and Allison's shirt were indescribably filthy but Dr. John's was clean. Even dirt wanted nothing to do with him. He adjusted his telescoping walking stick and waited for my answer. He pulled off his boots and socks and massaged each toe. He sighed repeatedly, increasing the loudness and pitch of each sigh until he sounded like a hydraulic bus door. "Well," Doctor John said, "I'm still wondering where you're going to camp tonight, Dan and Allison. Also, I'm wondering why you aren't wearing your sunglasses, Dan. The sun is going to burn your cornea if you're not careful. I'm also wondering if you dropped an orange peel a mile and a half ago. I saw it on the trail."

"Yes, yes," I admitted, trading down, because it was better to confess littering than tell Doctor John where we were going to camp.

"Do you want to guess how long it takes for an orange peel to biodegrade in a desert?" he said.

"A week?"

"Try a hundred years," Doctor John said.

It was now 4:00 P.M. The sun was lazy-hot; its heat stirred and thickened the air around the trough holding runoff from Golden Oak Spring. Hills the color of pumpernickel rose above Doctor John, with fuzzy plants and oaks on the tops. "I'm still wondering where you're stopping for the night," Doctor John said.

The truth is I didn't know where we were going to camp. At the moment, I wasn't even sure where we were. Technically speaking, though, I knew the answer: 5,480 feet above sea level, 22 miles from the Tehachapi turnoff, and still within 2 hours' driving distance of downtown L.A. I even knew where we were relative to the rest of California; imagine the Golden State as your left arm raised up, elbow slightly bent, palm opened forward in surrender. Picture a vein or tendon from the center of the wrist to the base of the arm. Now picture a pair of moles or freckles halfway between the shoulder blade and the elbow. That was our exact location, and yet I'd never felt so lost, unable to find my bearings.

Doctor John snorted with impatience, bringing me back to reality. "Where are you camping?" he said in a remedial algebra voice.

I looked up at him. My tongue was still swollen, my mouth puckered from remnant spines, but I forced my lips to enunciate.

"I don't know where we're camping. I don't know how long we're gonna go. I have no idea . . ."

"It's true," Allison said, roused from her nap, looking back and forth between me and Doctor John. "We have no idea." If Allison was angry with me for trying to eat the cactus, she showed no sign of it then. Perhaps her annoyance with Doctor John trumped all other concerns. At least for now.

Ignoring Allison, Doctor John gazed intently at the man

who had risked heat prostration to escape from him, at the man who had gotten out of a motel bed at four in the morning, dragged his girlfriend along with him, hitched a ride with a near-total stranger, dumped his water on the hard parched ground, and then staggered through gulches and hibachi-hot canyons just to stay away from him. Doctor John stared down at that man, and he said, "Dan? I'm starting to think that you don't want to hike with me."

"That isn't true," I said.

I don't know what possessed me to lie now, with nothing left to lose. I don't know why, just once, I could not be frank and earnest with a math Ph.D. who had taken forty-eight hours to put two and two together. I suppose I just couldn't bear the idea of making somebody feel bad about himself, no matter how obnoxious he might be. Allison piped in, trying to flummox him. It's a tag-team skill we'd honed together.

"It's not that we don't want to hike with you," she said.

"It's just that we have . . .such different hiking styles," I said.

"Oh, come on," Doctor John said. He looked stricken. Then his eyelids drooped. For a moment he just stood there, slouching, and I felt terrible. But then he shrugged, and a wicked grin creased his face. "It's really fine, Dan and Allison," he said. "I'll go on without you. But . . .I thought it would be a good idea that we all stick together because, as I've said before, we're such slow walkers."

The words *slow walkers* might not seem like a slap in the face to people who have never tried to hike a 2,650-mile trail where speed and endurance are the most important skills. But it's one of the worst things you can call a through-hiker. It's like calling a surfer a "barney" or a "kook." You just don't say it, or even think it. Ever.

"It's true," he said again, "we're the slowest walkers, Dan. That's why we're last in the season. But never mind! I'm gonna fill my bottles here. And maybe I'll see you all later." He filtered his water, ignoring us. Allison and I watched, dazed. Then he cinched up his pack, loaded his bottles, and shuffled north, toward the bald-faced forms of the Piute Mountains and the scrub oak. But just as he was starting to go, he turned back at us, smiled, and said, "Oh Lois and Clark Expedition? Be sure to prepare a report to Congress."

"Prepare a what?" I snapped.

"A report to Congress. The Lewis and Clark Expedition. Didn't you study them in high school? Lewis and Clark? Crossing the wilderness? They sent a report back to Congress. A joke isn't funny anymore when you have to explain it."

He took one look back at us. He wished us well and headed north.

After he left, I sat there staring at the dust. I could feel Allison looking at me as if she didn't know me. Nothing felt the same. It changes you when you bite your first cactus. Foothills sneer. Vultures smirk. Quails ask unanswerable questions. Lizards take their measure of you, appraising you like little insurance adjusters. Something shifted when I chewed that prickly pear lobe. I'd thought an impermeable bubble of safety had formed around me and Allison after we met the Gingerbread Man. Now I was beginning to have serious doubts. The Gingerbread Man had told us that nature wasn't so mean. He had chanted about the desert's benefits, about how you could dry your clothes out here so quickly and didn't have to carry a tent. Now I wondered if it was all a big lie. The desert had turned on me, just when I had started to trust it. The trail, and the desert, had drawn first blood. In that moment of pain, it never occurred to me that I might be responsible for biting the cactus. As far as I was concerned, the cactus had ambushed me. Out of sheer maliciousness, the plant had uprooted itself from the ground and taken a flying leap into my mouth. I thought that Allison should be ashamed of herself.

She had failed to stop a sneak attack by an angry and embittered plant.

Of course I blamed her. Wasn't it her idea to get water from a prickly pear? Considering she was a plant enthusiast who knew all kinds of arcane information about herbs and weeds and could go into detail about the "fairy ring" root systems of mushrooms and redwoods, she should have known better. I felt misled. At her prompting, I'd fallen from the garden. It may sound obvious to make an analogy between us and Adam and Eve and their expulsion from Paradise, but the similarities are uncanny. We lost our innocence when I ate that prickly pear. Here is an exact quote from God, straight out of Genesis: "Because you did as your woman said, and ate of the tree about which I commanded you, you shall not eat of it. All the days of your life, thorns and thistles shall it sprout for you."

I wanted to talk to her about my resentment, but right then she was not in a receptive mood. In fact, she was looking at me as if I'd lost my mind. That afternoon, she accused me of being fuddle-headed, of misplacing the compass and dropping our headlamp and shit shovel into a ditch. "Why are you always losing everything?" she snapped. "Why can't you get it together? When you do crazy things like that, it makes me not feel comfortable around you. It makes me feel like I can't trust you."

"Crazy things like *what*?" I said.

We were so sick of each other, so fried and frazzled, that part of me even regretted my decision not to hike with Doctor John. He drove me out of my mind, and yet he provided a distraction for the Lois and Clark Expedition. As long as we had to think about Doctor John, we didn't have to think about *us*. So much of our relationship was built around opposition. Many of our best memories had some element of us against everyone else. One of our first dates was a performance of *Macbeth* by a group of novice actors—including a police detective—at a local community college. Macduff was played by an enormous man whose oaken performance, his meter-and-a-half-wide rear end, and his Miles Davis–like habit of performing with his back to the crowd provoked shrieks of laugher that Allison and I had to repress by stuffing our hands into our mouths. The venue was small. The pressure to be polite was maddening. I was trying so hard to stifle my spasms when Allison pointed to Macduff, nodded gravely, and said, "He's very talented." We fell out of our chairs and had to run from the auditorium. Now whom did we have to laugh at, to resist, criticize, and conspire against?

We pressed on in silence, past a group of wind turbines and straight up a sunburned crest, where we saw the painted rocks of Jawbone Canyon below us to the west. We walked for hours to a blue oak savannah with a crystal fire ring in the foreground, as if a race of giants, with diamonds to spare, had used a row of them to hem a fire. We climbed through a homely expanse of scrub oak as the heat burned down on us. And just when I was about to say, "Screw this, no more, I've had enough," the landscape did something cruel.

I wanted the landscape to be as ugly as my mood. But suddenly, fourteen miles from Golden Oak Spring, it turned beautiful. Shadows made a black mantle of the closest peaks to the north. A sudden light rose from the black wall, throwing streamers of color across the sky. I'd never seen a sunset like this one, a horizontal band of yellow beneath a row of purple clouds with wings rising off of them. I saw bands of cinnamon and sulphur, and below them, an oblivious strip of blue, straight out of an ordinary day. We spied for the first time a massive rock formation, five mountains, their arms linked together and a white skullcap on the top. This was our first tantalizing glimpse of the High Sierra.

We walked, if not in peace then at least in silence, as we chewed gobs of "desperation fudge," blobs of peanut butter mixed with dehydrated milk and hot cocoa powder. Though my tongue still throbbed, it occurred to me that we'd almost made it, that it was beautiful here, that it was close enough almost to touch, and that perhaps the cactus was a blessing, for now things could not get worse. In the desert, every little trickle, every effluvial blat from a drainage ditch, has a grand name. Up there, in John Muir's Sierra, there were so many glaciers with cold water melting from them. In the mountains, some rivers, streams, creeks, and lakes had no names at all. If only we could get there.

I wonder what Clinton Churchill Clarke, reputed "Father of the Pacific Crest Trail," would have thought to see the Lois and Clark Expedition on the path that day, staring down lizards, guzzling water, passing out on the ground, and getting back up again. I suspect he would have been pleased. Clarke believed that backpacking trips were supposed to be a character-building struggle. One part John Muir, five parts General Patton, Clarke wanted to preserve the high wild country along the crest of the western states, then set it aside to beef up the bodies and morals of America's sow-bellied youth.

Clarke was an advocate for the forests, but he was as far from a backcountry bohemian as you could get. In a portrait shot taken in his early fifties, the great man is stiff and unsmiling, his hair slicked back, his neck folds creased above his bowtie and tuxedo collar. In the picture, he looks like a well-off blueblood—and he was. Clarke could trace his lineage to the earliest settlers of New England. He claimed Cotton Mather, the fiery seventeenth-century Puritan leader, as a direct ancestor. He held a bachelor of arts degree from Williams College, where he was a proud, paddled member of the Delta Upsilon fraternity. Clarke lived with his wife, Margaret Ruddick, in Pasadena's palatial Hotel Green, and was one of the first men in his town to own a car.

But Clarke's nearly forty years of service to the Boy Scouts, including a seat on the Eagle Scout Examining Board, reinforced his notion that the wilderness was a testing ground. Clarke did not come up with the original idea for a Pacific Crest Trail. Apparently, the first person to broach this subject in public was a Miss Catherine Montgomery of Bellingham, Washington, who spoke in 1926 of her dreams about a "high trail winding down the heights of our western mountains . . . from the Canadian border to the Mexican Boundary Line." But Clarke was the first to fight for the trail and articulate a clear PCT philosophy. Born in 1873, Clarke lived at a time when America was still trying to figure out how to use the forests and parklands it set aside for preservation, distraction, and amusement. In the early days of "ecotourism," most tourists didn't venture very far into the backcountry, perhaps out of laziness, but more likely because of lousy equipment. Their hiking gear was even more awkward and clumsy than the irksome loads I shouldered on the Pacific Crest Trail. As recently as the 1920s, tents were white canvas monstrosities that weighed fifty pounds. "People slept in bulky woolen bedrolls fastened at the end with giant safety pins," wrote Roderick Nash in *Wilderness and the American Mind,* his history of America's relationship with the great outdoors. "Food came wet-packaged in cans. . . . Wilderness travelers who carried their equipment on their backs were so rare as to be considered eccentric."[*]

Because there was so little access to the forest, hucksters filled the void by creating entertainments that reduced tourists to meek observers and wilderness to empty spectacle. James McCauley, perhaps the creepiest showman in the history of cheesy backwoods tourism, amused late-nineteenth-century Yosemite visitors by flinging various objects—including, by one account, a live chicken—off the 3,200-foot-high drop-

---

[*]   Roderick Frazier Nash, *Wilderness and the American Mind*, fourth edition, New Haven: Yale University Press, 2001, pp. 317–18.

off at Glacier Point. A San Francisco reporter filed this eye-witness report: "With an ear-piercing cackle that gradually grew fainter as it fell, the poor creature shot downward; now beating the air with ineffectual wings, and now frantically clawing at the very wind . . . thus the hapless fowl shot down, down, down until it became a mere fluff of feathers . . .then again dotted the sight as a pin's point, and then—it was gone." The story could be apocryphal, considering the newspaper reporter claimed the chicken survived the fall and climbed back up the cliff to be hurled off again, but McCauley certainly flung burning bushes and other detritus to amuse the masses, while shouting, "Let the fire fall!" The tradition survived through the 1960s.

Empty spectacles and tourist coddling irritated Clarke. He loved to take forays through the woods near San Gorgonio Mountain in Southern California. With each exploration, he noticed more concession stands, roads, and development ruining the "primitive" feel of his beloved mountains. In the back-country it was becoming impossible to escape "the honk of the auto horn or the smell of the hot dog," he said. "Our wildernesses are about gone. They have been driven to the high mountain divides where runs the Pacific Crest Trail System."

His disaffection gave birth to his PCT vision. The West Coast, he said, must have a long trail that melts flab and serves as a watchtower from which day hikers and long-distance backpackers can keep a careful eye on excessive logging, modern conveniences, and development. Without such a trail, primitive areas could be lost altogether, and so would the souls of California's youth. Seventy years before Keanu Reeves played an anti-robot resistance-fighter in *The Matrix,* Clarke warned Americans of our "enslavement" by radios, automobiles, and film projectors. "Make a ratio of the number of motors, of the number of tickets sold for movies, the number of radios sold, compared to our popula-

tion, and compare these figures to any nation in Europe . . .
and we see what an appalling over-mechanization has done to
enslave the people of the United States."

In 1932, Clarke lobbied the U.S. Forest and National Park
services to support the construction of his "continuous wilderness trail . . . maintaining an absolute wilderness character." To
plead his case, he warned the government about "a marked
deterioration in the physical, mental and spiritual caliber of our
youth. The medical report of the U.S. Army on the physique
of 5,000,000 young men taken into the armed forces shows
a serious deterioration in . . . their legs and backs, causing a
misplacement of the internal organs . . . In a word, too much
sitting on soft seats in motors, too much sitting in soft seats in
movies . . . too much lounging in easy chairs before radios."

Taking his cue from Benton MacKaye's blueprint for the
East Coast's Appalachian Trail, Clinton Clarke articulated his
cure-all for America's oppressive softness: a 2,650-mile trail
linking three countries—the United States, Mexico, and
Canada—while spanning the length of California, Oregon,
and Washington. Clarke, at first, was dismayed by the rights-
of-way issues that stood in his path. The trail, even now, crosses
a hodgepodge of private and public interests, and some of the
owners aren't thrilled about bearded smelly Wookies like me
trudging across their ranches and grazing fields at the behest of
the federal government. Fortunately, by the early 1930s, various
trails along the route were already established, and could easily
be subsumed by the PCT, including the Tahoe-Yosemite Trail
and the spectacular John Muir Trail, which plunges into territory so remote that hikers don't cross a road, or see a powerline,
for two hundred miles. At the time, the proposed route was
the longest scenic trail in America, five hundred miles longer
than the Appalachian Trail. Clarke envisioned a path on a Cecil
B. DeMille scale. In one of his writings, he said that the PCT
might one day be part of an even more gargantuan footpath,

"The Trail of the Americas," ten thousand miles long, from Alaska's Mount McKinley to Chile's Mount Aconcagua, the highest mountain in South America. This übertrail would use "ancient mule trails" and the shoulder of the "Pan-American Highway."

I suspect that Clarke would have enjoyed seeing the Lois and Clark Expedition rise up, the day after the cactus-chomping incident, and hike to an overlook where we saw our first snowy glimpse of Olancha Peak, to the north. He would have liked to see us grimace beneath our pack weight as we climbed steep hills, each with a tiki-shaped dolmen on the top and, out of nowhere, a row of foxtail pines. Fallen needles softened our steps. Pain and reward were Clarke's mottos, although he never put those philosophies to the test on the PCT. There is no record of him even taking an overnight camping trip on it. It saddens me to think he fought so fiercely for something that he didn't get to enjoy, but maybe it's for the best. After all, his hiking philosophies were so weird that I wonder how he would have held up out there. "Always rest by standing on the trail in the sun," he once wrote. "If you sit down you will lose pep. Drink little water. A raisin under the tongue will help. Do not eat when overtired." Clarke also advocated bringing almost seventy pounds of pack weight into the forests, not including water. With that much weight on his shoulders, he may very well have given himself a Pacific Crest coronary. And Clarke was deep in his middle age before he even started thinking about the trail. When he took up the PCT's mantle, he was already fifty-eight years old, and trying, with mixed results, to drum up publicity. He asked the Boy Scouts to do a "team relay" in which groups would hike small chunks of the trail in tandem, to help map the route. The Boy Scouts turned him down flat. His second choice, the YMCA, reluctantly agreed to help. The mapping didn't exactly light the headlines on fire. *The Los Angeles Times* of 1932 hardly even mentioned his efforts. But through the relay, Clarke met Warren Rogers, then secretary of the Alhambra YMCA, and another unlikely advocate for the longest trail in America at the time. Like Clarke, Rogers was a native midwesterner. Stricken with polio as a child, Rogers suffered from the nickname One and a Half Step, because one of his legs was half an inch shorter than the other, forcing him to walk with a gimp. Years of playground teasing drove him deep into the forests and up the faces of steep peaks. He wanted to prove that he could go where anyone else could. Rogers bagged 11,502-foot San Gorgonio Mountain when he was only fifteen, and in the course of his lifetime, he scaled 19 peaks over 9,000 feet "and never had so much as a sprained ankle."

It seems inevitable that Rogers would pair up with Clarke to develop the Pacific Crest Trail. Clarke was the visionary, and Rogers was the leg man, willing to walk vast distances to help chart the trail. In his mid-twenties, he led teams of boys to hike and help map out the proposed PCT route in relays over three years. There's a photo of Rogers from that time, eager and gawky, with a goofy smile, hiking with a fuzzy beard, jeans, work boots, and a heavy pack. Thirty-four years younger than Clarke, he handled most of the field work. The federal government helped out with groups of Civilian Conservation Corps workers, who burned connector trails on the footpath. Then the Japanese bombed Pearl Harbor, America took up arms, and federal trail funding came to a dead halt. The PCT withered. By the time Clarke died, in 1957, at age eighty-four, the trail had fallen into obscurity. Clarke's hometown newspaper obit did not mention the PCT in its headline, which read, "Cotton Mather Descendent Dies Here."

But Rogers kept rallying for the trail, and he never compromised Clarke's original vision. In a newspaper interview, Rogers made it clear that his dream trail was no place for tenderfeet or casual pleasure-seekers. The trail, he said, would be an "authentic" experience that would test the resolve of everyone who traveled on it. "It isn't like going through a path in the city among the trees," he said. "We never intended to stick mileposts up on the damned thing and destroy the wilderness. You're supposed to be enough of a backpacker to follow the maps."*

Rogers's perseverance paid off in the 1960s, when America was finally ready to support the PCT. Backpacking, once considered a "marginal" activity, started to boom then. The other development was gear. World War II nearly killed off the PCT, but the accompanying technology boom helped the trail in the long run. The war led to the proliferation of lightweight plastic, nylon, aluminum, and foam rubber gear, some of it spun off from state-of-the-art military rucksacks. Freeze-dried rations helped inspire the stomach-turning, flatulence-inducing "foods" that made the Lois and Clark Expedition possible.† Backpacking's new convenience and popularity emboldened PCT advocates, who lobbied Congress to pass the National Trails System Act in 1968, placing the Appalachian and Pacific Crest Trails under the care of the U.S. Department of the Interior, and the Bureau of Outdoor Recreation. Congress declared the Appalachian Trail and the PCT the first two official national scenic trails. By 1975, about thirty people had through-hiked the PCT. Interest fell in the 1980s but rebounded in the 1990s, with the advent of the light packers, led by backpacking guru Ray Jardine, whose once-ridiculed ideas about ultra-minimalist loads are now common practice on the trail. Another breakthrough came in 2004, when Scott Williamson—who had already hiked the trail six times—became the first person in history to through-hike it twice in one seven-month slog. Interest in the trail remains strong—

---

*   Alan Parachini, "A 2,606-mile Odyssey Through Wilderness," *Los Angeles Times*, p. G 1, October 30, 1983.

†   Roderick Frazier Nash, *Wilderness and the American Mind*.

these days, roughly 125 people a year complete it—but the PCT brought no such stability to its cocreator, Rogers. For the last twenty years of his life he tried to build a living off the PCT, producing food packs and maps, but could not get the business off the ground. Rogers eventually lost possession of his 850-square-foot redwood house in Santa Ana.

"He just could not keep it together," his son, Donald, told me. "There is no money to be found in the Pacific Crest Trail, and it just bankrupted him. He always gave so much more than he got in return."

The last time Rogers set foot on the Pacific Crest Trail, it was 1991. He was in a wheelchair. A photo shows him cutting the ribbon at a ceremony dedicating a new trailhead for the PCT at Walker Pass, California. His smile looks strained. He's wearing a plaid windbreaker and a scarf around his neck. Because of a bureaucratic holdup, Rogers did not live long enough to see the official completion of the PCT route. The last major snag was the privately owned, 275,000-acre Tejon Ranch in Southern California. The ranch's recalcitrant owners, fearing litter and fires, refused to let trail planners chart a course through their land and posted armed guards to keep hikers away. Those who dared trespass on the property complained of sentries taking potshots at them. Finally, the trail's managers started condemnation proceedings against the ranch. The owners relented, but the trail through Tejon is ugly and waterless.

This holdup robbed Rogers of a moment he had been waiting for most of his life. He died in April 1992, after making one last push to set up some much-needed water supply stops in the Mojave Desert section of the footpath, just north of Tejon Ranch. The final "golden spike" was pounded into the Pacific Crest Trail in June 1993.

Chapter 16

Wilderness Voodoo

One hundred miles south of the High Sierra, we entered a buffer zone between the chaparral foothills to the south and the highest peaks to the north. It felt as if the desert and the mountains were casting spells on us from opposite directions. At the same time, I entered a buffer zone between actually speaking with my girlfriend and merely grunting at her. In retrospect, this was understandable. She no longer trusted me because of the cactus incident. Because of the same incident, I no longer trusted the outdoors. The day we entered Jawbone Canyon Road, south of the Piute Mountain range, I gesticulated a lot, and sometimes snorted. Sometimes she tried to engage me in conversation, but I refused. Throughout the week, instead of saying, "Allison, would you please hand me that bottle," or "Allison, would you offer me a bite of that lemon-ginger Pemmican Bar?" I'd point and say something approximate, such as "Unk."

It's not that we were fighting, exactly. It's just that we were slipping backward into a Pleistocene frame of mind, our hair matted, our body odors indescribable. I tried to bond with the woods, the way the Gingerbread Man did. But what did I get for my bonding attempt, save for a row of perforations on my tongue and a lot of strange notions in my brain? Life out here was becoming too random. I was on high alert now, edgy and anxious. For this reason, I began to modify my notions about God and spirituality, and wonder if paganism was my only protection from the chaos and overwhelming power of nature.

As a Jewish man, I knew that pagan worship was an offense serious enough to merit inclusion in the Ten Commandments. God, in a quote from the Torah, reports that he is God, and that there is "none else." That statement provides no wiggle room to worship Buddha, Krishna, or the sprites that inhabit twigs. And yet, as we marched, I thought it might be smart to diversify my belief system. Maybe if I prayed hard enough to *all* of the spirits, I could get Allison, and the wilderness, back on my side again. At the same time, I was scared to pray to the one and true God of my Jewish beliefs. After all, why would a God who self-identifies as "awesome" care about our walk to Canada? Why not appeal to something lower and more accessible? It would be hyperbolic for me to say that I became an actual pagan out there, but I certainly flirted with this belief system. While I didn't entirely believe in the wraiths and faeries of the wilderness, I wasn't about to discount them, either. After making sure that Allison was too far behind me to see me throwing food away, I reached into my fanny pack and removed the best of my remaining snacks: a small stick of Dove Bar dark chocolate. I unwrapped the chocolate and rolled it around between my thumb and forefinger, until I had formed a glob. Though I wanted, desperately, to eat it, I chucked it off a sandstone cliff as a sacrifice to whoever was listening.

"Oh, spirits," I cried. "If you are out there, I call upon you from the rocks, the sand, the creek's sandy bottom. Take this snack and enjoy it. I offer this food to you with the following beseechment. No more sun, no more bugs, no more uphill. Please show mercy on us, O spirits, for we have had enough."

I threw the snack over the cliff, watching it bounce into a shrub with a "plop." This strategy did not work. I prayed for downhill but got uphill. I prayed for shade and got sun.

A few miles later, Allison and I found ourselves at a spur trail mentioned in the guidebook as a route toward fresh water. We took the uphill turn, climbing a path full of dried-mud hummocks, and a few oak trees drooping along the sides of us, until we reached a trough of reasonably potable water. I decided to filter and purify a few liters to drink on the spot, but when I set myself up, and put the filter intake valve in the water, I heard a splash. Allison had sat down beside me, taken off her boots and socks, and plunked her black-bottomed feet in the water I was trying to purify. She sat with a beatific expression, massaging her calves. I threw her a look, but she did not notice. She sighed and swabbed her feet, and palmed the cold water all over her toes and heels. Soon her feet were as white as frog bellies. They left a film on the water. "This does not augur well for us," I said to myself as I continued to filter the water. "This does not speak of our ability to compromise."

Late that afternoon, we descended along the steppelike rock formations known as St. John Ridge, a rolling set of bowls and humps. The ridge overlooked a valley strewn with mining debris. Here among the bitterbrush were boulders shaped like human molars. Some of them had cavities so wide I could have placed my fist inside them. The land looked like the aftermath of a fight between giants. I was daydreaming, walking way out in front of Allison, empty of thought, floating, when I heard a sound like a hundred maracas, so clamorous that I leaped. Ten feet in front of me, a rattlesnake coiled. Only the tongue and rattle moved. The serpent was fat in the middle, suggesting it had just eaten or was in the family way. My fear was like a mild form of electrocution, and yet the serpent was beautiful: the diamond pattern of its skin, the parallel segments of its rattle, the languorous curves of its coils. In my diary I would note that my fear of the snake was "undeniably primal, pulled straight from the unconsciousness of my ancestry," though that observation, in retrospect, was peculiar, considering my ancestry lies in Eastern Europe, where my forbearers were bakers, butchers, and rabbis who lived in Cossack-haunted shtetls where Jews beyond the pale were shot for no reason, and where the absence of rattlesnakes must have been cold comfort.

And yet the noise triggered something buried—dare I say, primitive—in me. Allison finally caught up and saw the snake. She looked nervous but restrained, taking a step back and then freezing. The effect on me was much more powerful. I was scared and yet I had an unexplainable urge to jump on the snake, wrestle with it, maybe even fling it around my shoulders like a feather boa. I did not know it at the time, but my reaction was perfectly normal and reasonable for a man. A snake researcher at the University of California at Berkeley told me later that rattlesnakes often trigger an aggressive behavioral response in men, but not so much in women. Most female snakebite victims get chomped on the ankle or foot because they stumble across the creature. But scores of men get bites on the neck and the hand, the elbow and shoulder, because they pick up the snakes, dance around with them, toss them in the air, or start throttling them. I restrained myself from embracing or strangling the snake, but the adrenaline stole through me with no release. In a few moments the snake became tired of us and poured itself into a hole in the ground. With slow steps, we passed its hiding place and continued on our way. But the uncomfortable feeling would not go away. We hiked almost nonstop that day, until the sun was all but gone.

It would have been smart to search for a campsite before dark, but hunger for Canada made us push on. We found ourselves high on a windblown ridge long after sunset, watching the tops of distant peaks turn to fins in the twilight, floating over the cloud banks. Soon we could not see where we were going at all. Even our flashlight did nothing but poke holes in the black. Allison chose the surface of a flat, cliffhanging boulder as our emergency camp. Instead of protesting, I just went on autopilot, knowing I was still in trouble and should keep my mouth closed. I started pitching the tent, throwing down my gear. Allison chose the left side of the flat rock, and unrolled her sleeping bag, her foam pad, her trail pillow. Somehow I got the side with the bump, which smushed against my face, even when I plumped and fluffed my Therm-a-Rest pillow, and set it on top of the protruding rock.

That evening, during a flashlight-assisted bathroom break, I made a few other discoveries about Allison's chosen camp. Allison had selected a spot near a hole in the ground overflowing with ants. The boulder seemed unstable. I could not tell if our rock was anchored to the cliff. For all I knew, if we fidgeted too much, or crawled to the end of the boulder, the rock might unfasten itself and drop into the black, taking me, Allison, the lump, and the ants with it. I woke up several times that night. Allison's stomach made cracking sounds, like a boulder loosening itself from a mountainside. Morning came after an eternity. Allison woke up long after I did. She crawled out of the tent. Through the tent's open vestibule I could see ants in our stockpot, nibbling the cremains of our pilaf supper. I had no idea how the ants had worked up the appetite to eat our food. Along with our communication skills, our cooking prowess had deteriorated over the past few weeks. I drowned our meals in too much water, while Allison sometimes scorched them. In my diary, I noted that she was becoming "more of an arsonist than a chef." Irritation rose inside me. Adrenaline from the snake encounter still pumped through my bloodstream. After days of near-silence and monosyllabic grunts, spiteful sentences came out of my mouth.

"Wow," my mouth said. "What an unbelievable camp that was, on the edge of a cliff face, with a big rock sticking into my head. That's what I would call a desperation campsite, when there's *no* other option, even though there were a hundred other spots where we could have camped." I said a lot of other things about the ridiculousness of our tent spot, and how a thousand other places would have been more suitable. I also accused her of being a slowpoke, of "always wanting to take it easy," of dragging down the expedition. I said all these things in a sarcastic tone that reflected my exhaustion and irritation. I knew full well that these accusations would hurt her pride, and yet I couldn't stop myself.

Even as I muttered these things, I blamed the snake. If we hadn't encountered the serpent, I wouldn't have been so agitated. The snake hadn't bitten me, and yet I was in the throes of its psychic venom. But it was impossible to explain this to her, so I didn't even try. Her face had already gone blank, and she turned her back on me. She squashed a bunch of things into her pack, tossed the pack on her shoulders, tightened her support strap, straightened her back, and starting running northward, away from me, down the trail, toward Canada. I could not believe what I was seeing. Yes, I had spoken out of line, but Allison was overreacting. Besides, she had taken some of the best snacks. "I am sorry, I take it back!" I shouted to the wind, but she could not hear.

Working as fast as I could, I took down the tent, mashed the tent poles together, grabbed the rest of our camp, and stuffed it into the pack. Without even buckling the support pad, with the pack hanging off my right shoulder, I started running after her, hollering for her to wait up a bit. "All-lisss-onnn!" I roared, but she was tearing down the ridge, kicking dust, knocking over stones. I hollered for her to stop or at least slow it up a bit. She did neither. Now, since there was no way she could hear me, I could say exactly what was on my mind. "You're not being rational!" I screamed. "Come on! You can stop running now!" She merely accelerated. Insects ticked in my ears. Down I jogged under Pinyon Mountain. She was out of sight now.

Plants threw fork-shaped shadows at me. A desert owl swooped above me, wings spread, its head a tufted discus. Down I ran, on a trail crisscrossed with dirt bike tread, to a place where the Pacific Crest Trail met a dirt road. There, at the bottom, was Allison, in a crouch, laughing inexplicably. She was resting there, hands on her knees. I took a step forward to see if she would retreat, but she acted as if she did not notice me. She was smiling at a note that seemed to be addressed to her. I got close enough to read over her shoulder. The note was scribbled on a torn-out page from a Gary Larson *Far Side* desk calendar. The cartoon showed a man, bearded and thin, clawing his way over sand dunes, tongue lolling, his body dragging. A billboard taunts from a distance. It shows a picture of a canteen, sloshing with water. "Hey, Lois and Clark Expedition," the note read. "I miss you guys. Hey, Clark, I miss your stories of newsroom life in Connecticut. Lois, I miss your pathetic blister walk. If you guys need water, tank up at the seeping spring. Take a left on the dirt road and walk down canyon for half a mile. The spring flows just under the road near the first tree you will see. To get to the water you'll need to push aside the cow chips."

I knew we could use the water. I hadn't filtered much at the water source, and we'd consumed most of it. The two of us said nothing as we pushed our way down the path to a lone tree. Though Allison did not look at me, and though she walked close to me, but separate from me, I was grateful to the Gingerbread Man. He'd created a distraction, forced Allison to stop, made her laugh, disarmed her, and told her where the water could be found. Perhaps she was biding her time, or she'd used up her rage on the run, but she spoke not a word against me as we walked.

We hadn't gone for very long when we saw two sun-blackened towers of black dried cow patties, four feet high. Each pile was a feat of construction, the larger pieces anchoring the structure, the smaller and svelter pieces of crap adding a tapering effect, reminding me of the towers on Antonio Gaudi's Church of the Holy Family. Beneath one of the larger and fatter cow chips, the Gingerbread Man had placed yet another note addressed to us: this one had a drawing of an arrow, and one word: *Water!* We walked in the direction of the arrow. There, just a few feet from the note, fresh water shone through the invasive thistles. We laughed at the sight of it. We did not say much for the rest of the day, but I thought we were on the road to making up, until late that night in our tent, when Allison was writing in the pages of her diary, pressing down so hard I could hear her pen tearing the paper. "Can't we get along? Can't we?" I asked myself before I nodded off.

When we rose up the next morning and continued our trek through hard, hot country, we were too tired to keep fighting or make up in earnest. The days continued like this. At last, we reached a strained détente. I knew we would be fine, that the insanity and magic thinking and weirdness should be over soon.

But one afternoon, on a spit of sand along a creek, Allison stopped to cook a meal in the middle of the trail. She sat on the hard-packed dirt and sand. She removed the cooking unit, pumped the fuel with a hand crank, twisted the intake valve, reached down, dropped a match, and watched the orange flames rise. She lowered a pan of water onto the flames and covered it with foil to trap the heat. There, in the half shade, she started to cook a packet of vacuum-packed gnocchi. She sat there, rocking in contentment, watching pasta bob and pitch. As she studied the bubbles, a swarm of meat bees descended, cumbersome creatures with a green cast to their wings. Allison ripped them from the sky, making a popping noise, like bubble-package wrapping, as she crushed them one by one. She did this in an angry but graceful way, reminding me of King Kong's final scene, when he's standing on the Empire State Building tearing biplanes out of the sky. Allison took three dead bugs and arranged them facedown in the dirt on the creek's bank. The backs of their wings, and their rear legs, pointed toward Heaven. "I put those bees there as a warning to the other meat bees," she said. She smiled, as if it were obvious. "See," she continued, "the other meat bees are gonna fly over us and see the bodies of their friends. They'll be so scared they won't want to bite us anymore."

She may very well have been joking around, but in the state of mind I was in, my first reaction was, "Wow. Way to go, Allison. What a smart idea!" In fact, I helped her, killing five meat bees and arranging them in the dirt, in a rough pentagram. It seemed perfectly rational, even necessary at the time. I thought, "We're sending a clear message that we will not tolerate being attacked by meat bees for one minute longer."

Chapter 17

Betty the Whore

Out on the Pacific Crest Trail, I gave a personal name to every piece of our backpacking gear. This was necessary for the Lois and Clark Expedition's survival. My flirtation with paganism had gotten me only so far, while my spells and incantations wore off quickly. Even the meat bees eventually figured out our ruse and began to attack again, sucking more blood as if to make up for lost time. I decided to try a different strategy. It was time to make our gadgets human, so we could communicate with them more effectively. By giving each gizmo a personal moniker, I could coo at it and cajole it into doing its job well and never stabbing us in the back when we needed it on our side.

Each piece of gear had grown into its name as we hiked along. Odie was our odometer. R2-D2 was our "rolling resupply bucket," which we mailed ahead to ourselves at every post office along the trail route. An emptied-out frosting container liberated from a Safeway supermarket in Prunedale, California, R2-D2 carried the Excedrin, foot ointment, powdered

Gatorade, sanitary napkins, guidebook chunks, and condoms we needed for each section of the trail. Even my backpack had a name: Big Motherfucker, or Big Mofo, for short. He got his name because he had 5,925 cubic inches of manly packing space. Big Mofo was so damned big you could stick a toaster oven, two photo albums, a Sparkletts bottle, and a Waring blender in his belly and still have room for seven sacks of Cooler Ranch Doritos. My special favorite was Betty, a leakproof fabric water container, able to hold as much as four king-size canteens. After I bought her at an outdoors store, I took her home and filled her with tap water. She puffed up, getting big out in front and sticking out in the back in a way that somehow reminded me of Betty Boop. I always knew we could rely on Betty. Her manufacturers said she was 100 percent guaranteed. I trusted her so much that I filled her to the brim and let her ride inside Big Mofo, right on the top, above our food bags and clothes.

It happened one late afternoon while Allison and I were walking on a trench on the bottom of the ocean. That is what it looked like on the flats south of the Scodie Mountains. Sand bars branched into the bushes. Wiry plants waved on the sides of the path. Lizards darted from rock to rock like sculpins. I was feeling pretty good about the trail that day, joking around, and Allison seemed to have forgiven me for the snake-induced "this campsite sucks and why are you so goddamned slow" incident from earlier in the week. In fact, we were throwing around the terms of endearment we used only when on very good terms. I called her Ratface. She called me Fishbody. To us, these were encrypted declarations of true intimacy and affection, made more meaningful by the fact that an outsider would have thought these names degrading.

The foreign environment entranced me. We did not belong here. Without sunscreen, survival hats, or water, we would have perished soon. Betty, our water bag, was our diving bell, a ballast to stop us from floating up into the sun. It amazed me to think we could travel unscathed through a place like this as long as our bottles stayed full. Since our water crises were over for good, I could now enjoy the beauty of this place on its own terms. Swallows knifed the air for insects. Piñon pines formed islands of green. As we rose up a hill, Allison noticed a stain of clear water on the back of Big Motherfucker.

"Hey, Fishbody, you're sweating like a pig," she said as we made our way up a steep trail on a mule-colored foothill, a featureless hump that looked just like the entrance to a municipal landfill. I smiled at her "pig" reference. Our first date just so happened to be at an agricultural fair in Goshen, Connecticut, where the two of us spent the afternoon watching the greased pig races, eating funnel cakes, and riding the pukers. Allison was so beautiful at the fair, with her glowing eyes and her blond hair blowing all over the place, that I could not look her in the face. I had to excuse myself a half-dozen times and visit the Porta-Cans because my heart was pounding and my nervous bladder kept filling. Who would have guessed that two years later I'd be walking up a steep ridge with the same woman, our breath smelling just like the Goshen Fair poultry enclosure, our shirts looking as though we'd used them to swab down the contestants in the 4-H heifer exhibition? Allison, as usual, was right. I was sweating to an unusual degree. I stopped and took off Big Mofo, who was sopping wet and strangely light. I looked inside. Water covered our food bags and our clothes. Water dripped on my sleeping bag compartment. Somehow, that morning, Betty's screw-on cap had popped off. Now it would not screw back on again. Two thirds of our water was gone, and the next reliable water was fifteen miles away. It was late in the day, so we would have to bed down for the night, conserve water, then make a push for it next morning. Besides, everything was soaked. I grabbed Betty by the neck, lifted her out of Big Mofo, and started to throttle her.

"How could you do this to us?" I screamed. "How could you?" I called Betty a stinking hag and a worthless piece of crap. Finally, I called her a whore. The name stuck. Betty the Waterbag, from there on in, would be known as Betty the Whore. This new name made me and Allison feel a whole lot better about the situation, but the name did not erase the fact that we were in danger again. For the next hour, we made Betty the Whore the scapebag of all that had gone wrong in our journey. I grabbed Betty the Whore by the neck and held her aloft, partly to keep the remaining water from dribbling out and partly to strangle her, to make her scream with pain.

We had another four hours of daylight to go, so we marched on. I started to lose the plot after a while, to thunder at no one in particular, and tighten my grip around Betty's nylon neck. Allison tried as hard as she could to distract me. We often filled the trail hours by talking about old jobs. Long before we met, she'd worked as a waitress in the kind of restaurants where waiters kiss their fingertips while telling customers about the specials. Allison told me all about the way she used to gargle red wine, swishing it from cheek to cheek as it changed flavors in her mouth. "You know how to tell a lousy bottle of wine?" she said. "That's when you sniff it and you detect barnyard." She explained to me that good vines must be "tortured in subsistence soil to grow the best grapes. They must suffer to thrive." It started to get dark. The air had a citrus-salty smell, slightly carbonated, with notes of sagebrush with yeasty overtones. We walked through scrub brush. The light was red and faint. Our water bag was running so low we would have just enough to get us through the evening and the next morning.

At times like this, you'd think deep thoughts would come to a man's mind. You'd think he'd get right down to business and start asking the big *whys* and the big *ifs* and the big *whats*. You'd think he'd take this time to inventory his list of sins and get right with God. But, no. Inanities enter the human brain.

You may try to will deep thoughts and important questions into your head but they just won't come. Instead you start analyzing the lyrics of the Eagles' "Hotel California," though you hate that song so much that you once fled from a diner where it was playing on the jukebox, and were almost run over by a truck. Walking up a windswept hill, you are troubled by the fact that the guests at Hotel California can "check out" anytime they like but they can "never leave," which implies a 100 percent occupancy rate, so it makes no sense that there would be "plenty of room," at the hotel, or any room left at all. You wonder if the Eagles had a game plan for all those extra guests. You figure there must be foldaway beds, but it torments you that Don Henley never mentions this in the song.

It also occurs to you, somewhere on this windblown ridge, that there are people in this world who really love backpacking. There are people in this world who go backpacking by choice. And it occurs to you that you and Allison are here by choice.

We were still hiking at the time of day when shadows lose their shape and run straight into one other, making one big shadow. We hiked toward a phantom radio tower, due north, saucer-equipped, high on a crag. A stripe of quartzite ran across a hill near the trail. In the almost-dark, minerals in the quartzite glowed like white teeth. As we passed the hills, I looked to my right, due east, at the glowing dunes of the desert, the great big swallowing nothing out there. The view was lovely enough to make me stop in my tracks, and yet it chilled me to stare at eastern ridges marching toward the Nevada border. "It could get me just like that," I kept muttering to myself. "It's gonna get me just like that."

"What's gonna get you?" Allison said, squeezing my arm. "Nothing's gonna get you, Fishbody."

A bluish light settled on the top of the tallest dune, and the light rose, wavelike, from the sand. The glow receded. My mouth felt as though it had just bit into an underripe per-

simmon, that suck-mouthed feeling, as if every bit of moisture were receding. We walked in the moonlight at the time
of night when every twig looks like a snake. The moon turned
pines into penitents frozen in their stations, arms bent in front
of them. Allison picked a spot of flat earth beneath a pine and
declared it ours. There, under the branches, we pitched Freddy,
the Bullfrog tent, and found enough string cheese to make a
rough dinner. Seam-sealed and vacuum-packed, the cheese had
lasted several days in hot weather without going bad, though its
texture was snotty and unpleasant. Allison took out our headlamp, fastened it to her skull, and flicked it on. Light shone on
our thumb-stained maps. The next unreliable spring was five
miles away. The moon was bright that night; it washed the stars
away on all sides, but a few of them had escaped to the outer
edges of the sky. Allison stared at a fixed point beyond the stars.
I looked at her and wondered if this was the wrong dream. If it
was the right dream it wouldn't be this hard.

I tried to cheer myself up by glancing up at the Big Dipper, glow dots in cruciform. Allison leaned into my shoulder. I
remembered what a teacher had told me, long ago, about the
Big Dipper. As long as there have been people on Earth, and no
matter where they were living on this planet, it's always been a
good sign. The Big Dipper is the one superstition that everyone can agree on. If you're in a desert somewhere, and you
look up and find the Dipper, it means you'll wake next day and
find good water. You might be thirsty, but the Dipper's always
full. It's a universally accepted concept.

I found out years later that everything I knew about the
Dipper was wrong. The Big Dipper, in various parts of the
world, is not thought of as a dipper at all. In modern Europe,
people think the Dipper is a cart. Egyptians look up and see a
bull's thigh. Others think it's a bear. And the Dipper changes all
the time. Human beings have lived on this earth in some stoop-
shouldered form or other for millions of years. At the dawn of

evolution, the Dipper formation didn't look anything like it does now. Timothy Ferris, in his book, *Seeing in the Dark*, says that the Dipper, a hundred thousand years ago, had a "squarer bowl and a straight handle like a primitive implement." In a million years, when Allison and I will have ceased to exist even at the microparticle level, the dipper won't exist, either. I crawled in our tent and cuddled with Allison, then uncuddled, because her bare legs, smooth in Tehachapi, were getting stubbly. We slept on different sides of the tent. When I woke up, the Dipper was gone. The white sky had washed it away.

We rose up that morning and walked into the foothills to look for the water for the better part of the morning, on dirt roads. We searched under rocks, behind piñon pines, and under hills. I don't know how much time passed, and when at last we found the meager water, it wasn't much of a relief. The two of us were sticky and tired, and the usual silty water was only a puddle, barely enough to quench us.

"It's our dream," Allison said, staring at the murk. "But it's just not worth this amount of anguish. You know what just kills me? We did everything right this time, and it's not good enough."

This time we hadn't screwed anything up. Equipment failure is an act of God. If we were going to quit anywhere, this was the logical place, right here, near a grove of thirsty pines. The Lois and Clark Expedition had gone far enough, it seemed. Eventually, we'd have to emerge from the woods and get jobs again. And did we really want to spend our vacation time bent over at another water hole, slurping mud, while mean greenies chewed holes in our legs?

But the two of us could not will ourselves to quit. It is possible to make a momentous decision without knowing why. Perhaps we feared that if we quit then, we would leave the trail before figuring out why we'd tried to hike it in the first place. At the time, Allison, sitting by the waterhole, said that we had been "shamed" into sticking with our plan, but I now suspect she had other motivations. As I've mentioned, she was a feminist of sorts. Perhaps her trail was a kind of protest, a boot kick in the crotch of backcountry patriarchy. Allison was one of only a half a dozen women walking the PCT that year, and dozens of men walked it that year. She often wondered out loud about all the "sexism" and the "macho shit" that pervaded hiker culture.

She had a valid point. A woman came up with the original idea for a PCT, and yet the trail, in some ways, was a sausage party. Even Allison sometimes talked about her experience from a masculine perspective. She spoke of the asceticism and humility that comes from walking a hundred miles a week and eating dried-food meals that she called "C-rats," a military term. She was coming to appreciate the discipline that the trail was giving her, and the way the trail helped her draw from reserves of feral flintiness. Her body, once soft, was finding its true shape. The hike changed her every day. She often said she was "amazed at the transformation" when she looked in a motel mirror. She was surprised at her resiliency, and so was I; in spite of her cranky knee, which still caused her pain, she just kept chalking up miles. California was helping her claim something for herself. "How many women can say they've walked across California?" she told me one day.

I had my own reasons for sticking to the trail. I can't boil it down to any one thing, either. The trail still seemed better to me than an occupation. In fact, it was becoming my life now, Velveeta, horseflies, sunsets, and all. The trail made me feel like an iconoclast, zigging when the rest of the nation merely zagged. The national recession was only a seedling when we dreamed up our plan to walk the PCT. Now the bad times were in full bloom. There's nothing like an economic slump to remind you of the chances you might have taken, if only you had found the cojones. I had some friends at that time who were becalmed in the Horse Latitudes of diminished expectations, even before the economy begun to plummet. They were stuck in the same small towns for years. Only their hair moved away, marching off their scalps and taking up residence on their backs and asses. All around me, men stood meekly as life's changes ran roughshod over them. Prospects diminished while guts enlarged. Every year gave shape to new unspoken horrors: maxed-out credit cards, mortgages, children, male pattern baldness, and they didn't even get to choose the pattern. I knew I had break out *now* or it would never happen. I needed find out what I had before the time was lost.

It was July 6. Twenty-four days had passed since we first set foot on the Pacific Crest Trail. After resting up for the night, we rose up the next day and made a vow to march on as far as we could toward Kennedy Meadows, while drinking cup after cup of sun-brewed Twining's Ceylon India blend, so strong it gave us cottonmouth. As we headed into the Domeland Wilderness, caffeine sang in our veins. We hiked, jogged, and sprinted through green-grass meadows, past tall trees that blocked the sun that lit the tops of rock giants above us. We ran until the landscape grew lush. The Lois and Clark Expedition hiked past a tilted shack, complete with a crone in a plastic chair out front and a pit bull at her side, but we paid them scant attention. On we walked until we reached a place where wildflowers grew to our waists, and the sound of something static filled our ears. It was water, more than we could ever need, flowing by the side of us. The Lois and Clark Expedition had crossed its last stretch of dry terrain. The first time we saw the Kern River, it seemed a dreadful waste, all of that moisture slipping past us. We also felt small beside it. In the desert we were the tallest things. Here, even the rocks on the meadow's edges were bigger than single-family starter homes. Mountains moved in closer, until I realized they were not independent of one another, but were towers on a connected wall. The closer we got, the more the wall seemed to wrap around us.

In a field, we found a Pacific Crest Trail journal in a weather-proof metal container mounted on a pole. Todd the Sasquatch had signed the trail journal in bold letters. "Am I the last through-hiker?" he had written. "NO YOU'RE NOT!" a message beneath it said. The spidery script was the Gingerbread Man's. We whooped. Maybe the Gingerbread Man would catch up to Todd the Sasquatch and leave him in his dust. But that wasn't all. Beneath his addendum to Todd's message, GB had written a missive for us:

"Hey, Lois and Clark Expedition," he said. "You made it. Welcome to the family."

Allison and I did a spontaneous jig in the tall grass. Now every bit of our hike added up to this moment. We could not stop jabbering about how our feet alone had brought us here as we high-stepped through the meadow and stomped onto a two-lane blacktop to Kennedy Meadows. Get me to a hamburger stand. Get me to the nearest phone booth. I could hardly wait to call the people who thought we would die. And then I remembered that Kennedy Meadows had no phones. It was one of the last "off-the-grid" towns in America, with ranch homes, scattered stores, and two restaurants—Irelan's Home Cooked Meals and Grumpy Bear Retreat, restaurant, information center, and home of Mountain Beef Jerky—all running on generators. The only way to call loved ones was to stand outside and yell. That, or you could borrow the emergency radio phone at the fire station for five dollars a call, but it was a long walk down the road. Oh well, we couldn't brag to our loved ones after all, but at least the locals would hear our stories. We'd be kings for the day.

The Kennedy Meadows general store was closed when we got there. Allison stuck her thumb in the air and waved it in front of the road. Minutes later a brick-colored pickup stopped. An old man and an old woman sat in the cab. A German shep-

herd crawled all over the bed. Its name, according to the owners, was Jake.

"Where to?" the driver said.

"Food," I said.

"Bath," Allison said.

"Painkillers," I said.

"I know the place," the driver said. "Get in. Don't mind
Jake. He won't bite you."

Jake curled his lips and showed some teeth as we climbed
in beside him.

"Jake," the driver said, looking back, out the window. "*Don't*
bite them."

The truck sped up, with us and our things in the back. Poly-
morphic rocks in the distance held their shape. The landscape
slipped back, cows in the foreground, dust on the cows, and
the highway behind us. Ranch houses flashed red and white.
The truck came to a stop in front of a bloated tan dog snoring
in the road. He looked like a hair-covered sausage. We climbed
out of the truck, shouldering our packs, and stepped over the
dog, which didn't flinch. The café doors were open. We looked
through the crammed aisles: beer, tackle, Advil, muffins, salsa,
banana chips, fishing lures, powdered Gatorade. Near the door
was a barrel of sour fruit gumballs that squirted goop in your
mouth. A middle-age woman regarded us with no facial expression. Her hair was curly, her body small and stocky. Standing next to her was a handyman, in his mid-thirties, plump,
with splotchy stains on his overalls, a tool belt around his waist.
"Hi," I said, hopefully. "We're Pacific Crest Trail hikers looking
for a bite to eat."

"We get a lot of those," she said, and did not smile. "Some
of you are okay. Some of you haven't been so nice. You steal the
salt shakers."

"We what?"

"And the pepper, too. The salt I understand, but I'm not so sure what you do with the pepper."

The handyman smiled at this. His eyes were bright marbles floating in an oil slick.

"Did you say Pacific Crest Trail hikers?" the handyman said. "You hikers shit all over the woods around here. The coyotes get the turds, and then the toilet paper dries up and blows around. And one time, this hiker tried to burn his toilet paper after he took a crap in the forest. He burned the toilet paper all right, and he burned the trees down, too. Five thousand acres."

"Well, I'm sorry to hear that," I said. So much for my king-for-a-day fantasy. Now, after walking 245 miles from Agua Dulce, I was just another potential condiment-swiping dead-beat, and an arsonist to boot. The woman's husband, Frank, came out, sweaty from the burger grill set behind the store. He held his arms to his sides and yelled through the door at the dog, which had risen from its slumber to bark at cows. We were starving. The woman, whose name was Virginia, took our orders. Cheeseburger, cheeseburger, sundae, sundae.

Allison and I walked out front and sat down. Virginia came up with our orders, one at a time. I fell all over that burger, biting wet chunks out of it, wanting more. The homemade ice cream was so cold it made my neck cramp up. We killed our sundaes with long glinting spoons shaped like swords. I was starting on my second when I noticed a dented exclamation mark of a man, skinny and stooped, walking toward us. He could have been fifty. He might have been eighty. The man had a ragged beard, jeans, a ripped shirt, and an expression of stupefaction. Frantic motions, absent teeth, and yet I was happy to see him at first. I needed a bit of attention from the outside world. Besides, he seemed like a friendly fellow. He kept on smiling. I smiled back.

"Damned Pacific Crest Trail hikers," he said. "You're not one of them, are you?" He let loose with a harrumph and shook his shoulders. The shake traveled south, down the length of him, like snake twitches. I no longer wanted to talk to him so much, and yet a talk was about to happen, perhaps a long one. He pulled up a chair and scooted up close to us. "You hear my question?" he said.

"Yes, I heard," I said. "And yes, we're Pacific Crest Trail hikers."

Virginia came up, smiling. "Ahh," she said to Allison and me. "So you've met Hiram?" Her eyes darted between me and the stranger, as she set down another sundae.

Hiram scooted up close to me. One of his eyes was all squinched up. His yawns smelled like liquor. He waited until I'd scooped deep into my sundae. Another spoonful of cold ice cream was starting to press against my tongue when Hiram gave me a jab on the shoulder and said, "The best way to eat a goat is when it's right out of the womb. It melts right in your mouth. Best fuckin' thing you ever tasted."

I just about spat out my sundae.

Hiram cackled, slapped his knees, and fell all over the place. He kept getting up and sitting down again. He laughed some more and pointed at my shocked expression, as if gesturing to an imaginary crowd. He let out a long blast of language about everything and nothing. He did a twitchy sort of jig as he moved all about that porch, circling us, regaling us with stories and anecdotes that I could only half hear. He moved with a peculiar grace, holding his arms to the sky. If he were capable of quiet, Hiram would have made a fine mime. He told us that he was a retired beryllium miner. As a recovering high school nerd, I knew a bit about beryllium. Among other things, they use beryllium in guidance systems for weapons of mass destruction, which is odd, considering that Hiram had no guidance system to call his own. He caromed from place to place on that porch.

"Want to know what really pisses me off?" he said. "On all

the land around here, you can't build new roads because it's federal wilderness designation. They're shutting down the jeep roads around here, and for what? The Sierra Club asks you, 'Don't you want to save the wilderness?' What they don't tell you is they're closing it off from everybody, including you, too. What about the cripples who can't go in with backpacks like you? What about everybody else?"

"We're just walking," I said. "We don't represent anything."

"You packing heat?" Hiram asked. "I tell you, there's so much meat running around out there, you're wasting your time with all that dehydrated shit. You wouldn't believe all the animals. You could shoot your way across the trail. You know, speakin' of animals, I was hanging out with a group of guys once, not far from here, and we ran over a bobcat—didn't kill it, though, only stunned it—and what we did is we put it in a briefcase. We left it outside, on the side of the road, and what do you know, a Cadillac comes cruising down the road, and it's full of niggers, you know, black people. So the Cadillac stops and pulls over, and of course they stole the briefcase—what else are they gonna do?—and opened it and drove away with it. They only made it a short while, and sure enough they slammed on the breaks and every single one of them ran off in a different direction."

Allison and I looked at each other, stunned. Hiram wheezed, and then he started in again. He asked us if we were carrying a rifle to help us get food on the trail. He asked us if we were even carrying a fishing rod. When we shook our heads both times, he laughed again. "Such a waste," he said. "To be out here and not carry a fishing rod. You got some of the best fishing in the country right here!"

Virginia cleared out the dishes and presented us with the bill. As she came around to take the water glasses, we asked her where we might find a bed. She pointed to a dirt road leading, across the rocks, to a hill, on which sat a gleaming aluminum trailer. The rent was thirty-five dollars a night, in advance. Allison and I paid in cash, and Virginia handed us the keys. We were just about to leave when we noticed the handyman chatting with Hiram, and looking at us with suspicion and amusement. Hiram explained to the portly fellow that we were out hiking the Pacific Crest Trail, but we weren't hunting or fishing because we were environmentalists. As he said this, he tilted his eyebrows in a dismissive way, and the handyman chortled.

We hiked onto the pebbles, leaving Hiram and the handyman sitting there gesticulating to no one. Out on the rocks, we found our trailer. Before we went inside, I shot a picture of Allison, holding a jawbone she'd found. All the teeth were intact. "Maybe it's a deer," she said. "I can't tell." The bone was a stained crook, curved in the middle. I have the picture still. Allison looks weary but lovely, her blond hair flying everywhere. She's flexing her right bicep, and in her left hand she's carrying the bone, white from the sun. Allison appears to be flying, her arms in a cloud bank.

The trailer was small and tight. Allison fell asleep on a simple bed in a dark room with wallpaper that looked like knotted wood, next to a tub with a hot-water faucet whose thin drool felt like a sacrament. The tub was narrow and short, and I had to contort myself, sticking my legs up, to fit, but I let the water coat me and watched the dirt rise along with the soap scum. It felt wonderful. The sun went down behind the mountains through the window. The trailer didn't have a generator, so I leaned from the tub to light the lamp on the floor; it hissed and gave off a greasy smell that filled the room. Light from the lamp revealed a row of other lamps on the floor, each made of glass of a different color: yellow, orange, pink, and blue. I lit them all. Our strange room glowed. Allison slept while I looked in a mirror. The wind picked up and shook the walls while I studied my bristle beard. My hair has always been brown, and yet my beard was red. My face had narrowed. Circles had grown under my eyes. I kidded myself that I looked like van Gogh. In truth, I looked a lot more like the cavemen in a diorama I'd seen, long ago, at the American Museum of Natural History, in the Hall of Evolution. I looked so hard in that trailer mirror, and at the man staring back, that it gave me vertigo; the more I stared, the more I saw someone with a dim glint in his eyes and a beetling brow. He looked so brave and mean and dumb, but mostly dumb. My mouth was closed, but the image in the mirror bared its teeth. I had to brace myself, my hands on the wall, and it felt like I was falling into the mirror.

Next morning, I couldn't get Hiram's harangue out of my head. I felt he'd misjudged us. It irked me, to have come all this way and have people get the wrong idea about us. And it occurred to me that this experience might not necessarily fill other people with awe after all. I could no longer assume that walking the trail would change the way people regarded me or, if it did change the way they looked at me, that the change was necessarily a good thing. If this was so, it was silly to chalk this up as an achievement to inspire other people. Was that the point? As my dad liked to say, "This trail is yours alone, young Daniel. You can't put it on your résumé."

If that was the case, we might as well enjoy it more, especially now that the desert was over and the mountains had begun. And so, when Allison expressed interest in buying a fishing rod, I backed her up enthusiastically. Hiram was right. Why rush this, and eat lousy food, for the sake of wowing everyone when they might not be wowed? Let's take it easy and live off the land. Besides, we'd packed too many baggies of homemade granola. It was delicious straight out of the oven. Now, one month later, I dreaded the kitty-litter clumps of oats, the terse raisins, the bitter elbows of old cashews.

And Allison loved fishing, though she barely knew how. She associated it, for some reason, with her father. They squabbled sometimes, but it was something they enjoyed doing together.

She wanted him to teach her to whip her line in an S-curve over her head and make the fly alight on the lake like a real bug. We were going on about all this when Virginia overheard us. "I'm going down to Bakersfield today anyhow for supplies," she said. "You want to come along? We'll stop at this fishing place I know."

Allison looked like a child then. She smiled in a way that still fills me with an ache when I think about it. Before we knew it, we were bouncing along in Virginia's sod-colored Blazer, down a road above a vast drop, no guardrail in sight, speeding down mountain roads above the copperhead curl of the Kern River. We stopped at the fishing place by the riverside. Allison searched the aisles. The owners indulged her, thinking she was Virginia's daughter, and Virginia said nothing to correct this. Allison found a black shiny thing, four segments folding into themselves like an opera spyglass, so compact you could barely tell it was a fishing rod. "Look at this," she said to me, holding it close to my face. It was her first telescoping Shakespeare pole. After we drove back to camp, without another thought, I took the granola from our backpack and threw it straight into the nearest Dumpster. We wouldn't need that crap anyhow.

Everything was going to be slower, and Allison would catch fish every night. That is how it was going to be, I thought, as we lit out from Kennedy Meadows the next day, toward a snowbound horizon, passing fishermen up to their waists in the Kern River, then up into a scorched wood, a forest of poles and skeletons with no arms. So the handyman hadn't been lying. The smell lingered in our nostrils. So one of our kind had done this to the forest? Allison and I vowed not to strew toilet paper all over the place, not to burn the woods down. We decided to be ambassadors for the PCT.

Once we made our way out of the forest of ashes, the trail changed. In bare feet to spare our socks, we stepped through cold creeks and walked across meadows full of shooting stars and toad song. As a precaution we'd packed ice axes, two and a half feet of blue aluminum with metal claws. You can use the duckbill part of the handle to dig stairs in a snow wall. You use the sharp end to bite into the ice if your legs slip out from under you. The new gear and clothes made me feel like a beetle, wobbling on stumpy legs. Big Motherfucker sagged with the weight of himself. Swaying on his hinges, he groaned.

But the land is beautiful enough to make you disregard gravity. One day out in the mountains, you are halfway across a meadow, and something comes creeping. You glance at the muscles in your lover's right calf and notice, for the first time, the length of her sunburned neck and the way she lopes when she walks across a meadow, the way she presses her nose into every mountain aster and columbine. You pull her toward you. Before you know it, the two of you are falling, just off the trail near the edge of a forest. Dried sweat makes your clothes stiff; you take them off. Your feet are swollen from the elevation; it takes too long to remove your boots so you give up; you leave them on. Soon you're on your back; your head is resting on a sequoia root. Her eyes are closed now, and her hair is blowing all over the place. A pine cone presses your back, then rolls up your neck and works itself into your hair. You are together just off the trail that has confused you, forced you to fight, and led you to a poison spring with uranium in it. All the worries about mile-bagging, all the obsessive thoughts about reaching Canada: your lust crushes these things. You lie in uncomfortable pebbles afterward. For a long while you stay where you are, on the ground. Lying there, dazed, you snap away at the telescoping branches of the trees above you with your Pentax K1000 camera because you want to preserve the way you looked up through the trees and into the blue, from this exact angle. You don't want to forget again, the way you forgot in the desert.

We lost Allison's fishing rod somewhere in the high country. I can't remember where the hell we lost that thing. Most

likely it was out in a backcountry camp near a row of boulders
and a ribbon of clear water. It would be easier to remember
where we lost it if she'd ever had the chance to use it. That way
I could look back on the maps and remember such-and-such
lake, where she caught a trout, and come up with a rough ap-
proximation. I have little to go on, but I remember the moment when she discovered it was missing.

We were a few miles north of camp one day. On a whim,
she'd searched her pack and found it gone. We backtracked to
our camp or the place she thought was our camp, for there
were dozens of tent-flattened spots like the one we'd used for
the night. When we got there, we found nothing but thigh-
high grass, boulders, and a stream full of thimble fish, the sun
shining clear to their bones. She searched one row of sites while
I searched another. "It's black, remember," she said. "The rod is
black. I might have lost it in the dark." I watched her down-
turned eyes as she scanned the landscape. "Are you sure we lost
it here?" I said.

She said nothing. Neither one of us knew for sure that she'd
misplaced the rod here, and we both knew why. I'd promised to
slow the pace, let her take afternoons off and fish, but it never
happened. I said we'd "slackpack," but old fears and ambitions
came up. I was concerned that steep snow, slippery glaciers,
and rough climbing would impede our progress, so I'd tried
to compensate by rushing us through the flatter terrain. Since
she'd rarely even handled the fishing rod, we could not say for
sure that it went missing in this place, instead of a hundred
other places. We searched for a half hour. A ranger went past,
then another hiker. Allison told them that it was a "telescoping
Shakespeare, brand-new," and to "look out" for it. She turned
to me. "You told me we were going to take it easy," she said.
"You told me I was going to catch fish for supper." Judging
from the just-so tone of her voice, this was a declarative statement, not an accusation. "I wanted it," she said. "I thought we

were gonna go fishing out here." I had no idea what to say, so I shrugged. She took one last look at the place she thought might have been our camp, and then she cinched up her pack and headed north on the Pacific Crest Trail.

"I'm sorry," I said.

She said nothing.

I followed close behind her.

Chapter 18

The Way of the Wolf

One week in the backcountry, close to the most popular base camp for Mount Whitney, Allison and I were sweating our way up a long set of switchbacks, our eyes on a diamond patch of sky above the treetops, a sign the climb would be over soon. We walked all day up steep ridges, then marveled at the views from the top. Directly in front of us, to the south, the tallest peaks caught the drifting sunlight. Scattered lakes in the foreground lay in shadow; they looked like holes punched from the scenery, through which the sky above the distant peaks shone. In the forest that day, I tended to lose myself in thought. I had been to these woods before. After one more week of walking, we were set to arrive at Mammoth Lakes, the resort where my family vacationed for one week each year. I came to think of this area as my refuge, sealed away from the rest of my adolescence.

I came of age in a chichi golf and beach town in California, a Jewish boy trapped in a blond eugenics experiment. Socially awkward, smelly, and bitter beyond my years, I spent large amounts of time in the basement of our house conducting unclean experiments on high school classmates, rendered in modeling clay. I would sculpt body cavities in the Play-Doh figures and stuff them with Play-Doh spleens, intestines, hearts enclosed in toothpick rib cages. Then, after a trial by a kangaroo court, I would sentence the green and purple homecoming queens, football players, surfer dudes, and stoners' wall denizens to have their insides torn out by my plastic Yoda action figurine. Disembowel them he did. I formed an alternate world in my family home's dank basement, where I constructed a balsa-wood dollhouse and placed a bread-dough figurine of myself in a balsa-wood BarcaLounger. While normal kids were heading to the prom, my alternate-reality Dan watched television and listened to XTC's "English Settlement" with his harem of scantily clad bread-dough lady friends, who would scratch and cat-fight and compete for his attention in ways that struck him as inappropriate but flattering. "Dan, oh Dan, would you like some more ginger ale?"

Aside from my Gumby killing sprees in the basement, and my imagined marathon sex binges with my stable of Play-Doh princesses, my family's annual trips to the Eastern Sierra became my greatest joy. In those years, the woods became my counterlife. My father would pack up our striped bile-colored Ford station wagon full of external frame packs, sucrose pellets, Tang, squeeze cheese, and freeze-dried astronaut ice cream. The road trips up to Mammoth Lakes were often frightful. Coyotes, with murder in their eyes, walked across the parking lot of the Carl's Junior in Mojave, sniffing Dumpsters, eying young children and dogs. On one trip, the car's radiator gave out on the long crawl up Highway 395, emitting a rancid-butter smell like burned Pop Tarts. But the mountains, when we reached them, were unlike anything I'd seen, great blocks of unbroken stone on dun-colored platforms with rusted rubble on their shoulders. They seemed to shoot vertically up above the Owens Valley. In the distance, cinder cones loomed red and sinister. Mount Ritter and the Minaret Mountains broke the sky with their black spires.

How I loved and despised those trips. The Sierra dished out delights and torture in equal proportions, in a system so carefully calibrated that I learned to regard intense pleasures with wistfulness. Every lovely lake and tarn concealed colonies of mosquitoes, warm clouds of them descending from nowhere. They lit on my calves and shoulders and wrists to punch my flesh with their twirling stylets, to suck and poke and gouge. Those clouds chased me from camp to camp as if linked to my head like speech bubbles in a cartoon.

No moment in the High Sierra went unpunctured. There was always a twist, an irony, a catch. During one of my reveries, on a scenic pullout on a high trail, where the air had a tangy Pine-Sol scent and views dropped away to a V-shaped valley full of wildflowers, a pack mule farted in my face. The foul whoosh went on for about fifteen seconds. I could not take it. And yet I learned to live with the balance, the yin and yang of comfort and pain, pleasure, smells, and disappointment.

It's not that the woods made me feel competent; quite the opposite. It's just that the woods made everyone in my family feel like an idiot. They were a great equalizer. Even my older brother, a strawberry-blond sadist with a weakness for Ayn Rand, was reduced to a wood louse by the sequoias. Out in the woods, he screamed with fright when yellow jackets swarmed around him. Once, while he was already panicking, I informed him that these stinging creatures were attracted to the glare of his brightly colored windbreaker, though who knows if this was true. I never claimed to be an entomologist. Out in the forest, during a sudden storm over the Minarets, my brother scanned the sky with rabbity eyes, searching for the lightning bolt I dearly hoped would roast him in his boots. That's what I loved so much about the High Sierra. It was a reliable producer of long-lasting and delicious memories.

I recall long nights eating crunchy dehydrated meatballs, which amazed and disgusted me: Who knew that scientists could freeze-dry gristle? Dehydrated carrots grew to four times their normal size in hot water. My father flinched when he saw the carrots, for they reminded him of his childhood, in which he was forced to eat slimy root vegetables. The carrots scared me, too, because they looked like mutant orange leeches flinging themselves from the pot with crazed insistency. Sleeping was fitful, and for good reason. In those days before ultra-lightweight North Face equipment, we used cheapo nylon deathtraps known as "pup tents," with not one but two poles propped—for reasons I still can't understand—on the inside of the tent, to hold up the roof. If I so much as rolled over in my sleeping bag, or even fidgeted, the heavy steel poles would come crashing down on my skull.

Mornings, however, were bright and pleasant. Skies were pink and purple and shot through with blue mist. Father would crawl out at seven thirty in the morning, in near-frozen temperatures, exposed knees knocking as he crouched in his mummy jacket vest—which, strangely, left his hairy arms completely bare to the elements—and light the fire. Then he'd stumble around for wood to make the fire larger. How strange to see him there, this streetwise New Yorker who grew up to be an electrical engineer and a wealthy man, who spent so many daylight hours away from home, troubleshooting or out on the road, now playing paterfamilias in Stone Age conditions, subjecting himself to inconveniences and low-level discomforts. "Young Daniel," he would say to me, in a booming voice, "get a log," and I'd make my way through the underbrush in search of kindling. For a shining moment I felt like a Walton. We had prunes, Ritz crackers, vacuum-sealed hash browns, and a stick of Hickory Farms smoked summer sausage big enough to inflict blunt trauma. For a short while, I had all I could ever need.

Distracted and nostalgic, I led Allison to a wrong turn,

down into a pine forest, which turned out to be an equestrian route to a trailhead, where some PCT hikers try to hitch a ride out to Lone Pine for supplies. We had just discovered our error and were turning around, hiking back to the place where we lost the trail, when a skinny man hurried toward us with a baffled expression on his bearded face. From a distance his legs looked hairless, as if he'd Naired them down. They flashed in the sun like scissors. On his back was a pack not much bigger than your average weekend warrior's, but filthy. I figured he would blow right past us. Instead he stopped and stood in the way.

"Hey you," he said when he saw our packs, ice axes lashed to the bottom. His skin had a dull sheen, slimey from sweat. "You the couple in front of me?" he said. "The Lois and Clark Expedition? Hiking the Pacific Crest Trail?"

Allison and I looked at each other. I nodded warily at the stranger. We were no longer very surprised when people we'd never met knew our trail names. The PCT has an amazingly proficient telegraph of gossip and innuendo, fueled by trail journals and occasional southbound hikers who tell the army of northbounders about everyone they've met en route. In a sense, the PCT has its own Internet.

"Mmm-hmmm," the stranger said, sizing us up. He had a tight little fuzz beard. His small eyes squinted through spectacle frames. "Tell me," he said, "did you lose a shit shovel seventy-five miles ago?"

I felt my face turn crimson. Yes, as a matter of fact, we'd lost that cat hole shovel somewhere in the southern Sierra, forcing us to scratch out our constitutional trenches with various branches and rocks. I nodded sheepishly.

"Huh?" he said, as though he hadn't heard me. "You lose some toilet paper, too?"

I blushed again. Well, yes, as a matter of fact, we'd also lost some toilet paper quite a while ago, forcing us, for a brief period, to scratch our bottoms with various leaves and branches.

"And a bedroll?"

"No," I said. "We did not lose a bedroll."

"Huh?" he said. "Okay, so the bedroll isn't yours, but you should be more careful next time. It's not good to, you know, toss your stuff all over the place. This"—he interrupted himself, gesturing toward the foxtail pines and their jigsaw puzzle bark the color of chocolate—"this is not a dump."

"I will be more careful," I said.

"What? Okay, yeah, you should try to be more careful."

We all stood in awkward silence for a while. Then he smiled. "So . . ." he said, "anyways, everybody calls me the Wolf. You heading to Canada?" After hearing our answer, he jumped in and continued. "Yeah, I can walk forty miles in one day. We're late in the season, I know, but I'll push on through even if it's snowing in the north, even if I've got to do the trail in snow-shoes. And when I get to that finish line, I'm gonna drink a dry beer." Wolf meant this literally; he insisted that he was in possession of a dehydrated "malt beverage" that foamed up when you added water.

Allison smiled. "You can't dehydrate alcohol," she said calmly.

Wolf would not be dissuaded. He insisted that it was an actual beer. He kept staring at us, smirking, tilting his head in bird-like motions. I could tell he was waiting for something to happen. I felt like I was on a stage, unable to remember my lines.

"You're overpacked," he said at last, pointing at Big Mother-fucker.

Oh, so that was the cue. I was supposed to comment on his puny backpack. Not wanting to be a Grinch, I played along. "Wow. It's amazing to me that you can hike the PCT with that little pack," I said. "How do you do it?"

He handed me his pack, which weighed next to nothing. In it I found a weatherproof bivouac sack, a fistful of Dots candies, marshmallows, and cinnamon bears in a Ziploc bag, a few packets of regular-flavor Top Ramen, and several squashed Snickers bars. I kept pawing through his pack. He had no tent, no sleeping bag, no Ridgerest, not even a compass. He didn't have maps, either. "What the hell?" I said. "Are you crazy?" It's one thing to hike the Appalachian Trail mapless. It has easy-to-find markers on trees. But the PCT is not nearly as well marked, with many confounding intersections. What if he got stranded or injured? "Where's the guidebook?" I said.

"I hate the guidebook. It's expensive and a waste, so I typed up this thing." Wolf reached into his shorts pocket and handed me a well-thumbed booklet of data, crudely stapled, with mileage figures in rows and basic information about water sources. "I'm thinking of printing up copies so other people can use it. So. Anyways. As much as I'd love to chat with you guys, I've got to get to Lone Pine and back. Chances are I'll sneak past your campsite in the middle of the night and you won't see me. That's how I got my name, Wolf. I can hike forty miles day if I want, but sometimes I get turned around and end up going in the wrong direction. One night, on the Appalachian Trail, I got so lost I snuck into camp at midnight. Some lady saw me and got scared. She thought I was a wolf."

"So . . ." I said, "You must be one of those crazy Jardi-Nazis."

He smirked. "Not one of those," he replied. "That Ray Jardine is way overpacked."

He waved good-bye and raced down the horse trail and was out of sight behind the trees.

The next day, Allison and I set off on a seventeen-mile round trip to the top of Mt. Whitney and back, four thousand feet up, four thousand feet down again. The Whitney round trip is not part of the PCT route, but we couldn't resist. Those who hike up the summit from Crabtree Meadows need no technical skills. You just walk up. It is, as John Muir said, a mule road. First the two of us put up the tent and stashed our gear at the lush base camp. At the time we just wanted views and the bragging rights. But Mount Whitney has always been one of my favorite peaks for psychological reasons. Unlike Mount Hood and Mount Rainier, Whitney doesn't try to be showy or bossy, dominating the landscape for hundreds of miles. Whitney has no fetching pyramid symmetry, no shapely figure that might look good on a beer can or pop bottle. Whitney isn't even the tallest mountain in America. It's merely the tallest in the contiguous forty-eight states. That qualifier condemns it to eternal also-ran status. As magnificent as it is, the mountain is also a little pathetic. On top of this, the mountain has been subject to one indignity after another.

Seventy years after white explorers had named most of the dominant West Coast peaks, Whitney sat in the darkness of obscurity, waiting around for someone to notice. Part of the problem is its location and surroundings. Unlike Mount Hood, which has no competition for miles around, Whitney is nothing but the highest spoke on a range of sawteeth. From the San Joaquin Valley, you can't see the peak at all. In the past century, many a man has tried and failed to reach its summit, not because the climb was all that difficult, but for the simple fact that they could not find the goddamned thing. Clarence King, celebrated geologist and outdoorsman, made a two-day trek toward Whitney, past tumbling boulders, over hazardous slopes, shredding his shoes as he made his way to "the highest peak." He arrived on July 6, 1864, only to look up and see two peaks that were significantly higher. Seven years later, he dragged his sorry carcass up the "real" Mount Whitney and was, by one account, "immensely pleased with himself." For two years he glowed with the knowledge that he'd conquered America's loftiest summit. Then, on August 4, 1873, during a meeting of the California Academy of Sciences, he dropped a bomb: in somber tones, he reflected about the arduous trek, and the mules he rode to "the highest crest of the peak south-west of Lone Pine, which for over three years has been known by the name of Mount Whitney . . . I know this peak well." Unfortunately, he added, "This peak is not Mount Whitney."* On September 19, 1873, King stood, at last, on the true Mount Whitney, only to find that three local fisherman had beaten him to the task by a month. King, who went on to become the first chief of the United States Geological Survey, was not the only great Californian to get confused. No less an explorer and mountaineer than John Muir set his sights on Whitney in 1873, only to climb Mount Langley by mistake.

All of this is enough to give any mountain low self-esteem, but Whitney faced even more degradation in the last half-century. As recently as 1958, it was the undisputed highest point in America. Then, in 1959, Alaska became a state, which meant that the 20,320-foot Denali was suddenly part of our country. Then, in the 1980s and 1990s, people with too much time on their hands put forth the theory that White Mountain Peak, facing Whitney from the other side of the Owens Valley, was really a few feet higher than Whitney, and that White Mountain rangers had perpetuated the "Whitney is the highest" myth to keep tourist hordes out of White Mountain's delicate high-desert ecology. I asked District Forest Ranger Jan Cutts, a spokeswoman for the U.S. Forest Service, about this conspiracy theory. She suffered my queries with good humor. "We're rather low on the pecking order, you know," she said. "We only manage land. We don't determine tallness." In any case, a 1998 global positioning study put the matter to rest: Whitney conclusively dominates the lower forty-eight, and White Mountain is merely the third highest peak, at 14,246 feet.

---

*   Francis P. Farquhar, *History of the Sierra Nevada*, Berkeley: University of California Press, 1969.

Pushing our way slowly up the switchbacks, hiking fast above the timberline, I could understand all the confusion. Even when we made it to thirteen thousand feet, feeling nauseated and barely able to nibble our chocolates, the summit was nowhere in sight. We climbed, up talus slopes, past a platoon of marmots, and straight through the slush of melting ice. On rocky wastes where no trees grew, flowers bloomed through cracks in the granite. "How far are we from the top?" I croaked to a man with a walrus mustache.

"You're on the summit, buddy," he bellowed back, "I mean it. You're on top of it!"

An hour and a half later, we were still nowhere near the summit, and a second man, also with a walrus mustache, assured us we were still two miles from the top. It was pushing 3:00 P.M., and we had to allow four hours to get back. What if we got caught in the dark? I was tired, looking around, wondering why Allison was not in sight, when I heard a blast of "fucks" and "shits." I looked back and saw Allison fifty yards back, in a wet heap in a snowbank. "Do you want to get to the top so badly that you don't care if I break my leg?" she said, dusting off snow particles. I pulled her out of the snow and was about to apologize when a familiar figure came bolting down from the switchbacks. It was the Wolf, looking no cleaner from his journey to Lone Pine. He'd just scaled Whitney from the opposite side, out of Whitney Portal, and was now skipping toward us. "Hey," he said, looking at Allison, who was still shaking the snow off her haunches. "I'm worried about you guys. Take my headlamp in case it gets dark. It can be hard to find your way up there. If you make it down by dinner time, I'll make you eggs and bacon."

"You mean real eggs and bacon?" Allison said. "What if it leaks all over your gear?"

"What gear?" Wolf said, flashing a smirk. He waved and ran away from us down the switchbacks.

We turned to face the mountain and made our way up the last pitch. At last we stood on top, staring at flat-bottomed clouds and the shadows they cast on the Owens Valley, a sultry murk to the east. Below us, day hikers in orange, yellow, red, and blue formed a rainbow inchworm making its way up the switchbacks. On the mountain, no one was around, just a brick shack with a metal roof among the talus. We were standing on Whitney, savoring our triumph, when we saw a thin man, unshaven and puffing a cigarette, even as he walked into the shack and signed the guest register. When he was done scribbling his message, I bent down to sign the next available space. The smoker had written, "Jason," giving no last name. Under "Address," he'd written, "Wherever." Outside, he took only a sleepy interest in the peaks and clouds. Thinking I might get him to smile, I unholstered my Pentax K1000 monster camera and stepped up to take his picture. Jason From Wherever threw his hands in front of his face.

"No pictures" he shouted.

With vague thoughts of hidden bodies and the Witness Protection Program, we followed him as he trotted back down toward base camp, off the mountainside. The land unfolded, rock staircases dropping to a mandolin lake where a beautiful woman sat on a rock alone, peeling an avocado. Back at camp, Allison and I stopped to fetch some food from our tent, then followed Jason From Wherever through the smoke of burning logs. At dusk, Wolf sat in a clearing tending a fire, while making good on his promise to cook us dinner. After ensuring he had an audience, he set a box of bacon on the flames and stripped the lid off to reveal a pound of white fat streaked with red. When the bacon was good and bubbling, Wolf took out twelve unbroken eggs from a red shock-proof container and dumped them in the bacon, which received each egg with a haughty hiss. Jason From Wherever sat down with us; Wolf had invited him to share our supper. The eggs foamed and spat. When they were cooked, Wolf grabbed a gluey clump of eggs and meat and stuffed it down the hole in his beard. Between moans, he said, "I'm gonna catch that Gingerbread Man and pass him, 'cause no one keeps up with me for very long."

"I don't know about that," I said, reaching out with my Lexan camp fork.

"Oh, I'll get him," Wolf said through a muffler of eggs.

We sat there, hunched, and bared our teeth in the firelight. All of us grabbed fistfuls of the smoked-meat pudding. The fire gave off so much smoke, the moon turned yellow. I felt part of something larger than myself, a wolf pack, a clan. Eating this burned, wet food felt like the fulfillment of an unspoken promise, a backwoods communion. When the flames died out, the first stars showed through the trees, and Allison announced it was time for dessert. She took out a brown Ziploc bag full of dirt-brown powder, spiked with a pinch of powdered espresso, added some filtered water, twirled the mixture with a stick, and, voilà, there was a pot of chocolate mousse so thick it clung to the stockpot's sides. Those with bowls made use of them. Those without them ate like bears. Wolf was speechless. "Fucking awesome," said Jason From Wherever.

We sat there most of the night, having the kind of loopy conversations that might sound intelligent in college, when all the dorm mates sit in the stairwells draining twelve-packs of Black Label, smoking impotent Samoan skunkweed, and pronouncing it "kind," then analyzing Peter Gabriel lyrics backward for an hour or two. "Followed the Grateful Dead for a while," Jason From Wherever said. "The thing about the Dead is they never fuckin' moved. Oh yeah, they sorta pivoted sometimes, but they mostly just stood there. Went to a concert once when Jerry moved, just a bit, I mean, he kinda shook his shoulders or something, and the whole place just fuckin' exploded."

The whole night went like that. Wolf talked to Allison about an "easy" way to cure her blisters. "Don't pop them 'cause they'll grow right back," he said. "What you want do is take a hot, clean needle with the thread still attached, and run it through your blister and let the pus wick off it." In the woozy haze of fat, sugar, and exhaustion, this sounded like a brilliant suggestion. And the night kept stumbling along until, at last, Jason From Wherever stood up and let loose with an extravagant belch. He took a tug off his cigarette, bathed us all in blue smoke, thanked us all for the free food, picked himself off the log, dusted off his bottom, and bid us farewell. He walked out into the woods and the forest swallowed him up.

Allison and I were about to take off, too, when Wolf, poking at the burned crisp of the bacon box, called out to us. "Listen, you guys. You want, we can hike together a while if you like," he said. "I could use the company."

Allison and I looked at each other. We hadn't seen this coming. The Gingerbread Man had proven to us that these speed-demon hikers could make good conversationalists, and could guide us over dangerous terrain. On the downside, speed demons could make us collapse from exhaustion with their relentless hiking techniques.

"You don't have to answer now," Wolf said. "I'll be in the lake near Crabtree Meadows tomorrow at ten thirty, taking a bath. If you want to hike, come looking for me. You'll find me."

Allison and I lit up our headlamps and made our way through the meadow, while considering his offer.

"Forty miles in the wrong direction?" Allison said wistfully. "No map? No tent? No guidebook?"

I didn't know what to say. He did seem a bit wacky, but I liked the knock-kneed coltishness that made me forgive the know-it-all smirks. More than that, I was curious. But I slept fitfully, knowing what lay ahead. Forester Pass was slippery and dangerous. I'd never hiked up and over an icy pass before. Suppose I split my skull? Allison had grown up in the frozen

Midwest. She understood how snow behaved. I'm a Southern Californian, born and raised. The first time I saw snow falling, while going to college in Connecticut, I thought there had been an explosion at a detergent factory. Besides, I hate slippery surfaces. Sure, we had ice axes, and everyone said they could save our lives. Back in the desert, the Gingerbread Man had tried to show us how to use them by throwing himself on a mound of dirt and stabbing it with his hiking pole. But his display wasn't all that helpful. The fact was I'd never practiced a self-arrest before. But not hiking with Wolf would have seemed rude at this point, considering the feast he'd given us. And besides, backing down would have made me look like a pantywaist in front of Allison. The decision was made. We would walk with Wolf over dreaded Forester Pass, the highest point on the Pacific Crest Trail.

Next morning we found Wolf floating in water so cold it made him howl. He put his clothes on, and we hiked into a deep wood where spider webs drooped in hammock shapes. Shelf mushrooms grew in plates so thick up the sides of trees I swore I could climb them and they would hold my weight. Wolf was patient and kind, indulging our slow pace. He walked in a birdlike manner, using his legs for the forward thrust while letting his arms hang to the sides as if they were incidental. He kept turning back to watch us waddle. "You guys need extra energy?" Wolf said. "I've got snacks." He reached in his pack and pulled out a baggie full of white glop mixed with red paste and blackish lumps. "You're welcome to eat as much of this as you want," he said. "It's cinnamon Gummi Bears, marshmallows, and raisins."

I thanked him but feared the snacks would make me heave. By my own calculations, we had plenty of food. I asked Allison to hand me the food bag. But when I looked inside, there was almost nothing left except some crumbling oat bars. We had plenty of flatulent freeze-dried dinners remaining: Lipton's Noodles, space-age stroganoff, and Big Bill's Beans and Rice. What had happened to our crackers? Where were the string cheeses and Blenheim apricots? Suddenly I remembered, with self-recrimination, that I had thrown our five-pound bag of granola into a Dumpster at Kennedy Meadows. I had my reasons—the granola was sickly sweet and the cashews had all gone bad—but we needed the calories now. I felt my body starting to digest itself.

Wolf frog-hopped boulders. Slow and indulgent as first, he was racing along, as if making up for wasted time. And there was one more unsettling factor. This was clearly not the Pacific Crest Trail. The signs all read, LAKE SOUTH AMERICA TRAIL. Rushing to catch a glimpse of him, we had no time even to ask him why we were going this weird way, or to check the directions to figure out where we'd gone wrong. Tired and ornery, I began to wonder if our imperious leader had any sense of direction. I also wondered if he was aware of his surroundings. I once read that a certain species of European swallow can fly when it's fast asleep. Is that how Wolf hiked? Did the wilderness even register in his mind? He never commented on wildlife except the sort that could harm him: chiggers, blackflies, and the like. His pace was robotic, metronomic. No slope could tire him out. Wolf hurled himself over every steep thing we saw without comment. He seemed superhuman. And though we were out of breath, and worried we would never catch him at all, the pace made me curious. What was the source of his tremendous strength? And what sort of person can hike for a day in the wrong direction, get up the next day, find his way back to the trail, get lost again, and not go mad? Or was he mad already?

Allison caught him on a rare rest break and asked him why he couldn't stop hiking. He told her that one of his girlfrends broke his heart. "I've never gotten used to rejection. I've been hiking ever since." When Wolf surged ahead of us again, and was out of earshot, Allison and I privately discussed why he didn't just leave the trail and meet someone else. When we finally managed to sprint our way alongside him, Wolf gave us a few more tidbits of his life story. He was twenty-three. In high school, his classmates voted him shyest. His driver's license showed a confused-looking young man with hair that reminded me more of an alpaca than a wolf. Wolf had been a roofer, camp counselor, and, to my surprise, a trail guide. But his main purpose in life seemed to be walking vast distances to mend a fractured heart.

He did not go into any detail about the true love who had dumped him. He did not even tell us what she looked like, how old she was, or the state where she lived. He talked only about his many treks into the backcountry. On his first fateful Appalachian Trail hike, he carried close to eighty pounds. At one point, he carried two backpacks at once. He brought along a trail guide dating to 1978, no map, six pounds of pancake mix, and a bundle of clothes, all of which got soaked. Then he hurt himself and could barely walk. It took him a month to hike a hundred miles. He gave up early, called his mother, and said he was quitting, but she knew that her son was so reluctant to give up any goal that she thought he was just kidding around. She would not pick him up at the trail turnoff. Consequently he had to walk, and hitchhike, a hundred miles home. "I thought I'd give up hiking forever after that," he said. "But I tried the Appalachian Trail again. I hated it all over again, but then I went to a town near the trail, bought a gallon of ice cream and a can of fruit cup, the kind with the little half-cherries and all the syrup. I dumped it on the ice cream and ate the whole thing. I felt better after that and kept hiking."

This confession made me like him a lot more. We bonded over junk food. But his ice-cream confession only made my stomach howl with hunger. As we climbed higher, trees grew twisted and squat, bent to the wind, roots exposed. They were bare of foliage, except for a few tufts of green needles. Their hooked arms clung to the slopes. Soon there were no trees, just boulders and scree as far as we could see. At twelve thousand feet above sea level, marmots ducked in and out of rocky dens. One stood at attention, its mouth a black *O,* whistling in alarm. Breezes turned our sweat to ice water on the slopes leading up to Forester Pass, a monstrous gray shape protruding in the distance. "We're going up and over that?" I kept saying to myself, my eyes bugging out at the ominous zigzag of snow and ice that rose from the base to the halfway point.

All this time, Wolf barely took a rest, and when he did, he often cut the break short before we got there, meaning Allison and I were out of breath and soaked through with sweat at all times. When we finally caught him, resting on a slope munching Gummi Bears, I was out of my mind with hunger. Rocks took on the shapes of potatoes and bread loaves, hard-boiled eggs and cocktail pickles. Allison and I had decided to make our stand. We were going to break up with Wolf right now. Even our muscles were feeling woozy. This arrangement was not working out.

"Uh, Wolf," I said loudly, before I could back down. He whirled around and stared at me blankly. "Oh Wolf," I continued. "We . . .uh . . .appreciate the fact that you've been nice to us. Thanks for the bacon. The thing is, we can't take another step. We feel bad about holding you back. I'm thinking you'll just go on ahead. We'll do fine up here on our own. Cook some dinner. Figure things out from there, okay?"

"Huh?" Wolf said. "What did you say? Well, that's fine. Do what you have to do." He looked pinched for a moment, put-upon and wincing, but he regained his equilibrium. The smirk returned. "Yeah, that's fine, you guys. But let me ask you a question: Where's the trail?"

Allison and I glanced at each other and then at the landscape.

There was no trace of trail. All around us was a crust of snow, footprints full of ice water, leading nowhere. Now Allison and I were too scared to continue without Wolf. Suppose we never found the trail and wound up stuck on that mountaintop? Of course, we had no indication that Wolf knew how to find the trail, either, but it made sense to stick together under the circumstances. That settled it. There would be no mutiny. We had no choice but to press on together, with Wolf leading. Flat-topped rocks became crude altars, set up for a quick sacrifice, as larger rocks, round as Olmec heads, looked on. I pulled hard on the cold air, which felt like mentholated smoke. All around me was a haze that hung in the middle distance and mountains with snow shapes draped on their flanks, chalk hill drawings of horses and leopards as long as football fields. I noticed the oddness of the light up there, the bluish tint that hung in the air and on the rocks and creeks, monochrome except for the black and green in the trees far below us.

We were headed straight for the granite wall between Bubbs Creek and Tyndall Creek. Many PCT hikers dreaded this place. It was common to sprain a leg here. Every once in a long while, something far worse happened. In late July of 1940, six Sierra Club members tried to cross the pass in late summer. Altitude sickness overcame them, their breathing turned raspy, and their lips turned blue. Two of the party, H. M. Mergenthal and Vincent Smith, were barely breathing. Mergenthal died the next day, but Smith seemed to rally, showing signs of movement. His friends carried him seven miles down to a base camp twenty-five hundred feet below the pass. When Smith passed out again, the others tried to stir him with blasts from an oxygen tank. The group loaded him up and started to make the seventy-mile journey cross country over high terrain, knowing he had no chance unless they could get him to the Kern River Basin. Remoteness was the John Muir Trail's selling point. It was so far from towns that hikers who wished to leave the trail, resupply, and return to the footpath had to budget at least three additional days for each supply stop. Not a road crosses its 211-mile route through Yosemite, Kings Canyon, and Sequoia national parks. That's the problem with the backcountry. Isolation is romantic until something goes wrong. Smith died long before they got out of the forest.

"Um . . ." Wolf said, standing before me. "It's three o'clock. You'll want to get down off the mountain before sundown. It's gonna be cold up here when the sun sets."

He turned around and rushed the snow-covered slope as if laying siege to it. He dug steps in the ice, the two of us following close behind. I did not want to raise my legs and risk falling, but I knew what would happen if Allison and I just stood there; the longer we stayed in one spot, the more our weight would melt the snow beneath us, like a scooper left to sink in a gallon of ice cream. As best we could, we followed this Gumby messiah, climbing rocks and snowbanks, slipping and falling and getting up again. Gray rocks radiated heat, forming circles of blue shadow in the snow around them. "Don't step near the base of those rocks," Allison advised. "You'll slip and fall." Blue plastic snow pants hugged her hips. Her survival hat shaded her face, its brim drooping over her forehead. What struck me, more than all those things, was the calm of that face. She was surefooted and confident, while I found myself sinking waist-deep in snow, post-holing, and falling on my face.

"Jesus Christ," I roared.

"Yes?" Wolf said.

"God damn it!" I shouted.

"Don't take my name in vain," Wolf said.

Sandwiched between calm Allison, a few feet behind and below me, and smirky Wolf, I wobbled forward. An ice chute lay immediately to our left. If I fell into it, I would toboggan to the bottom, now twenty-five feet, now fifty feet, now seventy-five feet, straight below us. Wolf was still smirking but there was a strained, wet look in his eyes, a look of concern when he glanced at me. I could tell he was worrying about me. I froze, scared, before a gap between two rocks. "Take my hand," he said. He grabbed hold of me, yanking me across the gap with such strength I felt like a child. He offered the same assistance to Allison, who said no. She leapt the gap just fine on her own. I should have been grateful then, but his concern and help just made me feel weak. All the same, I knew there was no climbing this pass without Wolf.

The switchbacks narrowed until it seemed we were climbing a turret with an exterior staircase leading to a vampire's perch: a stairwell, sinister but beautifully constructed, suggesting a backbreaking effort among its builders, even as it extracted the same from us. To the south, I looked down on a bowl of blue-streaked ice spreading out as far as I could see and culminating in a black crust that rimmed the horizon. A sign read, ENTERING KINGS CANYON NAT'L PARK. FORESTER PASS. ELEVATION 13,200 FEET.

But this was not a moment to celebrate. Once you claw your way up the snowbound pass, you've got to claw your way back down the other side. Far below us, to the north, lay a bowl of dark water in the shape of a human foot. The lake had no name, only a number: Lake 12,248. It was so far below I couldn't gauge the distance. Snow obscured our descent, turning it into a madhouse of confusion. Even our pathologically specific guidebook took a laissez-faire attitude toward the descent. All we could do was face the downward slope and aim for the black lake's big toe. The only way down was to twist and squirm down a ridge covered with ice, rocks, and pebbles. Wolf plunged down the mountainside, tripping over sun cups, depressions in the snow shaped like the corrugations in an egg container. "Trust me, this is the easy way," he moaned as he fell against a boulder. This was not hiking, exactly. It was more like selective tripping. I had learned, by now, that when Wolf said something was going to be easy, it meant a variety of things, none of them "easy." It might mean "bound to inflict punishing blows all over your body" or "liable to knock the molars from your skull."

"Easy," Wolf said a third time, and that's when I knew I'd be fortunate to get out of this descent to Gangrene Lake without smashing my bones to atoms. By this time, I was a quivering Shmoo of fear, barely able to move. Allison was just behind and above me now, sliding down the mountain, inadvertently kicking bread loaf–size rocks toward me. One whooshed above my head. I skidded on my ass, with rocks and pebbles ripping at the seams of my electric blueberry survival pants. I was furious. How could Wolf have gotten us into this mess? How could Allison be so calm? It was all their fault, the fact that I was struggling and tired, the fact that I hadn't had time to stop and get a proper snack. Up there on the mountainside, pebbles beneath my boots, I managed to stop myself from skidding for one blessed moment. And as I clung to the mountainside, contemplating all the falling and shrieking I was about to do, my thoughts, at last, became focused and clear. "Come on now," I said to myself. "Get real." It was time to stop blaming everyone under the sun for the fact that I was here, falling down a mountain and fixing to split my skull. It wasn't Wolf's fault. Hell, he'd practically pulled me up the mountainside, giving me encouragements as I went along. And it wasn't Allison's fault, either. She'd tried to keep me calm and focused. I couldn't blame my upbringing, either. This wasn't my parents' fault. So whose fault was this, anyhow? Who was really to blame for the stupid and dangerous things that kept happening to me, over and over again?

I am talking, of course, about John Muir.

As I fought my way down the slopes, four words echoed out from my past: "Goddamn you, John Muir!" I said again and again.

Long ago, when I was only eleven, my father took me and most of my family on a two-night backpacking trip across a small portion of the John Muir Trail. Above Thousand Island Lake, where I thought an uphill climb would never end, I threw off my backpack in front of my parents and started shouting, "DAMN YOU, JOHN MUIR! DAMN YOU, JOHN MUIR," until my throat was raw. I was furious at him, even though, at the time, I had no idea who the hell he was. I had seen photos of the man, with his shag-moss beard and penetrating gaze, but I didn't know he was the fellow who had founded the modern environmental movement, or that he had lobbied successfully to establish Yosemite National Park. I did not know he was the founding president of the Sierra Club. I just assumed he was some silly tool who had built his own trail with a rusty pickaxe and named it after himself.

Muir didn't build the John Muir Trail; it is a tribute to him, not one of his projects. And yet my irrational impulse to curse him was more appropriate than I suspected. Muir was largely to credit, or to blame, for people like me who went to the western wilds in search of a salve for their psychic nicks and pains. Muir wasn't the first to rhapsodize about the woods and nature's redemptive power. In fact, his writings often repeated what Thoreau had said before. But Muir, unlike Thoreau, did not dilute his rapturous writings with descriptions of terror and frightful awe. To him, the woods were pure frosting, a celebration and tangible evidence of God's paternal kindness. Muir was the first to popularize the notion that forests are wild but friendly places where a man can become whole again. Because of his influence, he helped countless Americans shake loose the influence of a Puritan-Calvinist tradition that cast the woods as a place of devilry and mischief, a place to be brought under the yoke of agriculture. In doing so, Muir provided the philosophy that unified my contradictory views about the outdoors. The more I learned about Muir, the more my attitude changed from scorn to admiration and idol worship. Until I read about him, I thought of my suburban life and my annual forest explorations as separate realms. Muir sold me on the notion that a man could internalize the beauty and harmony he finds within nature and bring those qualities home with him. He might even use these qualities to mend the broken pieces of himself.

It may sound simplistic, and sentimental, to suggest that every hiker who comes to this place has a "defining wound" or loss that motivates his walk, like Wolf's heartbreak or the Gingerbread Man's implacable rage against the USDA food pyramid. Life doesn't fit into any neat *ABC After-School Special* packages. But Muir's wounds set the standard for those who travel to the wilderness to find the grace they lack outside the trees. Muir somehow survived not one but *two* beastly childhoods, first in Dunbar, Scotland, where his arch Presbyterian father thrashed him with a switch, even for minuscule offenses, and later, in Wisconsin, where that same father forced Muir to dig sandstone wells by hand. Muir passed out and almost died from inhaling carbolic acid gas—a condition called "choke damp"—at the bottom of a well, and yet his Grinch of a dad, after letting him rest for a couple of days, made him go right back down into another well. Muir learned to survive by guile and invention. His father was so controlling over Muir's time that the young opportunist invented a pulley device that raised his bed and tipped him out before sunrise so he could sneak in a few minutes of study. It's a lesser known fact that Muir also invented a machine that lopped the heads off gophers, but let's set that aside for a moment.* My point is that Muir never lost his practical sense of loony improvisation. Those impulses

---

* Years later, Muir expressed gratitude that this "horrid guillotine of a thing" didn't work very well.

could have helped him make a fortune in the industrial world, but a horrific accident changed his course.

In March 1867, while he was working in an Indianapolis carriage factory, a file flew up and punctured his right eye, leading to a "sympathetic" reaction in the other eye that left him temporarily blind. He stood near the factory window in the dusty light, dazed, as the vitreous humor drained into his cupped hand. At this point, Muir gave up the last vestige of conventional living. The Lord, he thought, had sent him a clear message: "God has to nearly kill us sometimes to teach us lessons," he remarked. Leaving the factories behind, he tramped across the South and the Southwest, and in 1868, ended up in the Sierra Nevada. By the time Muir arrived on the scene, the gold rush had already destroyed much of northern California's high country. Still recovering from his eye injury, Muir used wound metaphors to describe the landscape. He wrote that hydraulic mining had "scalped" the foothills and "disemboweled" the valleys.

To save what remained of the woods, he wrote voluminously about mountains and forests. His rhapsodic prose is often ridiculed today, but Muir's haters fail to understand the cunning strategy behind the rosy description: he was inviting readers to sympathize with the humanized trees, bears, and chipmunks, while placing loggers and shepherds in the role of serial killers. In the words of the essayist William Cronon, John Muir recast the woods as a kind of "domestic sublime," a safe place where the forest is church and the animals, gentle parishioners. In doing so, Muir also created the impression that the woods were a refuge, offering an escape hatch for anyone with sturdy legs.

Muir's writings made me feel better about the fact that I had no place in the suburban world, that I failed at sports, did not know how to talk to girls, and wore goofy ensembles: mixed plaids, Keds in insane colors, and corduroy slacks, long before their second coming and redemption. Muir's writings helped me forgive myself for being shy to the point of paralysis, wearing my hair in an accidental mullet, brown storm clouds drifting over my ears. Muir, as a young lad, wasn't much of a ladies' man, either. He didn't get married until later in life, and the thought of this comforted me at high school dances, where girls assembled in Conestoga wagon circle formations, Belinda Carlisle–style Go-Go's skirts flashing in the strobe lights, while I slouched alone, delivering lame pickup lines to any girl who dared to stray from her protective circle: "Would you like to maybe visit the concession stand for Reese's Pieces? Or perhaps, if you want, a soft drink?"

It was nice to know the Jeffrey pines, dormant volcanoes, and Belding's ground squirrels awaited my return every summer, offering strength and distraction, even in the throes of my obsession with Millicent Wong, who didn't love me in return, though I stalked her so diligently and gave her an avalanche of achingly nondemonstrative greeting cards—"I want to be friends with you, okay?" I even tried to ply her with decorative roses I'd made by hand from bread dough, Elmer's glue, red lacquer, paper, and toothpicks. The woods helped me forget my degrading date with Sarah Jane Hitt, who was willful and self-possessed, in spite of the cruel classmates who ranked her among the toadliest girls in the school. At evening's end I tried to kiss and paw her just because I thought kissing and pawing were what you had to do on a date, even when the revulsion was clearly mutual. This dream of wilderness stayed with me throughout college, and set the stage for my love with Allison, who shared my enthusiasm for all wild things, mushrooms, strange plants, sudden rainstorms, and open pastures under the Berkshire Mountains.

But that day, up on Forester Pass, I couldn't help but feel exasperated with my idol, and unworthy when I thought of him. I could not understand why his recipe for redemption did not work with me. His safe, domesticated woods were turning me black and blue. His calm benedictions could not stop me from getting bitch-slapped like raw pizza dough against the cold Sierra rock. My clothes were soaked through, and I had nothing to eat but nut crumbs, nasty oat bars, and dehydrated dinners in my rucksack. Mountains were bullies, the clouds overwhelmed me, and the trees made me feel like an ear mite. How could Muir feel so strong and proud in a landscape that only made me feel absurd? How could Muir survive on "essences and crumbs," with a pack as "insubstantial as a squirrel's tail," while I felt hungry and weak?

While I longed for lobster, Muir subsisted on rock-hard bread and tea, seeing no need for fancier foods, not when the glaciers all around him ate nothing but "hills and sunbeams." The woods were Muir's pleasure garden. Dangerous thunderstorms were "jubilees of waters." During a near-death experience on Mount Ritter, his life "blazed forth . . .with preternatural clearness." Hypothermic evenings on winter snowscapes were an excuse for Muir to dance the Highland jig to keep warm. He even enjoyed running around during earthquakes. Danger was his tonic. He never carried a gun, and he never suffered a snakebite, a bear bite, or a spell of sickness in the forests.

And that, I suppose, was the difference between Muir and me. I had wanted to follow him here but I didn't know how. My childhood miseries were ordinary. My sufferings were fairly standard. Muir had had all the physical and mental hardship he could stand before he ever set foot out here. I wanted to see what he saw, feel what he felt, but I just couldn't. If Muir were out hiking down Forester with us that day, he would have had a hard time comprehending my panic attack. He would have been up there tripping and falling and laughing it up with the Wolf, and if he had taken the time to look back at me, he would have snorted at my "morbid fears." Muir once derided those who become sick with fear "as soon as they find themselves with nature, even in the kindest and wildest of her solitudes, like very sick children afraid of their mothers."

His retreating vision escaped me at every turn.

His ghost was here, but I could never quite grasp it.

It was time to head down to Gangrene Lake. Halfway down the slopes, with pebbles in my socks, and my ears ringing from all the times I'd fallen through the melting ice, I came to the realization that things could not get any scarier, or more dangerous, on the Pacific Crest Trail. Then I had a realization: I could not remember if I'd paid my latest health insurance premium two months before. Had I or hadn't I?

Allison and I were self-insured through an expensive program called COBRA, available through the newspaper we'd quit. The program made me quite suspicious, and not just because it shared a name with the seventh deadliest snake on the planet. I also objected to the fact that the insurance covered almost nothing except hospitalization for grievous injury. Up until now, it had never occurred to me that COBRA could be good for anything. Now the likelihood of such injuries was increasing with every second as Wolf led us down a nonexistent steep pathway toward purgatory. Under the pale white light, chloroformed by ugly clouds, the dank lake winked like the eye of Beelzebub. Allison was still behind me, and now the rocks she was raining down were as big as bricks. Good God, I said to myself. Now I really mustn't get hurt. I prayed to God that Allison wouldn't fall down and crack her skull. If that happened, she would find out that I'd bungled the insurance and then there would be hell to pay. "Go down on your heels," Allison roared, and I had no idea what she meant. "Heels, heels, heels, walk on your heels."

"How?" I screamed.

In small increments, the bottom of the valley grew closer until we arrived at the slimy ice around the lake. Any hasty or ill-considered move would send us falling into its fetid waters.

We had to cross one last stretch of dangerous late-afternoon slush on a near-vertical stretch of slope. I slipped. My boots sank to the ankles in the dark lake, filling my socks with cold water.

When at last we arrived at the Pacific Crest Trail, Allison and I covered each other with kisses, wrapped our arms around each other, and roared.

"Welcome to the Range of Light," Allison said.

The two of us took a moment to stare down at the Bubb's Creek Canyon. Polished walls gleamed. There was a dry emptiness to the sky above the pink-brown mountains and the U-shaped sweep of pines between them. All around us was the rush and push of life in the canyon. This was the type of expanse that could move any heart, including Wolf's. He had a transfixed look as his eyes caught the orange beginnings of a Sierra sunset. I wondered what he was going to tell us. He sat on a slab of rock in the reddening light, his head bowed before the scenery's majesty. He alternated his gaze between the valley and us. I could tell he was winding himself up, choosing just the right words to pin down this golden moment.

"Know what?" he said. "Snickers taste like shit. Not just Snickers but all chocolate. But the thing is I still eat Snickers because they give me so much energy."

He reached in his backpack and offered us a couple of ass-squashed Snickers that looked like they'd been run over by an eighteen-wheeler. Some of the bars were hanging halfway out of their wrapping; they had that white, skanky look that chocolate gets when it melts and hardens a dozen times or more. If I had been anything short of starving, I would have rejected his offer. But Allison and I were tired, relieved, and glad to have survived the "easy" way. I grabbed hold of a candy bar and forced it so hard down my throat that I ingested stray bits of wrapper. Allison smiled through the lip gloss of low-quality melted chocolate. The sun was sinking. Rangers might be lurking here, ready to bust us for our lack of a wilderness permit.

We followed Wolf as he guided us down from the Gangrene Lake toward the dark forest where we'd camp for the night.

John Muir's Range of Light became a range of darkness as the sun fell through the gap in the valley. Through the pines, we heard a rasping sound as if the forest were clearing its throat. The noise came from a weak stream, boulders rising from its bed. The sunset's colors drained into Center Basin Creek. Reds and oranges swirled in the stream, even as the sky turned gray. Tired and disoriented, none of us wished to slosh through knee-deep water, but camp was on the other side. Wolf had a plan. Bending over in pine shadows, he lifted up a piece of twisted wood, nine feet long, and threw it over the water. It winged through the air like a javelin and came to rest in the mud, with opposite ends on either bank. "This will be our bridge," Wolf said. "I'll test it out first."

Wolf walked in spider steps. The wood boinged beneath his feet, but he made it across. "Now you go, Madame," he said to Allison.

"Mademoiselle," she said. "I'm not married."

Wolf looked stricken but held the stick as Allison walked in delicate steps. I watched with lustful intent. She now had incredible legs from hiking 323.4 miles so far in our journey. Sure, I was exhausted, but when you're in your twenties, no amount of panic, fears, stenches, muscle ache, or self-recrimination can dampen the need for sexual gratification. In your twenties you will always clear the table for sex, even if you've just staggered home from surgery. If only Wolf hadn't been there; we could have retired to some shady bower by the river and dispelled our tension.

Allison made it to the other side. My turn to cross.

"Is it okay to walk on this thing?" I said to Wolf and Allison. "It looks sorta sketchy."

Allison believed that people should make their own decisions without constant hand-holding from other people, and just shrugged. Wolf had a glazed "huh?" on his face. I stepped on the bridge. It cracked and splintered.

"Um . . ." Wolf said.

I wagged my arms to hold steady. The bridge buckled.

"Um, you might want to jump," Wolf said.

The bridge snapped like a pretzel stick beneath my boots. Down I went, chest first, into the water, my knees knocking into slimy pebbles, my backpack bonking my shoulders and skull. Water soaked my shorts. Wolf looked down at me, puzzled. For a while I lay there in the stream, drenched and angry. I got up and shook the water off me like a dog. "Look what you did! This is all your fault," I wanted to say.

Back on the trail, I passed Wolf, not speaking to him even when he asked if I was okay. We kept walking in cold darkness.

Allison was watching me. "You look terrible," she said.

I grunted.

We camped. Allison and I ate the last meal in our reserve, something sweet and sloshy, with tofu pellets and roachy raisins. She didn't like the fact that I was sulking and using my tumble in the creek as an excuse to take a long rest break while she cooked and cleaned. She didn't like the fact that I was snubbing Wolf. "You'd better check on him, make sure he's okay," she said, chafing the stockpot with a filthy rag.

I grunted again, and stood for a while at the edge of camp, watching the moon climb like a round white bear through the tallest branches. When I'd collected myself, I looked for Wolf, and soon found him sitting Indian-style in his windbreaker, leaning toward his fish-can stove full of burning leaves. He was eating Top Ramen, original flavor, the blue-white wrapper lying on his shoes. He hugged his knees.

"Hey," I said.

"Hey," he said.

There was silence for a long awkward while. Night birds filled it with their trills.

"I just wanted to thank you for all you've done," I said. "We never would have gotten down Forester Pass in one piece if it weren't for you."

"Mmm," Wolf said.

"I mean it," I said.

"You would've done the same for me."

"Yeah," I replied. "But really, I didn't do anything for you at all."

"Your thanks is enough," he said, as if to signal the end of this discussion.

The breakup moment came fast the next day. We arrived so quickly at the portentous intersection that I hadn't prepared a speech. Wolf wanted us to keep plugging along with him somehow. As he stood there, a bank of clouds passed over the cliff face, creating the woozy illusion that the landscape was about to fold over and topple on us. I was at a loss, so I thanked Wolf again. There is always an element of self-laceration and hairshirt-wearing when you give thanks. It's a way of recognizing kindness and, at the same time, expunging guilt. And there is always something about parting ways with someone that turns us all into Hare Krishnas for five minutes. When we leave someone behind, and know we will never see him again, we bathe that person in the perishable milk of loving kindness. Wolf, I now realized, was a brave and decent man without irony or cowardice, two of the mankind's worst afflictions. Wolf had tried to do right by us. Now he was about to be erased from our lives, and this knowledge made me appreciate the qualities that under other circumstances might have stung like nettles. He hadn't given us any trail names, or any particular comfort, but at least he'd shown me that you could take your life's disappointments with you into the forest and turn them into something else. Your heartbreak probably won't go away, but at least you can convert part of it into fuel to get you up and over the next mountain and back down again.

"Um," Wolf said, "you don't have to go down to Cedar Grove. You could eat my food."

"We'll only slow you down," I said.

"Well, okay then," he said. "But maybe I'll see you down the trail somewhere. Maybe you'll catch up to me."

"Maybe," I said. "We just might."

Allison, the realist, laughed. "Like that would ever happen," she said.

We shook hands with him. Wolf turned around to walk up a canyon wall. He was out of our sight in no time at all.

Chapter 19

Why I Walk

I walk because I want to be cool. I walk because I want to be a rebel.

All my life, I've shied away from doing cool things. I'm talking about swearing in public, taking drugs, slutting, and engaging in displays of primal rage. It's not that there was any law against doing any of these things, except the drugs. It's just that I was a nerd.

Growing up in a seaside town in Southern California, I had a large group of friends, all nerds. Studious and polite, they defined the boundaries of my world. In high school, we never got into any trouble. I thought we were being cheeky when we drove out to Spires, a chain restaurant in Torrance that stays open until midnight. Some nights, when our blood was up, we would stay out as late as ten thirty at night and eat a platter of popcorn shrimp. If we really felt like pressing the boundaries of societal norms, we ordered the Monte Cristo, which is basically a French toast sandwich, with ham, cheese, and powdered sugar on the top. Sometimes, we would stay out as late as eleven, sipping fountain drinks and ordering milkshakes, without even telling our parents, because, gosh darn it, they didn't need to know. At the time, I thought this was as rebellious as a teen could be. Consequently I was shocked—shocked!—many years later when I found out that all the other boys at my high school were smoking pot, snorting coke, and getting blowjobs on catamarans. How come they'd never invited me to even one of these parties? Where did they get the drugs? How did they keep the catamarans from tipping over? I tried to visualize these parties, but they were unimaginable. To me, a party was an occasion in which people gathered to play Pictionary or Yahtzee and perhaps consume some Hawaiian Punch. So how did these wild parties work? What did they look like? Did they start off with Pictionary and Hawaiian Punch and somehow transition, gradually, into the sex and drinking? Or was there no transition? Did some appointed person stand up at the party, in an awkward moment, and announce what was going to happen? "Hey everybody! It's eleven P.M. Put down that Yahtzee set. It's time for the drugs and the soulless fucking to begin!"

Don't get me wrong. I smoked pot a few times but felt nothing but forgetful, craving Beer Nuts, and convinced that everyone on earth was out to beat the shit out of me. In other words, it had no affect on me whatsoever. Once, at an outdoor music festival with my sister, Edie, I decided to join the counterculture once and for all. Unbeknownst to my protective sister, I bought a hash-infused granola bar from a freak in a dashiki. The granola burned in my stomach and made me dance shirtless to long-haired bands with names like Pele Juju and Leftover Salmon. Soon I was sitting in a lawn chair watching the landscape flash red and green and blue. Edie found me and stood over me shouting, "Dan, are you okay?" I might have asked her the same question, considering that my sister's head had inflated to twenty-five times its normal size and was rotating on its axis. Didn't that hurt?

I spent the rest of the festival hiding in my tent moaning and groaning. That day, the drugged cookie let me down. The next morning I was the same person I'd ever been, but with one more ridiculous new experience behind me. That's the problem with drugs. If you're a nerd, you might hope against hope that drugs will make you into something you're not. "Nerd plus drugs equals cool." But most of the time, there is no transformation. The nerd merely becomes hyphenated. "Nerd plus drugs equals drug-taking nerd."

But now, at last, I had reason to feel ecstatic. I was truly rebelling, like never before. I had stopped bathing. My beard was blood red and messianic. I had stories to tell. I had a gorgeous girlfriend, and with every sweaty mile, she looked more like an Amazon. The sun had bleached out every dirty part of her dirty-blond hair; it was pure gold and yellow now. Besides, we had reached central California, and had finished 12.1888 percent of the trip. Only 87.8112 percent remained. We felt unstoppable.

Still, I had no idea what to expect from Cedar Grove. The last time we'd left the trail for a supply town, the locals had treated us like rubes, thieves, and arsonists. We were hungry. Cedar Grove was a campground, hotel, and RV resort along the three-pronged Kings River. A sprawling wooden building housed a lodge we couldn't afford, a tasty if overpriced café/snack bar, and a grocery that was decent if you ignored the night crawlers that throbbed in plastic containers near the food items. A crowd gathered around us at the resort café, where we sat pile-driving pie, turkey, and ice cream down our throats. At first I wondered if they would mock us, but it soon became clear that we were rock stars. An old woman from Brooklyn in a black overcoat and pink scarf came up to see us. Our every utterance about trail life made her swoon with curiosity and worry.

"Oh, it's so interesting," she cooed. "My son did a cross-country bike trip once and it helped him get a job 'cause his employers all wished they'd done the same thing. But I worried about him all the time. I hope you're not being reckless. You drinking enough water? You wearing sunscreen? You're both so fair-skinned."

Allison laughed when the old woman went away. "New Yorkers are so fascinated with anyone who's not like them," she said, shaking her head.

It was true. The New Yorker regarded us as fascinating but not entirely sentient objects of curiosity, as if we were bioluminescent toads in a cardboard box. But I didn't mind being someone else's pleasure toad. All my life, I'd craved attention. Now so many people had so many questions that it became difficult to shove fistfuls of potatoes down my throat. Since we were so late in the Pacific Crest Trail hiking season, there were no other smelly through-hikers to elbow their way into our spotlight. Another couple was hanging out in the café, but few people were interested in them. For one, they were fresh-faced, not haggard like us. The young man and his girlfriend had heavy packs but looked like they hadn't spent much time in the woods. We'd overheard them saying they were walking from Mount Whitney to the Oregon border, laden with gourmet foods. They were taking it easy, going seven miles a day. Moments later, they slipped into the forest. Soon they left my consciousness altogether.

For once, I was full of stories, and everybody listened. Attention was like oxygen. I gulped it down so fast it made me lightheaded. Even Allison started hamming it up, believing in our legend. A pale-faced boy sidled over and asked for a look at her scrapes and bruises. "Look at this," she said, rolling up the sock of her right foot to show the boy her blood blister, red and livid, straight out of a medical textbook. "Nice, huh?" she said.

The boy's eyes opened wide. "Don't die," he said.

Everyone, all of a sudden, thought the trip was worthwhile and amazing, and we did nothing to discourage this view. So many people thought we were bad asses that I believed it, too.

A Virginia family, including three luscious Southern belles with creamy skin and tapered noses, walked over and mobbed me. The girls chattered and interrupted one another in catty but charming ways in an effort to talk to me. For a moment I wondered if Lee's Press-on Nails would be the weapon of choice in a blood fight for my attentions. Soon the hot girls found other amusements, and less attractive well-wishers took their place. "Back off. Pick a number," I wanted to shout.

Heady with the crowd's adoration, Allison and I retired to our tent at sunset, where we had wild, if muffled, celebration sex with the rain cover draped above the tent. Famous people need privacy, too. We filled my sleeping bag, and our Northface Bullfrog tent, with our egos and naked vastness. In my mind's eye, we were a pair of 757-pound Sumo wrestlers grappling each other in the darkness. The feeling that we were larger than life, and an inspiration for others, only got stronger when we were lying there afterward in each other's arms watching the sky go black through the mesh lining in the tent. Bit by bit, after Allison nodded off to sleep, I began to hear other couples across the campground groaning and panting with desire. We seemed to have triggered a bacchanalia of lust that blew through the grove. A geeky, standoffish Eurotrash couple, whom we had met hours before, now filled Cedar Grove with loud Esperanto grunts and gurgles rising from their tent. "Kwok, yok, yarooog!" they snorted. A few minutes later, through the opening in our tent, I saw that the Euro-couple, in a shameless move, had emerged, all sweaty, from their tents, well aware that half the campsite was watching them. They looked like a pair of contortionist dancers taking their sweaty bows in the moonglow. Allison lay mop-headed across my shoulder. She was bathed in the red tint of a Winnebago's beer lights. Children ran wild through the woods. Generators whirred. Out of the distance came the faint, amplified drone of someone giving a "ranger talk" at the outdoor amphitheater about "what animals do when people aren't around." The wind picked up. I fell asleep.

The next morning we felt so buzzed from confidence that we did something we dared not consider before: we streamlined the expedition. We took Draconian measures to lighten the pack load, getting rid of our inflatable Therm-a-Rest mattresses and our extra sweaters. If Todd the Sasquatch, the Gingerbread Man, and Wolf could hike with so little, then dammit, so could we. Feeling like Jardi-Nazis, we swaggered through the campfire convoys of Cedar Grove. I sat down on a bench and wrote a letter to my good friend James, the North Carolina journalist who had suggested we hike the trail in the first place. When he first said it, it seemed like a joke. Now I wanted to let him know that his grand escape plan had worked out after all.

I wrote:

> Hiking has given us a new perspective. We've climbed down an icy, snow-covered pass, probably the scariest experience of my life. We've met a lot of people, many of them truly friendly and giving, and others who are straight out of some Hangar 18 extra-terrestrial cover-up seminar. We met an aging cowboy who bought us biscuits and gravy. We met a toothless prospector who likes to eat newborn goats and basically frightened us. Adventure really is a good thing. In the past month, I've done a lot of things I've never done before, including hiking 26 miles across a desert toward a "reliable water source" only to find a piggly little mud hole waiting for me. All of this has made me a slightly different person. So then: What do I do when I return to civilization?
>
> 1. I'll probably have to shave my ever-growing brown-red beard. That'll take a week right there.
> 2. Clean my fingernails—that will take a month.
> 3. Have my belongings, and myself, dry-cleaned.
> 4. Perhaps seek employment.

5. *Eat nonstop until I gain back the fifteen pounds I lost.*
    (Not kidding. I look downright cadaverous.)

I'll write again after I get out of the Sierra. See you soon.

                        Your friend,
                        Dan.

After mailing the letter at the Cedar Grove resort, I came across the young couple I'd recognized from the day before at the café, the ones who were hoping to walk from Whitney to the California-Oregon border. Immediately I noticed that a small crowd had gathered around them. It made me envious and annoyed. Who the hell were they to steal my limelight? Suddenly I noticed that their once-bulging backpacks looked empty.

"What the hell?" I said. "What did this? And why are you back so soon?"

"Bear," the man said, shaking his head.

Chapter 20

The Hairy Other,
Part One

The man, tall, rangy, and handsome, in his early twenties, looked only moderately bummed out. He didn't act like a man who had just been mugged and humiliated by a mammal.

"So what happened?" I said.

"Well," he said, "I know we're supposed to only camp in places that have those bear-proof food lockers. But we overshot it and didn't feel like backtracking. We tried to hang our food up in a tree. We hung it up as high as we could, but I guess we did a bad job. The bear just climbed right up and knocked it down and ate our stuff. We banged pots and pans and screamed, and it just gave us a look like, 'What, are you crazy?' and took off with all the food. He got our organic cheese. Our breads. He got all our snacks." The man shrugged, sighed, and smiled. "That bear must've needed that food way more than we do," he said with a dreamy expression. "Lorraine and I appreciate our blessings. We aren't subsistence. We've got good teaching jobs. We don't have to eat grubs or go eating diapers to get by. The way I figure, when that bear came after our food, it was karma. That bear got some great stuff. I was just giving back something to nature."

While I appreciated his kindness, I wondered if bears would be quite so forgiving if they were to switch places with us humans. My general feeling is that the bears, given half a chance, would wipe us off the globe. A squirt of fear ran up my spinal cord. Suddenly I remembered all those warning signs posted throughout Cedar Grove. I didn't want to go out there and get my food swiped by a bear. I'd heard horror stories of bears chasing people until they dropped their backpacks. Allison and I had entered the realm of the Hairy Other, the dark master that lurks in the woods. The Hairy Other is bigger than you. He hides his bulk in the underbrush, or beneath a stand of pines, and though you may not see or smell him, he sure as hell sees and smells you. There are six hundred thousand black bears in thirty-seven states. Each one ranges over five square miles to gather its food. The chances of walking into any reasonably remote forest and not seeing one are slim. I knew black bears attack people rarely. They're too busy sucking down chipmunks, marmots, beehives, blueberries, thimbleberries, rose hips, hazelnuts, dogwood, and plums to want to take a bite out of our hairy asses.* But attacks do happen. A starving bear can and will administer a sucking chest wound. If a six-hundred-pound bear that can run as fast as a pony comes bowling after you on the trail, what the hell are you supposed to do?

"If the bear comes after you for your food, don't resist," the man said. "Sometimes the bear will do a fake-charge, to make you drop your stuff. They know what scares you. Usually it's just a bluff-charge, but you never know. Don't fight him off. Once the bear gets your food, it's his."

---

* List derived from Edward Hoagland's "Bears, Bears, Bears," from *Heart's Desire*, Tempe, Ariz.: Summit Books, 1988.

From that moment on, Allison and I could not seem to escape the signs of bears at Cedar Grove: hooded trash cans with security latches, written warnings, pictures of scraggly blackies all over the men's room, creating the impression that one of them might come up from behind you while you're taking a piss and scalp you where you stood. Quiet as a cat, the bear waits in shadows as you stumble around the bathroom, searching for something—anything—on which to dry your hands. You ask yourself: Where are the paper towels? Where the hell is the automatic hand drier? Thinking you are all alone, you don't feel the least bit self-conscious as you shake, shake, shake, then zip up your pants. Slowly, methodically, the blackie unfurls the two-inch nonretractable claws that will soon rip your face off. The last thought that goes through the oblivious murk of your mind, mere moments before your brains are scattered like confetti all over the bathroom walls, is "Why do those last drops always fall down your pants?"

I knew, in the rational part of me, that black bears got the worst of it in their stand-offs with humans. Among the many indignities they face: a multimillion-dollar black market trade, originating in Asian countries, trafficking in black bear body parts. American poachers shoot black bears dead, then remove their gall bladders, which are shipped, via middlemen, to unscrupulous pharmacists, who buy them for as much as three thousand dollars a pop and use them in phony "cures" for impotence, cancer, and rheumatism. Bear bile, sold by the gram, has a higher street value than cocaine. And you don't need to be a poacher to harm a bear. Campers who toy with them by offering them food and garbage, and then snapping their pictures, seal their doom. If a marauding bear, enticed by human smells, loses its fear and starts prowling campgrounds, harassing humans, and busting into cars, rangers will relocate or "put down" the animal. But those guilty feelings did not make me less fearful. The fact was Allison and I would be helpless out there.

That afternoon I asked a frowning backcountry ranger about "bear troubles" in that area. He had a gigantic beige hat and Oakley-type reflective glasses. He kept a shotgun as long as his arm mounted in the dash of his patrol car. The ranger told us that bears can recognize the shape of a food-storage cooler. The object's particular look and color translate as food. This thoughtful abstraction can drive bears to bust open a window or unhinge a car door to get at its contents. I didn't believe the ranger until he showed me a fistful of photographs: a car whose insides looked like they had been attacked with the business end of an industrial food processor, and a van with fat hunks of upholstery puffing out of tears in the backseat. There were nibbles all over the furnishings. It wasn't hard to extrapolate. Those nibbles could be all over us. "The fact is [bears are] unpredictable, and a lot of 'em around here have lost all fear of humans," the ranger said. "And that's not a good thing when you're sleeping out in the woods. Never, and I do mean never, sleep in a camp that doesn't have bear-proof boxes for your food. And never, never take your food into your tents with you at night. They'll go after toothpaste. They'll go after underarm deodorant. They'll even go after bug spray. They'll eat damn near anything."

"So what am I supposed to do?" I said.

"Show respect," the ranger said. "Leave 'em alone. And stay out of their way."

That's all very well and good, I wanted to say. But suppose we blunder into a mama and her cubs? What then?

Back in the woods with Allison, farther north on the trail, in a dark stretch of a secluded section of the Sierra Nevada, I kept hearing burbling sounds all around me. No, it couldn't be a bear, I kept saying. Maybe it's just yesterday's rice pilaf. It was getting late in the afternoon. We walked through a stand of strange trees, their bases as black and plump as potbellied stoves. The slanted red light fell on the trees, making them look hot to the touch. Allison was not helping matters. To pass the hours in the forest, she'd started telling me a series of "Pacific Crest Tales," penny dreadfuls she invented on the spot. She made a good case that these tales helped us climb steep switchbacks. They took away the occasional pain and boredom of hiking. The trouble was, I was already on edge from fear of bears—and her tales were always horror stories, ending with geysers of blood. In most cases, the victims were insipid men. One of her stories was about a family reunion in a creaky old cabin on Michigan's Upper Peninsula.

"See, the family was drinking, having a great time, except for the crazy older brother. The family had him locked in a stinky basement with rats crawling all over it because he was so insane. So he's down there for twelve years, eating rats, going crazier and crazier. His skin is bright white 'cause he's never in the sunshine. So there they are, having a great old time, when the older brother starts screaming and begging for mercy from the basement. Won't somebody please help meeeeeeeee? So the family is getting really drunk, and the younger brother is going to the bathroom, where he hears the sound coming up from the floorboards—somebody pleeeeeeeeeeease help meeeeeeeeeeeee. I am so lonely. Would somebody come downstairs and keep me company? Please. I haven't seen the light of day for over a dozen years. I promise not to harm any of you.' So the younger brother can't stand the guilt anymore. What's the worst that can happen? He unlocks the deadbolt from the basement door. Then he takes down the main lock, and then the other lock, and finally the last latch on the door. His family has no idea where he is. They think he's on the toilet or something. 'Hello, is anybody down there? Hellooooooooooo?' He walks downstairs on creaky steps and he hears nothing at all. And he sees nothing 'cause it's pitch black. And suddenly he sees a glowing shape, glowing, moving toward him. And it's the white glowing skin of his older brother, smiling, smiling.

'Hellloooooooooooooo? Are you gonna hurt me?' says the younger brother? 'Are you gonna do anything mean to me?' And the older brother says, 'It's okay, nothing's gonna harm you, nothing's gonna harm you.' And then he grabs his little brother by the throat. Cuts his throat. Chops off every single one of his fingers. Cuts off his toes. Cuts off his nose. And then he cuts off his dick!"

Allison, it seemed to me, said that last line with an unnecessary amount of relish.

"Cuts off his dick?" I said. "Did you just say cuts off his dick? And that's the end of the story?"

"There is no more," she said.

I knew she was a big joker. I knew she had a morbid sense of humor that could surface all of a sudden, in the darnedest of places. But it was dark outside. And there was no one around but the two of us, and somewhere in the back of my mind was the suspicion that Allison, perhaps, was one truly sick individual, and now I was going camping with her. And it made me worry. Between bears and Allison, there was nowhere to run. Allison's imagination was a fertile crescent of disgusting images. She was a Scheherazade of horror. The scary stories just kept popping up out of her, fully formed.

That night, as we first started thinking about a potential campsite, I was pondering, in particular, the dirty basement and screaming brother, the flashing razor, the severed penis lying in the basement dust. I was pondering the rats that the pale brother ate for dinner. Suddenly a hairy shape broke from the bushes near the Pacific Crest Trail, a rolling shape, low, fat, ungainly, but moving with great speed toward Allison and me at first, then whirling away, so fast, in a blur of pine needles and dust. Its hair was black, but not all of it. On the tips of its back I spied a flash of cinnamon and a shade of murky gray near its wet muzzle. It took me a moment to realize this was not a figment from Allison's sick mind.

"Oh my God," I shouted. "Bear! Bear!"

And then it was gone. Quiet again. How big was it? I couldn't say. I caught only a suggestion of haunches, a trace of shoulder, but I'd seen my first wild bear, moving among us, a pair of eyes, a well of dark brown as deep as our ancestral past. It's just not the same when you see a bear in a zoo, bored, fast asleep, pacing, or sitting there belching and yawning. When you see one in the woods, it somehow makes the forest revert from background to foreground. The forest seems to rise and engulf you. Was he there all along, watching? As we hiked farther into the dark, we came to a campground with a bear-proof food storage locker for campers. We shuddered, for it was padlocked to a thick tree and covered with nasty scratches, top to bottom. Something big and hairy and hungry had really wanted that food. Should we stop here for the night? Should we call it a day? But somehow, when you're hiking a 2,650-mile trail, the greed for mile-bagging can get the best of you. You forget to stop when you really should. You press on and on.

And all the while, I kept thinking about the Hairy Other, the watcher in the woods. For as long as there have been humans in America, there have been bears in the forest. In the course of those fifteen millennia in which people of one sort or other have occupied this landmass, men and women have reduced our monsters and our wilderness with spear, repeating rifle, shotgun, ax, and bulldozer. The great forests are gone. The mega fauna are extinct. But the woods still had the power to resurrect a strange, almost supernatural fear. It must have been a familiar feeling to the cavemen equivalent of Dan and Allison, traipsing through these woods in the Pleistocene era in loincloths, while clutching bone-frame tents and spears made from flaked-off rock points. Cave-Dan and Proto-Allison must have been fucking terrified. Back then, the two-thousand-pound short-faced bear roamed freely across the United States. When it reared up on its hind legs and roared to the sky, the beast was 11.5 feet tall from his hind legs to his skull. That's twice the size of a modern Kodiak bear. Think of a carnivore at the pointy end of the food pyramid, a beast so powerful that nothing, except a mastodon, would stand up to him. There was something direct about these creatures. Unlike black bears or grizzlies, they were not pigeon-toed, which meant they didn't waddle. No, they just came right at you in a straight line, and they didn't mess around with nuts, roots, and berries, either. The short-faced bear ate nothing but bloody meat. A black bear would be no match for one of these goliaths, which could have popped one into its mouth like a petit four. But a black bear could still weigh six hundred pounds and climb a hundred-foot pine tree in thirty seconds flat. We had to keep our wits about us out here.

Every night in the Sierra Nevada we hoped to find another camp with a bear box. But on some nights we miscalculated. On one such night we wound up camped beside a creek beneath a high cliff. We built a fire. Bats hurtled through the twilight. We debated tying our food stash to a tree, so high up that no blackie could get at it. But then we thought about those two airheads back in Cedar Grove who did the same thing and got screwed. There is a documented case in Yosemite National Park in which a bear climbed a tree, jumped off one of the branches, grabbed a bear bag on the way down in midair, and then came to a rolling stop on the ground twenty feet below. For all these reasons, I did something you're never supposed to do: In open defiance of the scary ranger at Cedar Grove, I stuck the food bag between Allison and me and slept with my ice ax near the opening of the tent, with the following idea: if a bear stuck its greasy filthy maw inside our tent and tried to get at our food I would stand and fight, to the death if I had to. I got the idea from reading a section of *The PCT Hiker's Handbook,* by hikers' guru Ray Jardine, who said he slept with his food, though he was extremely cautious to stay well away from designated campsites that would attract bears. "In PCT environs," Jardine writes, "I sleep with my food, prepared to guard it without compromise. At night I keep my flashlight near at hand, lest I take a blind swat at porkie. . . . And I do not suffer the misconception that my nocturnal bliss is inviolate. I fall asleep prepared to rise and assert my position."

The branches blew and scratched at the tent that night. Out of the enfolding woods came the sounds of padding on bumpy feet. Pad pad pad pad. Gurgling stomachs waiting. Snoring sounds. Wet snurfling and belching. Watching us. Digestive noises, then something large, so close I could hear the sloshing juices in its gut, or was it Allison? Stomachs growling somewhere. Long shadows again. "Never again, no, never," I said to myself. "Never again." A pressing snout, a depression in the top of the tent, a scratch, and a distinct black shape—don't scream—then nothing. Just wind. A dent, a scratch, a thump that woke me up, though I was barely sleeping. Just a pine cone. Something sniffing again. Where's the flashlight? I pick it up, a Maglite, black and shiny, stuck between my front teeth and lit full blast. Is anything really there? Should I bop it over the head? Spaces compressed and expanded at night in camp on the trail. The flashlight seemed only to flatten the darkness. Then quiet. Nothing.

This pattern continued for some time: I kept hearing—or thinking I was hearing—gurgles, snorts, and scratchings. Allison's stomach would make a frightening sound in the dark at three in the morning. Then morning came, in the smallest possible increments of lightness. On one such morning, deep in the woods, we were just getting under way when we came to a steep, steep cliff, practically vertical, off to one side of the trail. We saw a scraggly deer charge straight up the face of the cliff, bursting out of the forest, scaring the shit out of us, then up, up, up, rocks skidding beneath its hooves but it just kept going, going, apparently not caring if it broke its little neck. I gasped as we watched it vanish up the wall. Then I turned to Allison.

"If the deer out here are this cocky, the bears out here must be tough bastards."

The two of us turned to face the granite wall. We climbed all day. Between Allison's stories and the valleys and shadow, the clouds and streams and days blurring into one another, I cannot pinpoint the day, the time, the week, or the exact spot that it happened. I can only say that a bear, some days later, burst from the trees to the side of the trail, about a hundred feet in front of us, making us both leap forward in surprise. It had the look in its eye. It saw and smelled us. The bear froze for a moment. I knew what would happen. It would chuff. It would paw. It would make a charge for our food. To my relief, the bear turned its back on us and started sniffing at the ground.

And then Allison ran right for it.

"What?" I screamed. "What the hell are you doing?"

She lifted her hands to the sky to make herself look bigger. She would not stop. She bowled herself straight at that bear, now about sixty feet away. Her backpack quaked behind her as she ran forward, boots kicking dust as she roared. "Git, git, git," she said. "Git the fuck out of here."

The bear looked like it didn't even have a chance. It tore off through the woods so quickly that it hip-checked a sapling, making the tree shake like crazy.

The bear made a break for it, and melted like a ghost in the thicket.

Chapter 21

Macho Me

We were almost through with our first month on the trail, and making headway, aiming north toward Yosemite National Park. We hiked through creek-soaked meadows and corn lily fields, on soft ground. I felt entitled, comfortable, smug, and a little bit macho now. After all, we'd just walked four hundred miles into the High Sierra from Southern California in spite of all the dire predictions about us. Allison looked even more scrumptious than before; the trail had sculpted her body, firming up her buttocks so much they looked like oversized fists. Her back was strong, and her legs were steel pinions. I was skinny and strapping for the first time ever, and starting to understand what Eddie meant when he said my body would get so trail-hard I could hold a Bic lighter to my feet and feel no pain.

The footpath in this section was remote; Kings Canyon, Sequoia, and Yosemite national parks made up the largest road-free open-space expanse in the lower forty-eight states. Walking through the seemingly endless forest gave rise to the illusion that

America was untamed, although a mere 2 percent of the United States fit the category of "wildlands." Since we traveled cross-country on foot in the rawboned country, I felt a kinship with the snaggletooth mountain men of the nineteenth century. I'm talking about the first Anglo-Americans to reach this area in the 1820s, men with flintlock rifles as long as their arms, buckskin jackets, skinning knives, and hair that fell down their backs in braids. To the pelt-seeking profiteers of the western mountains, a balanced breakfast might include a root, a snail, leg of cougar, and a fine roasted dog. In these days of MapQuest, it's strange to think that most lands between Missouri and the Pacific Coast were considered undiscovered country in the early nineteenth century, at least as far as white people were concerned. Travelers who ventured west of the Midwest were said to be "jumping off," as if leaping from the far cliffs of the earth. Never mind that hundreds of thousands of Native Americans were pretty well settled in after millennia of living there, and never mind the leaky Spanish ships that had explored the coast of California as far north as Point Reyes, near present-day San Francisco, more than two and a half centuries earlier. As far as the Eastern establishment was concerned, the area where Allison and I were walking right now, and much of the Midwest, might as well have been on another planet. Thomas Jefferson, before the Lewis and Clark Expedition, speculated that woolly mammoths still tromped through the forests of Missouri, and no one thought he was insane when he wrote this in a popular book. Now there's no place left for a mammoth to hide. Everything has been pinpointed, explored, duly noted. Still, I liked to pretend I was a pathfinder, a mountain man, and gritty. The frontier had been closed for more than a century. There were no more empty places on the American map, but that didn't matter to me, not when there were so many empty places in the map of my brain.

I sometimes forgot that there was life outside the Pacific Crest Trail. I had everything I needed right here: female companionship, trees, stories, and even music. In the deepest woods, Allison entertained me with atonal renditions of death metal songs. One of her favorites was a Covenant song about Lucifer:

"Satan is his name," she screeched as she hiked through a waterfall's refreshing mist. "Across the bridge of death. There he waits in flames!"

Then she made a scary face. Sometimes she would bang her head, toss around her hair, or flash the sign of the Beast. Those were the good old times. In the midst of all this scenery and interesting music, I was starting to lose sight of the civilized world. But Allison sometimes ruined the spell by trying to engage me in serious discussions about our future in this "other" world, the one I could no longer picture. Lately, she could not stop thinking about jobs and other unmentionables.

"I miss the city sometimes," she said. "I get so bored. Where do you think we'll live when this is over? What do you think we'll do? I'm thinking it might be cool to live near Boston. I'm thinking we might get jobs at the Quincy *Patriot Ledger*. It's supposed to be a really good newspaper."

"The Quincy *Patriot Ledger*?" I shot back. "Why do you want to talk about that stuff now out here, where it's beautiful?"

"Whatever," she said. "You shouldn't make fun of me just because I know what I want to do with my life when this is over. I just want to go out and *do* things, you know?" We'd had this conversation many times before. "It's okay to have ambitions," she often told me. "I have a classmate from J-school, a friend of mine, who went to Germany to be a newsman and almost got blown up in a car bomb. The secret to that kind of success is drive." Sometimes her work ethic baffled me. Before we left on the trail, I eavesdropped on her having a phone conversation in which she scolded a friend for whining about working occasional twelve-hour days. "Working twelve hours is not *that* bad," she told the person on the end of the line. "It's not that much more than eight."

Unwanted talks about jobs and the future reminded me of a life I didn't want to think about. Worst of all, Allison intimated several times that we would probably have to get off the trail for an extended period in the next couple of weeks. Her anthology was about to be published. The book editors had warned her that she must be available off the trail to go over the final edits. This meant we would have to leave the PCT for at least a week. Never mind that we were running late, never mind that winter storms would crush us if we dallied. But I blocked out all she said. As far as I was concerned, the world of jobs and responsibilities was becoming an abstraction. She might as well have been talking about lizards on the moon. The journey, and Allison, were the only things I could picture. There was nothing to do but walk the trail.

We spent one morning climbing to Glen Pass. After slipping and sliding on loose pebbles and ice, we reached the top, where the pale blue sky faded to pastel-pink above the mountains. Hundreds of feet below, spyglass lakes gleamed from a hundred sockets. Loose bits of rock gave way to snowfields and sentinel rocks stacked on top of one another, forming an ominous ridge. It was hard to fix my gaze on any object. My eyes moved back and forth from scattered forests to white cones, and ink-dark ponds between them.

Climbing down the other side, Allison and I saw a few hikers slouching uphill. One man was painfully alone. On his face was a look of total resentment. Though Allison gave him a supportive nod, I could not help but judge him. Clearly he did not know the rules of the backcountry, I thought, and now the trail was taking a switch to his velvety-soft behind. A few minutes later, several Brownie-age girls tromped past us with exterior-frame packs on their backs and genocide in their eyes. No one smiled. In a shady glen, we met a sweet and aging couple carrying a gadget that emitted a shrill sound similar to the "voice" of a male mosquito. "Somehow it drives the pregnant girl mosquitoes away before they can bite us," the man said. "It cost eight bucks and it works just great." Allison and I were impressed, though I can't say the same for the mosquitoes, which crawled all over the man and his wife.

After meeting these other hikers, I couldn't help but wonder whether the age of access was such a good thing. Now that highways girdle America, it's easier than ever to get yourself killed in the backcountry. Sometimes I feared for the safety and well-being of my fellow travelers, but I also laughed at them. After all, the Lois and Clark Expedition had walked here all the way from Los Angeles. Though it pains me to say this now, I felt superior to the rubes who drove in their minivans. Since I'd already gone through what they were experiencing then, I thought I'd earned the right to snigger at their travails. I assumed my own initiation was over.

Meanwhile, we kept meeting unlucky and credulous people who transformed John Muir's Range of Light into their personal Mordor, a purgatory in the pines. One day, we met a sufferer who trumped all the rest.

We'd stopped for the evening in Woods Creek Camp, with several cleared tent spots close to the rushing waters. The camp was shady, under tall trees, with a view of the Woods Creek Suspension Bridge, which shimmied every time a hiker walked across it. The camp had bear boxes, so we didn't have to worry about a marauding *Ursus americanus* for one night. We were hanging out by our tent, tying the rain flap down over the top of it, when we heard moaning sounds emanating from a nearby tent. The panting got faster. The fellow, I assumed, was spending some quality time with himself, but when he emerged from the tent, it was clear that he was grunting out of misery, not pleasure. He was shaking all over.

"Is something wrong?" Allison asked him.

"It's not a question of something being wrong," said the man we would come to call Oedipus Rex, behind his back of course. Brown bangs winged into his eyes. "It's a question of everything going wrong that can go wrong, and some things going wrong that could not go wrong."

"Do you need any help?" Allison said. "We've got extra food. We were thinking of making s'mores."

"S'mores?" The man grunted. "All I've got is ramen crumbs—and I'm almost out."

Still shivering, he told us his sad story. He was from New York City. He wasn't much into hiking or survivalism, but he'd heard about the glorious John Muir Trail and was curious. A few months ago, he'd won a round-trip first-class ticket to California. "I figured it was my chance to see something pretty," he said, "so I decided to fly here and hike the JMT. The thing is I forgot my sunglasses. On Muir Pass, there's snow on either side for over a mile and a half, and if you stare at the glare it'll burn out your cornea. And that's what I did. I got snow-blinded temporarily, seeing white. I finally got the idea to hold a piece of paper in front of my face with a slit in it to see through, but it's hard to walk with a piece of paper in front of your face."

"I'm so sorry," Allison said.

"Anyways, I also realized that I'd forgotten my sunscreen, and another hiker gave me an extra bottle, but by that point I'd burned my hand so bad it got infected. After my hand got burned, I knew that things could not get worse, but guess what, they did. One night I forgot to stake my tent down. The wind swooped it up like a kite, and I had to chase it for a mile cross-country, over some steep shit, and then I scraped the fuck out of my knees."

"Um," I said, "we've got some disinfectant in a tube if you want . . ."

"Also, I didn't bring a goddamned ice ax, so I had to climb Donahue Pass on my hands and knees, barehanded, in ice and snow, 'cause I wasn't wearing any gloves. And then it turned out to be the wrong fucking pass."

"Well," Allison said, nodding her head in a sweet and encouraging way, while smiling and pointing to the man's fancy-looking bait-and-tackle stash. Nothing brought out the gentle side of her like someone suffering. She couldn't bear to see anyone in pain. "At least you're getting fresh fish for dinner every night."

"No, I'm not," he said, annoyed. "I never learned to fish"

"Isn't there anybody who can help you?" Allison said. "Don't you have a hiking partner?"

"Nobody," he said. "Ten days in the wild and I've lost my mind. I've started talking to squirrels. And the worst part of it, they've started talking back."

I stood there for a while. For just a fraction of a second, I wondered what might happen to me if Allison left me behind and forced me to walk in the woods alone. Would I start hallucinating and singing with marsupials? America's first Caucasian settlers thought the woods were a scary place where demons dwelled. Devils hid in the rocks. But I shook the thought out of my mind, reminding myself that it was this guy's fault for being here alone, having a bad attitude, and being so unprepared.

The conversation petered out, and Allison and I took our leave of Oedipus Rex. For a while we sat outside our tent in stunned silence. We wondered to ourselves: How much effort would it take to transform this gentle garden into someone's personal hell? Seeing Oedipus Rex made me redouble my efforts to enjoy every second of this experience.

The next day I felt sad that Oedipus Rex wasn't enjoying his adventure the way we were. Thinking of his sad example made me revel in every rock cornice, every diamond of scattered light. The Lois and Clark Expedition pushed on, over slopes without trees, past boulders and a troop of marmots in the sun. The marmots looked like guinea pigs but were the size of small dogs, with russet-colored fur and the ability to stand on their hind legs while whistling through *O*-shaped mouths.

At the time I was sure they were greeting us, offering up the forest's good tidings, but who knows what they were thinking? After all, marmots are inscrutable, and capable of rampages. They love to attack parked cars, gnaw holes in the cars' tubing, and drink the coolant and brake fluid. The deadly chemicals do not harm them. I didn't know this then.

As we continued our nature walk, Allison spied two Belding's ground squirrels, living Beanie Babies chickering in the bushes, playing tag. They were cute, with their sniffy noses, furry bodies, and little arms bent forward in repose. I wished I could be one of them, so free and happy, cavorting in the bushes. I did not know at the time that they were furry sociopaths who practiced infanticide just for the protein and whose females would sometimes take the nurslings of other ground squirrels and murder them on the spot.* I moved through the lives of animals and the forests that contained them like a stranger who knew nothing of the language. My ignorance was pleasant. The hiking was steep and strenuous, but the living was easy. We watched a rabbit-eared mule deer in a field at sunset, and walked along the slow waters that wormed through the meadow at dusk. The air was as cool and dry as John Muir had promised in his diaries. Even when Allison slipped and fell on a muddy bank, the land reached up to receive her body like a cradle; her landing was soft. Our lives were an indulgent fantasy.

Below Muir Pass, a rock bowl held our own lake. It had no name that I knew of, so I named it after the Lois and Clark Expedition. Clouds got caught in the bowl. They misted themselves across our tent. That night we discussed only our silliest dreams. "You have a gift for baking," Allison said. "You could

---

* Allan A. Schoenherr, *A Natural History of California*, Berkeley: University of California Press, 1992, p.217. *Sociopath* and *murder* are my words, not Schoenherr's.

make pies." She wondered if we might one day open up a bed-and-breakfast-brewery-bakeshop-bookstore and call it a B and B and B and B and B. I talked about dusting off a silly science fiction novel I wrote at sixteen, some dreadful *Narnia–Lord of the Rings* hybrid about a collection of magic books that control the Earth's elements. The evil Umglots steal the books and plot world destruction. "Why not go back and rewrite that book and sell it?" Allison said. "It could be huge."

Night bled into day, day into night, and before we knew it we had scrambled up and over most of the passes on the John Muir Trail. We were heading through the soft loam of a forest when we ran into two women with short-cropped hair and slender packs. They seemed to be in their forties. One stopped us. "Watch out for Bear Creek," she said. "It's fast and cold. It almost knocked us off our feet. Somebody told me there's supposed to be a bridge, but it's gone."

The warning unsettled me, although the idea of too much water seemed fantastical after all our dehydration crises in our first few weeks of the trail. Down in the hot country, I would have laughed in the face of anyone who warned me that rushing water could ever imperil us on the PCT. Danger from water? That would have sounded like dying of luxury, like choking to death on a Kobe beef and foie gras sandwich. When we got there, Bear Creek made a hollow sound like storm water through a drainpipe. The creek was fast, dark, and fifty feet across; leaves and twigs shot across its surface. Allison stood on the shore while I scooted my boots in the water to try it out. The creek was shallow near its banks, but when I took two steps forward, the bottom dropped until the water covered my ankles, my knees, my thighs. Soon I couldn't see the lower half of my body anymore.

The creek's bottom was a slick rock mantle. I tottered. Bear Creek smelled like algae, and Big Motherfucker bore down on me, shifting his weight from one shoulder to the other. I now knew it was foolish to lash my pack so tightly to my back. Now if I fell face-first, Big Mofo would pin me to the bottom of the creek. The water tried to pull me down, but I grabbed tight to a boulder. When I at last worked up the nerve, I made a break for it, pushing myself off from the rock, taking ten giant steps toward the shore, and falling to my knees in the shallows on the other side. Now it was Allison's turn.

I shouted at her to loosen her straps, but she couldn't hear me. Soon, deep green water covered her up to the waist. The creek was drinking her. She was teetering and starting to cry. I shouted at her to hold still. Throwing off my pack and wading into the water, I kept wondering what the hell I would tell her father and mother if she went down and her pack held her under and I couldn't lift her out of there. What would be the reason for her drowning? What, exactly, was in Canada? Without my pack, it was easier to fight the current. I splashed out to her, held out my arms, and she sloughed her pack off, right on top of me. I took hold of the bulky pack while she let go of the rock she was holding, swam with the current, and dogpaddled, in thrashing motions, toward the opposite shore. Without the ridiculous pack, she was buoyant, and crossed the creek without much trouble. In an instant, she was crawling up the bank, soaked and still crying. I put my arms around her back onshore.

"You saved my life," Allison said later on.

I did not know what to say. As she continued to cry, I told her that Bear Creek was not a reasonable test, that it was damned hard. Those women had warned us about it for a reason. There ought to be a sign posted about the place. Just then, two young hikers with chisel chins and stripped-down backpacks approached from the other side. They were heading straight for the creek. I bellowed at them. "Be careful!" but they stomped on in, waded in the water, and cut straight through Bear Creek as if it were a municipal kiddie pool. In a flash, they were finished, and marched right past us. "You're right, that was tricky," said the man in front.

Allison and I looked at each other in puzzlement as the cold sank into our skin and made us shiver. Was it just us, I wondered, turning every little inconvenience into a tragedy narrowly averted? If Bear Creek was so easy, why did those two women make such a fuss about it? We rested together awhile, and when Allison had dried herself, changed clothes, and thrown her garments in a fabric bag, we got as far from the sound of Bear Creek as we could.

On we walked, past nightfall. In our tent later, I could not help wondering if there was a tape-stop reality at work here, if Allison really had drowned and my unconsciousness, unable to process the truth, had manufactured a ghost-cloth Allison, quilted from memory. It occurred to me that my "knowing" of her was scattershot at best, that there were blanks. In a pinch I couldn't say very much about her. I knew she had a temper, and was neat, and that most of our fights were about dishes on the floor, mold on the walls, my losing the keys. I could say she loved Chianti Ruffino and brown Italian sodas that scorched your tongue. I knew she wanted babies someday but I'd never asked if she wanted a boy or a girl, or more than one, or if she wanted them with me. I knew exactly how to amuse her, to the extent that she once almost laughed herself to death because of me. I once did a crazy dance on her kitchen floor, making her choke on a melon wedge, which required me to practice the Heimlich maneuver on her. So I guessed I'd saved her life twice, though I'd instigated both scenarios that made me have to save her life in the first place. I might also say that I regretted the times when I yelled at her so much that I made tears fall down her face, like that time in Albany, when we were criss-crossing the country in a caravan to reach this trail and she was in the car in front, speeding through rain, and because I did not want to lose sight of her, I sped, too, and the cop stopped both of us, her first, then me. He gave us each eighty-dollar tickets, and I stood there in the rain, the water running down my face, yelling through Allison's open window until she shook and cried, and now I wanted to tell the real Allison, or the ghost one, that this was shameful and that I would never yell at her like that again.

But when the first stroke of sun hit the tent the next morning, and she did not vanish like a ghost, I could no longer remember what it was that I wanted to say to her. I remembered the gist of it, but the words were in the wrong order. I tried very hard to piece them together, but it would have sounded silly or ham-fisted and wrong.

I wanted to get it exactly right.

I decided, once again, to let it wait.

Chapter 22

Smedberg Lake

We stomped down to Reds Meadow and took a shuttle up to the condo village of Mammoth Lakes, a scruffy enclave eight thousand feet above sea level in the eastern Sierra Nevada. My father, a burly, strapping man of sixty-eight, greeted us at the Sunshine Village condo with his bald pate and gap-toothed smile. He was dressed in a oversize red T-shirt that read PICASSO in cursive lettering. My mother and father were still skeptical of the trip. "We're very proud of you," my mother said. "But, really, you've done *enough*. You don't have to do any-more of this to impress us." In spite of their trepidations, they stuffed us with wine and ribs, took us to the movies, and to my surprise, boasted about us to every waiter and waitress. "Can you believe what my son has done?" my father said to hostesses, gear-shop employees, and even random people in the street.

At a fancy restaurant, Allison lost thirty dollars in a bet with my father. I can't recall the subject of the bet, but my father told Allison that she would "never have to pay that money as long as you stick with my son forever." It was the first intimation that my family wanted us to get married. I could not help but look at Allison in a new light that weekend. I noticed the solicitous way she hiked up dusty switchbacks to Shadow Lake with my slow-moving father, staying close to him to make sure he did not topple—my father, like me, is rather top-heavy—and the gentle way she dealt with my nephews when they played roughhouse games with her, including Smell My Feet and No Mercy.

That week, wherever we went, everyone treated my girl-friend as if she were a part of the family. My sister-in-law winked and made rapid pointing gestures at Allison's ring finger.

I was only twenty-six, and the thought of getting married still petrified me, but perhaps my family was right to put the idea in my head. Allison was more than my girlfriend. She wasn't afraid of saying and doing most anything that came to her mind. She often did what I only thought of doing. It was like having a bullhorn attached to my head, trumpeting my interior thoughts to the world. Before we left Mammoth Lakes and returned to the trail, we stopped by the local KFC to for-tify ourselves on lipids and rubbery meat. When we ordered up a bucket to go, the teenage cashier smirked. She said, "It's dumb to eat this stuff. It's full of saturated fats." Allison looked at her, smiled, and said, "Yum. Saturated fats. Bring it on." The teen-ager winced. The strange thing is I was thinking those words at the same time Allison said them. It felt as if the speech had started in my brain and come out of her mouth.

After we said our good-byes to my mother, father, and neph-ews, we marched north toward Sonora Pass, moving through a dappled valley full of lakes, snowfields, and painted-rock caves. Below us was a highway in shadow and the frozen form of Or-phan Lake, black and blue with no creeks running in or out of it. Buzzards rode the thermals. They barely moved their wings as they wobbled above us. We pitched camp early and woke up the next day near Ebbetts Pass in a field of volcanic rubble forming outlandish shapes. Bat wings. Gorgon heads. Dream castles. All the while, she told me stomach-churning tales full of so much gore that I wondered where she came up with all of this stuff. Perhaps she was a Viking in her previous life. Allison got a fiery look as she recounted the story of a Nantucket serial killer/journalist who dressed up like a whaler's ghost so he could slaughter guests at a bed-and-breakfast with a rusty old harpoon and write about his own exploits for the local newspaper. At one point he impales a girl and boy in a claw-foot tub. Naturally, the journalist was never caught for his crimes. "In fact," Allison said, "he even finagled a job at *The Boston Globe,* on the police beat."

I could tell she'd made that story up on the spot. She never did any advanced scribbling. Maybe that's what drew me to her in the first place—the power of improvisation. I always have to chart everything out. Diagram it. Draw myself a map. She seemed to have the ready answers to every threat to her comfort, whether it was boredom, shyster mechanics, or bullies at work. But that week we ran into a situation so disagreeable that it tested her powers to respond.

We were enjoying ourselves in the wind, high on a set of bumpy peaks, where I was telling her some halfhearted story about a goat-eating giant, when a storm snuck up on us, a drooling dark one with tendrils draping down. The wind picked up behind the clouds, shoving them forward, and then the weather started blowing sideways, speeding our steps as we rushed down the path toward Lost Lake. The rain cloud's streamers were upon us now. Soaked straight through, we pitched an emergency camp at the edge of a parking lot on a dirt road near the whitecapped water. We knew it was stupid thing, to spend the night near a jeep track. If you camp near an access road, you're in striking distance of off-road vehicle enthusiasts, who are usually shit-faced and bearing small-bore firearms. But the rain was thrumming, and our exhaustion left us with no other option. A few campers were there already, quite drunk, blasting oldies. They sang along to the Beach

Boys' "Don't Worry, Baby" and Peter and Gordon's "A World Without Love." A red-faced man altered the words as he went along. Actually, he augmented them, by inserting the words *you bitch* at odd intervals. For example, he sang, "Don't worry, baby! Everything's gonna be all right . . . YOU BITCH!" Someone on the other side of the lake popped off three gunshots and hollered after each speeding bullet. The rounds made a metallic whoosh as they cut across the water.

"We should just pack our stuff and leave," said Allison, in our tent. "Nothing is worth this. We might as well hike in the rain."

"I think it's too late for us to move," I said. It was four, and I worried the path would shove us up onto the shoulders of some big mountain with no adequate flat spots. "I'm too tired to go anywhere."

The evening wore on. Much to our surprise, the revelers settled. By nine, it was quiet. The rain stopped. I stepped outside the tent. A young man and his father were gathering their drenched supplies, bunching them into their arms and walking toward their pickup truck. "It's about to get worse," the father said. "We're heading out."

"We're staying," I said.

"I think you should leave, too."

"There's room enough for all of us," I said.

The soft oldies continued, but the bitch-shouting man's voice gave out. Allison and I went to sleep, and soon the water, lapping against itself, was the only sound. I was glad we'd ignored the advice of the young dad.

Through my dreams, I heard a mechanical rumble, metal teeth on metal teeth, a trembling like thunder, then a jolt on my shoulder, and Allison staring me in the face, shining her flashlight down on me as she shook me awake.

"Mwwuuhh? Good Lord," I said, rubbing my eyes. "What time is it?"

"One thirty," she said.

"What's the matter?"

"We're about to get run over!"

I opened my eyes with a start, in time to see a red light flood the tent. "It's backup lights," she said. "It's a truck. Rolling right for us."

I rose up in my sleeping bag and turned around. The noise was deafening: the "chunka-chunka" sound of a massive engine, the crunch of thick tires getting closer. We should have cut and run then, but we were frozen in the tent, unable to act. The truck finally stopped, its exhaust pipes belching into our tent vestibule. The truck door opened. Out came the sounds of clomping boots, people stamping around our tent. "If anyone moves outta there, we'll hit 'em with this," one of them said. I gaped at Allison. Were they talking about us? Allison wondered if they were trying to provoke and smoke us out, rousing us out of sleep to beat the shit out of us, or worse. We huddled against each other, sipping our Sharkleberry Finn Kool-Aid and hoping to God that whoever they were would just go away. But they kept on shouting, and soon we heard a knock-knock-thumpa-thumpa-bonk-bonk nearby. "They're building something out there," Allison said. "They're putting up some big tent. All of them!" It sounded like they were erecting the World's Fair on the shores of Lost Lake. In between their labors, they made a point of trailing their flashlights across the camp, straight into us. One of the men cleared his throat and began to bray, "Hey you guys," he said. "I'm readin' a really good new biography of W. C. Fields. It said he started out in vaudeville. Did you know that?"

"No. I had no idear."

"Well, it's true. One day he was supposed to wrestle a real bear onstage. He's scared out of his mind, so the management gets this tough old guy to dress up as a bear instead. And the old guy starts beatin' the shit outta W. C. Fields! Just whalin' on him. After a while, W. C. Fields starts screamin' for mercy. 'Bring back the bear! Bring back the bear!'"

"I can't believe this," Allison said.

"Ya get it?" the man said. "Bring back the bear?"

"Oh man, I'm gonna get these idiots," Allison said.

"Oh, I get it!" another of the men said. "Bring back the bear. Ah-haw-haw-haw-haaaaah!"

"But they'll beat the crap out of us," I said.

"No, they won't," Allison said. "I'm gonna get them. But not yet."

"Did you know?" the first man said, "that a bear is a marsupial?"

"No, it's not, you fuckin' idiot, it's an omnivore," another man said.

We sat there, just taking it, while the redneck equivalent of the Discovery Channel kept blaring on outside. Allison was half Swiss, half Italian. The Swiss side of her was neutral, calm, nondemonstrative, but you did not want to fuck with the Italian side of her. When she made a vow of revenge against the cretins, you knew she'd follow through.

At five o'clock in the morning, it was on. By then, our tormentors had fallen into a drunken sleep. Allison emerged from her tent and let loose with the most horrible whooping cough I'd ever heard. "Brraaaaaaaaaaaaaaaackhhhh," she said, dredging up hidden reserves of imaginary phlegm. You might say this was an act of passive aggression, considering our tormentors were unconscious, but there was nothing passive about her behavior. She stood just a few feet away from their tent's zippered entrance, clearing her throat with as many decibels as she could muster. All at once, the thugs woke up. We could hear them rustle, and moan. Part of me wished to God that Allison had had enough, that her revenge was over—I was scared they were going to thrash us—but she was just getting started.

"Hey," she shouted. "Where are those goddamned tent poles? Where's my fanny pack?" She tripped—deliberately— over pots and pans, and I kicked a few pieces of metallic gear

around to show some solidarity, even though I was terrified. At
any moment the men could dog-pile all over us. Now she was
taking up tent poles, using them as bats, and pretending that
our pots and pans were softballs. "Pow. Plink." Then she began
to cough again, but much more violently, doubled over, turning red with the exertion.

"Oh, for the love of God," the W. C. Fields monologuist
moaned. "Doncha know what time it is? Lady, can't ya take a
cough drop?"

I could tell they were getting pretty riled up in that tent by
now, fixing to bust our heads, and I knew it was only a matter
of time. Allison paused for a moment, and we packed up our
things and got ready to go. But even then, she wasn't finished.
She turned around, stood in front of the tent one last time,
cupped her hands in front of her mouth, and bellowed, in the
deepest voice she could muster, "Thanks a lot for keeping us up
all night, you assholes!"

I braced for the worst, but silence followed. Allison stood
there as if hoping something would happen. And then it occurred to me: the miscreants were scared. They were not coming after us. In fact, I wondered if they expected us to come
after *them*. Perhaps they thought she was just crazy. Or maybe it
was the fact that they hadn't even taken a look at us. For all they
knew, we had a Glock in our sleeping bag. In any case, there
wasn't a peep of protest as we stormed past their camp and
vanished into the woods. Watching Allison stand up to the slobs
made me feel clean. I've always had a hard time with bullies. In
middle school, I tried to avoid them. I tried not to say anything
to antagonize them. Some of them had it in for me ever since
elementary school because I was part of the "Mentally Gifted
Minors" program, hanging out with the brilliant dorks in the
school portables, making stop-motion animated films, coming
up with my own recipes, and inventing machines to save the
planet, while my blond Cro-Magnon tormentors grunted and

pounded wooden blocks together in homeroom. But Allison never hid from bullies. The more I thought about this, the more I thought I needed her as my wife. If she wasn't scared of wild animals, newspaper editors, KFC clerks, or drunk assholes in a car camp, she would have no problem standing up to real estate agents, Montessori teachers, or annoying Lamaze instructors. And so, I was convinced. As we shuffled through the woods, I knew for sure that Allison would one day become my wife.

But there is one aspect of marriage that nauseated and frightened me, no matter how much I thought about it. That aspect is called "compromise." Allison and I still hadn't figured out what to do about the fact that she wanted to get off the trail to make last-minute revisions to her anthology about doctors. She'd told me that we would have to give up at least a week of hiking time to do this, in spite of the fact that we were a month behind schedule. She wanted us to get off at the next major supply stop—Echo Lake—hitch a ride to Lake Tahoe, and take a bus from there to her aunt's house near Sacramento. It was the one last significant interruption on our expedition to Canada. I dreaded this; we were in a groove, having finished 634 miles of trail. I still hoped Allison would just get off the trail by herself for a week and let me hike the next one hundred miles alone and then meet me in the next section. After all, it was *her* book, not mine. I knew full well that Allison had every right to work on her book off the trail, and that I *should* leave the trail with her. I fully supported her project. In fact, I had line-edited it. If I had been in her place, I would have insisted that she leave the trail with me to show solidarity. Walking the PCT did not diminish my ability to understand the difference between responsibility, compromise, and me-me selfishness. If anything, all those long hours in the woods had heightened my understanding of these things. It's just that I was finding it harder to make the "right" choices in spite of this newfound clarity. By then I had convinced myself that the Pacific Crest Trail was my *only* chance to feel mature and complete. Every step toward Canada was a step toward manhood. I feared that the trail, if I never finished it, would leave me stranded in a permanent kindergarten, like that freaky midget in *The Tin Drum*. But if the path was supposed to make me so "finished" and mature, how come I was starting to pitch fits and stomp around when I didn't get what I wanted? It did not occur to me then that the trail was becoming more than just a path toward possible wisdom. At the same time, the foot-path was turning into an alternate childhood and an extended leave of absence from rationality. The trail, in other words, was *trying* to teach me wisdom and mindfulness, but instead of listening, I was sticking my fingers in my ears and saying, "Blah, blah, blah." The more I walked, the more I seemed to stand outside myself, observing my behavior, duly noting it, judging it, but doing absolutely nothing to intervene.

One night we were camped out on the bare rocks on the shores of Smedberg Lake, a bowl of black gloss deep in the interior of Yosemite National Park. The words just blurted themselves out of me. We'd hiked all the way from Los Angeles County—and I didn't want to stop.

"I don't think it's right that I have to get off the trail with you," I said.

"What?"

"You heard me. I really don't think I should have to get off the trail because of *your* book."

The fight was on. We spoke in fusillades, words blasting into one another. To the bears and squirrels listening in on us, our fight must have sounded like one sustained sentence with no punctuation. We circled each other, with me baring my incisors at my girlfriend and jumping up and down. Both of us were convinced that the other party was obstinate, out-to-lunch, a mental homunculus devoid of fair play, reason, and rationality. *"I don't want to get off the trail,"* I shouted. *"You agreed to get off the trail,"* she shrieked. Clearly, reason was not working for us.

Compromise was not in the air. This was one of those fights that would have to be won by decibels alone. If she screamed at me, I'd just have to scream louder. There I stood, making sounds like lions and foghorns as I stood above Smedberg Lake, a water body I could not even begin to describe now because I paid so little attention to it, lest its natural beauty distract me from my yelling. After a while, she responded by getting quieter while I got louder.

"You knew I had to do this, Dan," she said.

"No, I did not. This is your book. You did not tell me this. You're ruining my dream for me. You're derailing my dream."

"So this is *your* dream now? Know what, Dan? You look crazy right now. You've been shouting at me over a stupid hike, and yes, you look insane, and you're freaking me out. You're scaring me and I'm *alone* out here. I don't have anywhere to go and you are *fucking screaming at me over a hike*. I just need you to stop it now. I just want you to get a hold of yourself or take a walk or go somewhere, but just *stop screaming at me*."

I stopped myself somehow, and the night got quiet. I heard nothing at all but the shameful ringing in my ears from my shouting. I walked away from the tent, just to get away from her, get away from us, and more than that, get away from myself. I stumbled around shore without a flashlight and watched the moon on the lake, bubbles on the surface, and something, a bug maybe, sending ripples through the moon's reflection. The water murmured on the lake's edges. When I returned to the tent, my voice had been stripped. I could not even bring myself to say good night. We fell asleep, but not in each other's arms. My dreams erased the memories of the fight, but just momentarily; the blotted-out memories of the night returned as soon as I woke with a scratching throat under the white sky over Smedberg Lake.

We got off the trail two days later, near Lake Tahoe.

Chapter 23

Bitter Fame

Allison was angry and silent, but she took the time to bathe me as we stood in the shade near the highway shoulder. She swabbed a washcloth over my face and neck. I don't know why she did this, and I didn't understand the look of maternal concentration on her face. The washcloth smelled of Stilton cheese, cat farts, and moldy strawberries. In fact, Allison had dubbed the cloth "the odoriferous skankrag." By now, I'd grown accustomed to our odors. They made me feel authentic. Our scents were like period costumes that gave us something in common with nineteenth-century pioneers. Some of those emigrants bathed only once a month. They must have smelled like us. I was squeamish when I started out on this trail. Now I was getting accustomed to filth. According to *Backpacker* magazine,[*] Pacific Crest Trail hikers are among the most foul-smelling things on this planet. Their "suffocating reek" comes

---

[*] Admittedly, I wrote the acrticle "Showdown: Who Smells the Worst?," *Backpacker*, May 2005, p. 44.

not from sweat itself "but from the bacteria that feed on the amino acids, fats, and oils found in human perspiration. The bacteria emit a putrid blend of chemical compounds including ammonia and methylbutanoic acid that cling to the clothes and body—and multiply with each passing day. Opening the car windows will only help so much, but at least it spreads the misery. Depending on wind conditions, someone could pick up this hiker's aroma from 100 feet away."

The fact that we had to scrub the stench away just to "fit in" outside the trail, just to hitch a ride to a supply town, filled me with disdain. And so I winced and made faces as she washed me, daubing my chin, anointing my forehead with redistributed sweat and dirt. Every time I swallowed hard, I felt the ache in my throat. My sore throat reminded me that I'd lost control forty-eight hours ago at the lake. I'd behaved boorishly. I couldn't even begin to apologize for all my gnashing and howling. And yet it was all I could do to keep my mouth shut during the cat bath.

We were close to the northern tip of the four-hundred-mile-long Sierra Nevada range, a short drive from the Nevada border, a few miles to the east. This was where the emigrants crossed after rolling westward from Kansas, Missouri, and Wyoming in the 1840s. The pioneers, like the Lois and Clark Expedition, were only trying to find something better. They dared liberate themselves from the banality of convention. And here we were, leaving the woods, but not by choice, heading straight for the banality we'd tried to escape. A young couple stopped to give us a ride that day. They were kind, and engaged us in small talk, but I could not help but notice when they rolled the car windows way down to release our stench.

South Lake Tahoe, on the California-Nevada border, was ten minutes by car from the trailhead, but it might as well have been on Neptune. We arrived at a long reach of strip malls, pizza parlors, KFCs, motels, and bars with the green foothills bubbling up just behind them, as if to mock them, and then the big-boned mountains, and there, in the middle of all this, the lake itself, sitting there like an afterthought, 1,643-feet deep, nestled in a valley between the Sierra Nevada and Carson ranges. Burned out, wanting fast food, we decided to spend a half-day in Tahoe before taking the bus to Sacramento, but we were at a loss, wandering the town in a haze, past a late-night carnival Tilt-O-Whirl, and a real estate office, with a rumpled man working the phones, his tie draped across his left shoulder. It seemed inconceivable that the world could contain the rumpled man and the trail, and yet we were less than ten miles from the trailhead.

We bummed around. I passed a shop selling T-shirts with almost incomprehensible sexual puns on all the shirts. One showed a cartoon of a leering man forming a hole with his right-hand thumb and pointer finger, and sticking his left-hand pointer finger into the hole. The caption read, "I don't know any women who cry, but I know a few who sure like to bawl." How stupid is that? "The pioneers didn't have to deal with all this materialistic crap," I thought to myself. This world is not real. Only the mountains above this town are real. With misanthropic relish, I imagined termites nibbling down the faux-Alpine motels, and casinos tumbling in the lake. I'd been to Tahoe once before, with my mother and father. They took me to see Tom Jones at Caesar's Palace. I remember the wind machine, and Tom Jones wiggling through a fake fog that was really just liquid nitrogen, and the vixen-in-estrus yelps from the women, who were probably just making fun of him. Now I was walking in Caesar's Palace once again, this time with Allison, past a false waterfall and plaster frescoes, electric pyramids, and a Cleopatra impersonator who looked and sounded as if her ancestral homeland were Sheboygan, Wisconsin. When we'd had our fill of casinos, card sharps, and the all-you-can-eat stroganoff buffet, we jumped on the Greyhound bus. It was a two-hour ride in black darkness on I-80 at sixty-five miles an hour. I did not bother looking out the window. Why look out

at all that inauthenticity? Allison saw me looking glum and she
nudged my shoulder. "Next stop, Excremento," she said, and
we both laughed.

I was feeling glum, in withdrawal from the trail, when we
holed up at her aunt's house. I paced the hall, gnashed my teeth,
and tried to give Allison space, because she was under deadline
pressure and I didn't want to upset her anymore. To give her a
break, I wandered the deserted streets of a nearby town. While
Allison faxed messages to her editors, I sat around at a diner
drinking sour coffee and chewing *Exxon-Valdez* hash browns.
Later, I stared for fifteen minutes at a closed-down movie theater with an existential message on the marquee: COMING SOON
TO A THEATER NEAR YOU! How, I wondered, could a theater
come to itself? At least Allison got her work done, while I was
able to keep my hair-pulling to a minimum. But my feelings
built within me, a surge of mute nostril agony that I could not
control. With no other option, I vented my primal despair to
my diary. The result was a passage that continues to amaze me
with its primitive yet graceful display of incandescent rage. It
ranks among the purest things I've ever written:

> *I want to be back on the fucking trail. It's not fair that I'm*
> *willing to make the big miles and work my ass off for this trip*
> *and morons [bastards here has been crossed out, with morons*
> *written across it as a replacement] from NYC are just shavin'*
> *time off it. I want to get to the Oregon border. Here's the deal.*
> *We got thru the Mojave, the Sierras and wouldn't have made*
> *it unless we want it very badly, well, now coming off it's like*
> *cold turkey heroin!*

I hid this blast of poetic fury from Allison. All told, we were
off the trail for about a week. Thank God for Allison's cousin
Tom, who lived in a nearby town and gave us an unexpected
gift before we returned to the trail: two Day-Glo orange vests

Actual Diary Entry

and baseball caps saying LOIS AND CLARK EXPEDITION with stick-on black letters. My hat said CLARK. If only the Gingerbread Man could see us now! It's one thing to get a trail name. It's another thing to accessorize. For a shining moment I felt famous, the vest and hats' loud colors shouting our greatness and glory. But Tom warned us that the clothes would serve as more than fashion statements. Bear hunting season was almost upon us. He didn't want some drunken hunter with a sporting rifle blowing us all to hell.

After taking a bus from Sacramento back to South Lake Tahoe and hitchhiking back to Echo Lake, we returned to the trail, wearing our bright orange outfits with pride. We were part of a team again as we passed into the Desolation Wilderness, hiking past Aloha Lake, a flooded valley with lodgepole pines protruding from the middle. The wind made the bare snags tremble. Once more I thought of the pioneers and what it must have been like to roll through a landscape that seemed to laugh at human ambitions and dreams. But we were beating that landscape now. After going this far on the trail, nothing seemed undoable. Near Blackwood Creek, we were in an expansive mood, feeling giddy and determined. We decided that someday we would open a bookstore together and name it for a literary suicide. We agreed, after much consideration, to call it Sylvia Plath's Oven. There would be a sign out front saying, EVERYBODY, STICK YOUR HEAD IN HERE. There is something about a mountain setting that makes such ideas seem good at the time. As we entered the Granite Chief Wilderness, my calm, and hopes of success, returned in full. It was August 25. By my best calculations, we had two months to walk a thousand miles—and no more interruptions. As the trail reached a mountain crest, we looked above the clear-cut slopes of the Squaw Valley ski area and saw a pair of eagles launch themselves off a pine bough. They looked clumsy at first but found their momentum and rose up weightless.

The trail followed a rock spine on jumbled crags with granite spokes. Just north of where Allison and I were walking that day, an emigrant party steered their wagons across a treacherous pass. They were the first such group to cross the Sierra Nevada. The leader was a fellow I'd never heard of, named Elisha Stephens, forty years old and ugly as a possum. His neck was crooked and his beard was a tangled mess of tufts. You could hang your hat on his nose. In spite of his looks and lack of leadership experience, he'd been voted the captain of twenty-five men, eight women, nine girls and eight boys, all in eleven wagons that left from Council Bluffs, Iowa, in the spring of 1844. His destination was Sutter's Fort, in New Helvetia, California. Why did he set off on this journey? It's hard to say. A taciturn man, Stephens left no diary behind. He must have had strong reasons to take a journey to the West when such ventures were considered insane or at least stupid. Maps of America stopped dead at a blank space from the Rockies to the one hundredth meridian, an expanse so empty there were no railroad tracks or roads, not even a telegraph wire.

What, then, was the appeal? Perhaps he wanted to get rich, but the gold rush was five years off. Maybe he craved free land or was as sick of his old life as we were when we ditched our jobs and left for the trail. As he headed west, Stephens suppressed a mutiny, drove footsore cattle through creeks, and felt the sun burn down on the misnamed Forty-Mile Desert, which was twice that long. After all that hardship, Stephens and his party entered the Sierra Nevada. They arrived at a granite ledge very close to where Allison and I were hiking that day. The ten-foot rocky barrier blocked the way. The Stephens party could have panicked or given up. Instead they emptied their wagons and hoisted each one up the ledge, using a rope pulley chained to the backs of their oxen. This emigrant party was resourceful as well as lucky; the group lost no members on its journey westward. In fact, it increased as it went along because of two babies born en route. Stephens and his crew opened up a mountain pass that became indispensable for thousands of other emigrants, including the forty-niners, not to mention the railroad and freeway that would both breach the pass, sending millions more people through the mountain notch.

I wonder if Stephens fantasized about fame and glory when he made it through this stretch. I, certainly, had such fantasies. Sometimes, at the end of a trail day, I pictured Allison and me finishing the trail and becoming highly paid motivational speakers, teaching self-esteem to addicts and fatties. But Stephens, if he had such notions, was in for a jolt. After his trek, he lived in obscurity in what is now Cupertino, California, and ended his days as a reclusive beekeeper and chicken farmer in Kern County. In the late 1860s, after thousands of Chinese and Irish laborers finished laying out the Central Pacific Railway route across the mountain pass, no one thought to invite poor Stephens to the ribbon-cutting ceremony. He became the town grump, bitter and grumbling. One day, he had a stroke and ended up paralyzed in a local hospital. Soon after, he dropped dead. Gravediggers planted him in a potter's field in Bakersfield, with no headstone. The cemetery lost his internment records. Silicon Valley landmarks perpetuate but misspell Stephens's last name—among them, Stevens Creek Boulevard and Stevens Creek Auto Mall.* But when you drive on Interstate 80 from Reno to Sacramento, you will not see Stephens's name on the signs along the pass he opened. Instead, the signs pay tribute to another group of emigrants who crossed the pass two years after Stephens rolled through. Their western journey would have little historical significance if not for some of the emigrants' unprecedented barbarism and savagery.

The name of that group is the Donner Party.

On August 27, three days after we returned from our Tahoe interlude, we hiked on a rocky hump on the Sierra Nevada's northern tip. The trail, a foot-wide strip, approached Tinker Ridge, a hatchet-shaped rock overlooking Donner Pass. Old Highway 40 was a short way downhill from us, so we were only slightly startled to see a family approach from nowhere, a man, woman, their young daughter, and two coiffed Afghan hounds. The dogs walked close enough for me to smell their rosy perfume and admire their bright ribbons. The girl gave us a hateful wince, perhaps because of our Day-Glo reflective outfits. Down we walked through fir and pine as we crossed the

---

* Phil Sexton, interpretive specialist/Web manager and Elisha Stephens aficionado, Tahoe National Forest, provided me with the details on Stephens's post–Donner Pass life. Other materials are from Fradkin, *The Seven States of California*.

flanks of Mount Judah, the crag the pioneers spied from Nevada to the east as they neared California. We dropped to the highway near Donner Summit, on a strip of black gravel under tall trees. Here, the south-to-north Pacific Crest Trail came within screaming distance of the Donner Party's east-west route, though it is hard to pinpoint where the wagons crossed; earthmovers have widened the pass so much that the Donners might not even recognize it now. Standing near a DONNER PASS sign, Allison placed her right wrist in her mouth and chomped down hard enough to leave pink marks in her skin. I photographed this. Then we traded places, and I pretended to eat my left forearm. In the trail journal, I jotted the lyrics of a spontaneous song we sang there in honor of our arrival that day. It's sung to the tune of "Yesterday" by the Beatles.

> Pity me
> I had to eat my friends so violently.
> They're not half the men they used to be . . .

My amusement faded when the singing stopped. In my diary I recorded an "inexplicable sadness and irritability that rose out of nowhere, as if the grave past of the place made me feel that way." At the time I wondered if these emotions were something received, as if the thoughts were floating in the air above the highway long before we got there. While the feelings were real enough, I now wonder if the word *Donner*, emblazoned on the highway signs, was enough to set off an emotional depth charge. Perhaps my brain was responding to a name that forces travelers to remember when most of North America was a trackless expanse of trees and mountains, so vast and hidden that devils and serpents could conceal themselves there. A man passing through this terrain would fear for his life and sanity. The forces there might kill him or turn him into something less than human.

The Donner Party—actually, several families traveling together—rolled west from Little Sandy River in July 1846. Their starting place was present-day Wyoming. Not all of the emigrants fit the stereotype of cash-strapped pioneers hoping to improve their fortunes. Some rode in wagons bulging with silks and mahogany cabinets. One wagon was pimped out with a sheet-iron stove, a browsing library, a full-length mirror, and a second story containing a bedroom. Most wagons needed two or three oxen to pull them across the prairie, but this "Palace Car," a kind of Big Motherfucker on wheels, required four. Tamsen Donner, the family matriarch, stowed a ten-thousand-dollar nest egg in her quilt. She wanted to use the money to found a school in California. Patrick Breen, a well-to-do farmer, rolled with an entourage of fine horses, cows, and Towser, the family dog. Poor Towser! But I'm getting ahead of myself.

Though Allison and I had laughed at the emigrants in our song, the more I learned about them later on, the more my giggles became stifled. The Donner Party tests the theorem that tragedy plus time equals comedy. Consider that they were credulous and overpacked small-town dwellers who had no outdoor survival training. They left too late in the year and yet they took long rest stops and tried to make up for this by taking an unproven "shortcut" that wasted even more time. They fought needlessly and thuggishly, exploding into rages when they should have stayed calm. All I can say is, "Sounds familiar." Historians believe the Donner Party was doomed the moment they decided to follow the advice of Lansford Hastings—a lawyer, naturally—who told them they could chop out three hundred miles, nearly a month of travel time, by taking a "cutoff" that would route them through the Great Salt Lake Desert. Hastings wasn't rolling with the party, so he wasn't there when the emigrants were hacking their way through the trackless and damned-near-impenetrable Wasatch Mountains, cursing his name all the while. Pushing west, they left the Palace

Wagon to rot in the sand, but it was too late. By the time they reached present-day Reno, it was late October, and the emigrants looked up with foreboding at the Sierra Nevada massif, and the ominous gray clouds above it. Instead of rushing west to stay ahead of winter, they rested for five days at Truckee Meadows, then headed up into the mountains, running into an unseasonable storm that forced them back from the summit where Allison and I now stood. Up to their shoulders in white, the travelers decided to bivouac for the winter, not as one unit but in squabbling factions camped along an eight-mile stretch of forest. Hunger gnawed at them as they settled into shanties and lean-tos left by the Stephens party. To hold off hunger, they devoured pack mules, oxen, grass, pine twig soup, shoe leather, wagon axle grease, and ox hides boiled down to a nauseating paste. They consumed all the dogs, including poor Towser.

Strange, how infamy is such a prodigious diarist. The Stephens party left behind scant records of its exploits, but the Donner Party members either kept journals or submitted to extensive interviews about their ordeal later on. That is how we know that the trapped emigrants first entertained the notion of cannibalism on, of all dates, Christmas Eve. In late December a group of pioneers sliced the meat off the arms and legs of Patrick Dolan, already dead of exposure and hunger. As they ate him for supper, they held their gazes away from one another and cried in the firelight. Cabins turned into charnel houses. Human brains boiled in a cauldron. Two Miwok Indians named Luis and Salvador were part of a relief party sent out to help the stranded emigrants; they were shot at close range and devoured. Only thirty-nine of the eighty-seven party members survived the six-month ordeal. The rest perished en route on the trail, in the frozen mountains, or on the way out of the wilderness.

I found it hard to get the Donners out of my mind in northern California, not because they were monsters but because they were not. For the most part they were ordinary people.

In the words of California historian Kevin Starr, "Taken collectively, the Donner party was Everyman in a morality play of frontier disintegration."* Unlike Ed Gein, Jeffrey Dahmer, and other cannibals who haunt our popular culture, the Donner Party members weren't crazy. If they were capable of atrocities, any one of us is capable of those same atrocities, under the right circumstances. "Cannibalism is not a psychology that erupts in psychotic individuals but is a universal adaptive strategy that is evolutionarily sound," writes Lewis Petrinovich, UC Riverside professor emeritus of psychology. "The cannibal is within all of us."

Allison and I were weary and grouchy after leaving Donner Summit. Seven miles later we arrived at a clearing beneath a steep and wooded hill. There we found an unlocked and unmanned Sierra Club hut, set aside for long-distance hikers and cross-country skiers. The windows of this A-frame had a baleful look, as if they had borne witness to tragedy. We had to enter the hut on a staircase that bypassed the first floor and rose straight up to the second story; I later found out that the builders added this unusual design feature because of harsh winters, when snows almost always swallow the whole first floor. Shelters are rare on the trail; the elements are so harsh out there that most shacks would get knocked down in a year or two. But this one had strong bones. It was thick and sturdy, though the inside was dingy and uncomfortable; previous occupants had trashed the place and left graffiti, or dopy self-affirmations, on most of the walls. Cans and squirrel baffles dangled from ropes nailed to the roof.

Soon it was dark out. There were no lights in the hut, so we bumbled about with our Maglites, constantly bumping our

---

*   Kevin Starr, *Americans and the California Dream*, New York: Oxford University Press, 1973.

shins into things. Allison sat for a while in front of a latticed
window staring at Cassiopeia, the star formation named for a
treacherous queen. She insulted Neptune when she claimed
her daughter, Andromeda, was more beautiful than the Sea
Nymphs. The gods tied Andromeda to a rock and sent out a
sea monster to devour her. Perseus showed up just in time to
kill the monster, but the gods weren't finished with Cassiopeia.
When she died, they flung her up in the sky and turned her
into stars—but with a catch. Sometimes when you see her,
she's upright and proper in a chair. Other times, the chair is
upside down. In those moments, Cassiopeia is in disgrace, with
the blood rushing to her head. She's remembered, but for the
wrong reasons.

While Allison stared at the stars, I went downstairs to check
out the basement. I found more graffiti, a long table, and a
dog-eared Bible. My fingers settled on the following passage:
"A man's life consists not in the abundance of things which
he possesses, for what shall it profit a man if he shall gain the
whole world and lose his soul?" I kept my finger on the passage for a while. The quote struck me as relevant but for murky
reasons. It applied to me, but I did not yet know how or why.

That night we slept in bunks pressed close to the roof. We
killed our flashlights and lay there in the darkness on wooden
platforms in our sleeping bags, our heads lying inches away
from the rooftop. "To lose his soul." The words kept repeating
as the night went from dark to black and the sounds began.
I heard rumbling, scratching, rustles. Sometimes I thought I
heard footsteps. I sat up on the cot while Allison kept on sleeping. Ghosts to me are not an abstraction. I don't believe in
them, but I fear them. As a boy on vacation in the High Sierra,
I once stole a rock from an abandoned mine near Mammoth
Lakes. From then on, twice a month for a year, miners visited
me in my sleep, and even in my daydreams. Their eyes were
rotted out. I shut my eyes to block them out, but I still heard

their bones clank. This kept happening until I actually returned to Mammoth, the very next summer, and put the rock back where it belonged. The visions stopped. They say ghosts want our attention. Ghosts are like stars. The light source died long ago, and yet you can still see them glowing. Chances are it was probably just squirrels, raccoons, or opossums moving through the hut that evening. My rational mind knew this. It was just varmints, nothing more, and yet I kept thinking there was a person outside, or what used to be a person, standing there, just a few feet away from where we were sleeping that night, fiddling with the knobs, trying to get in.

Chapter 24

The Hairy Other,
Part Two

The Lois and Clark Expedition was on the move. We splashed through streams, made our way through a clear-cut forest, and entered a land that smelled like rotten eggs. In Lassen Volcanic National Park, steam rose from vents in the banks of Boiling Springs Lake. It was the second week of September, and time to celebrate. We had walked just under a thousand miles together, in seventy days, since leaving Agua Dulce. A butterfly lit on Allison's head and rolled out its tongue like a party streamer. "I love it here," she said.

Some tourists stood next to us, gagging on fumes, putting hankies over their faces, but we didn't mind the smell. We couldn't believe that our feet alone had brought us here. Now we had nine supply towns behind us: Agua Dulce. Tehachapi. Kennedy Meadows. Reds Meadow. Tuolomne Meadows. Echo Lake. Sierra City. Old Station. Belden Town. Next on the list was Castella, close to Mount Shasta. Allison wanted to linger in Lassen, but there wasn't time. Though we were making great progress, it was early fall, and we had good reason to move fast.

The weather was just starting to turn. By the time we crossed into the South Cascades, it was late September, and the sky had a gray pall. And we weren't the only ones hurrying. Bears were out there, getting ready for winter. Everywhere we went, I sensed them watching.

Out in a desolate part of the Modoc Plateau, in a place called Hat Creek Rim, the water tasted of cinders. We walked among the stilt-legged ruins of a fire tower. We were hurrying toward Canada, taking shorter breaks. Once, that week, we were walking through a meadow; wild onions splashed pink and red, giving off a strong odor. Allison picked a sprig to save for our mac-and-cheese that night. That's when we saw a bear in repose, two hundred feet across the field, head down, back arched, a cinnamon stripe on its fur. I stepped on a twig. The bear whirled and ran away. We followed to get a glimpse. He ran up the nearest tree, hook-climbing it with his two-inch claws. After making his way thirty feet up, he stopped dead, all three hundred pounds of him. The bear held fast to the trunk and bundled his rump against the air. Allison stepped into his shadow. The bear could have dropped down and squashed her then, but he did not move. I aimed the telephoto lens at him and clicked, again and again. When I was finished, we left him hanging in the tree.

Bears once frightened us. Not now. The more I studied them, the more they seemed ridiculous. In a letter home that week, I wrote that bears "look like bloated overfed Labrador retrievers. We're not that scared of them (anymore). They are oversized raccoons with fat asses." I felt sorry for black bears, and sometimes pitied myself for being born too late. The last wild wilderness was just about gone. California was once home to a hundred thousand grizzlies. They lived in chaparral foothills, on mountains, in deserts, and out on the beaches. Native Americans forged an uneasy truce with them. Some tribes thought the grizzlies were just another variety of human being. Then came the Californios, forty-niners, and ranchers, who fought wars against grizzlies with rifles, lassoes, whaling guns, and lances dipped in strychnine. *Ursus horriblus* lived in California for millions of years. It took six decades, the lifespan of a single bear, to wipe them all away.* The last known Golden State grizzly was gunned down in 1922 in the foothills of Fresno County, apparently for sniffing too close to a sheep enclosure. Nowadays, California is the only state whose official animal is stone dead within its borders. The grizzly was a menace and pest when he lived. Now that he's gone, he is a totem on savings-and-loan buildings and Hollister Brand fashion T-shirts. If you glance at the Great Seal of California, the griz looks like a neutered Chihuahua. He's bending in front of Minerva with an expression of accommodating weakness. He looks as if he expects the goddess of wisdom to drop-kick him into the San Francisco Bay.

That day we headed north toward, of all places, Grizzly Peak. On the one hand, it was comforting to walk without worrying about an animal that could strip the bones from our backs without provocation. On the other hand, the grizzly's absence made the forest feel like a terrarium with the disagreeable elements removed. If black bears—those wimps—were the standard-bearer of hairy otherness in this wilderness, what kind of wilderness was it, anyhow? And did *wilderness* have meaning anymore? And so I became a quiet stalker of black bears, convinced they were tame and silly, not truly wild.

It happened on September 17, north of Lassen, in a logged-out section of trail. I was hiking ahead of Allison. As I rounded a curve in the trail, I arrived at a sculpture of an adult bear. The statue seemed to be made of marble. It had a vacant expression.

---

*   Susan Snyder, editor, *Bear in Mind: The California Grizzly*, Berleley: Heyday Books, 2003. Courtesy of the Bancroft Library, UC Berkeley.

The poorly designed artwork was the biggest non sequitur I'd seen on the PCT. I was deeply offended. Why would someone take the time to sculpt and sand down and set up this marble lump and plant it right in the middle of the PCT, where a hiker might run right into it? And what, exactly, was the sculptor trying to prove? Was the artwork an expression of guilt? I was getting myself all worked up and annoyed when the statue, suddenly, moved. Then it turned to look at me. Glare at me. Snort at me. The statue was not a statue, but a *real fucking bear* who had been resting in the middle of the trail. He was not polished stone, but flesh, hair, and black eyes filled with something between hatred and mere annoyance. The bear huffed once, then dashed into the woods.

"Oh my God," I cried out.

Allison caught up to me. My breathing was fast and sharp. It was hard to speak. I explained to her what had happened.

She looked disappointed. "I didn't get a chance to see it," she said. "You're always out front. You always scare everything away."

She was right. I felt guilty about frightening away all the quality wildlife. And so we decided to stalk that black bear on the Pacific Crest Trail. We got very quiet. We tiptoed through the woods. I'd heard many ranger warnings against this behavior. Never sneak up on an animal. Never enter its "defense perimeter." But I didn't care. At the time, my behavior did not seem, in the least, retarded. I thought we were just being cheeky.

On we walked, in search of the Miracle Statue Bear. The trail cut across the side of a steep and pine-covered hillside. To the left of the trail was a slanting forest. We walked for fifteen minutes and saw no sign of the beast. Allison took the lead. She saw nothing; she was getting frustrated, so we called off the search. "Forget it," she said. "Let's just walk on." And so we did. Allison stayed about ten paces ahead of me, to make sure she got the best look at all the good fauna. Suddenly, she stopped and stared at something I couldn't see. She smiled. She was looking down, off the left of the trail, at something just below her in the forest, about twenty feet away. "How cute," she said. Then the color drained from her. I heard a sound like a bloodhound, but louder and full of reverb, as if the dog were baying into a hollow tube. Something just off the trail was calling out to us in a rage. "Ha-ruff-squonk," it said. "Huffa-huffa SQUONK. Ha-ruff-SQUONK!" Allison turned to me and said, in a soft and wavering voice, "We'd better get the fuck out of here."

"What do you see?" I said.

"Let's just get out of here," she said. She started shaking. She walked backward, slowly, while keeping her gaze focused on the copse of quaking trees just below the trail, and a huge brown shape just behind it. The thing kept snorting, the trees kept quivering, and I knew, all at once, that we were about to get mauled. Thrashed. Bitten everywhere.

"What are you doing?" I said. "Why are you walking? Let's run!"

"No," she said. "Don't. They can run faster than us. *Don't* try it. They can't resist a chase."

"But I don't want to just stand here like a fucking idiot . . ."

"*Don't run,*" she said again.

Fine. I did as she said. I took several giant steps backward, slowly, methodically, still staring at the trees, and lifting up my arms so the bear would think I was larger and would be afraid. Then I took another giant step back. So did Allison. We did this for several minutes. Then, we ran. We ran like crazy. We ran as if someone had set us both on fire. We tore up that hillside, running until our lungs ached, running until the lactic acid burned in our legs.

"So," I said, between gasps. "What the hell did you see?"

"Cute cubs," she explained as she ran. "Two of them. Cute little furry things. Round little fuzzy ears. And then . . ."

That was all I needed to know. We kept running. "This," she exclaimed, "is the most frightened that I have ever been because of an animal."

When we arrived at the top of the steep slope, we were out of breath. We glanced down at the forest far beneath us, to see if the bear was pursuing us. She wasn't. In fact, it took us a while to spot her. Allison saw her first, below us in the woods beside the trail. She was nosing her cubs one by one up a tree, her vast and hairy rump pointed in our direction, as if inviting us to kiss it.

So maybe I was wrong. Maybe the woods were sending me a little message. "Back the fuck *up*," the forest seemed to say. "Perhaps we're not as wild as we used to be, but we're wild enough for you." I sat there with Allison in a pile of wet leaves, still pumped with adrenaline, but relieved that the forest had let me off easy. I vowed to be more respectful next time. I vowed not to mix it up with any more woodland creatures until we hit Canada. From now on, I'd avoid confrontation with the mindless fauna of the forest.

But it was already too late to avoid confrontation.

A much smaller monster, one we couldn't even see, was lying in ambush for us in the woods of the Pacific Northwest.

Chapter 25

Attack of the Pain People

In late September, we entered the kingdom of Shasta, a sleeping stratovolcano in the South Cascades. We were now just 230 trail miles south of the Oregon border. Allison and I were entering a time of year when the weather was getting colder. The sky swirled with odd colors: gunmetal gray, off-white, tooth-plaque yellow, brown, and blue, and yet this did not bother me. In the past few weeks, we'd faced down near-horrible disasters, and some deus ex machina always showed up at the last moment to save us. Allison had taken some severe headers face first into the rocky soil, but she'd always caught herself in time. In another instance, hogging the map and directions, she was so spooked by a gaggle of wicked quail that she very nearly fell off a cliff. But she somehow caught herself. Nature could be frightening and unpredictable, but we seemed to have luck on our side. How else could we have escaped from Mama Bear? Now, in Northern California, I just wanted that luck to hold out for a while. The kingdom of Shasta was our final obstacle before we finished all of Northern California. By every indication, our journey was going smoothly now. Never mind the disturbing legends I'd heard about Shasta. According to Native American tradition, it's taboo to cross into the mountain's sacred kingdom. Vengeful beings occupy the waters and rocks, where they stand sentry against any human who dares to trespass on or desecrate the land. Wayfarers who travel above the tree line are especially vulnerable to this race of spirit beings. The name Native Americans gave to these little people is the same word they used for "pain."

According to author and California cultural historian Philip Fradkin, Shasta crowns a region that attracts more myths and legends than any other part of California. Allison knew a bit about the stories. She'd mentioned a thirteenth-century mystic named St. Germain, whose wraithlike presence haunts Panther Creek near Shasta. Allison and I shared an interest in the occult. When we were first dating, in rural Connecticut, we gave impromptu tarot readings at parties. With our limited knowledge of tarot rules, we misinterpreted the cards, which led us to tell my already anxious downstairs neighbor that he was going to die very soon. Allison and I once traveled to the remains of an allegedly haunted settlement called Dudleytown, near Cornwall, Connecticut. The silence was unearthly there. Even the birds were quiet. Allison discovered a tree with a human face—a lump for a nose, two knobs for eyes, and sap crying out of them. It made me wonder if trees could imprison human souls. Allison had asked me, that day in Dudleytown, if I believed in the landscapes of evil. As we left the ruins of that colonial town, we talked about the powers of good and ill that resided in certain forests.

I have always been superstitious. I suppose, in the back of my mind, I was concerned about the region of Shasta, and whether the powers within the landscape would work for or against us. Still, I felt nothing but hope and excitement as we hiked into Castella, a former lumber town and railroad settlement in the heart of the Sacramento River Canyon. Castella is exalted by hikers because of Milt Kenney, the most famous "trail angel" to live near the trail. Milt earned his reputation as "Mayor of the Trail" by helping an average of sixty hikers per season for the past twenty years. We were looking forward to meeting him. Allison and I were also aware of Castella's reputation as a place for the "halfway blues." Although it's only 210 miles from the Oregon border, many hikers get demoralized because of a sign at the Castle Crags Campground saying MEXICAN BORDER, 1,487 MILES. CANADIAN BORDER, 1,113 MILES. Something about the sign can make a man feel small; the task at hand is nearly as enormous as what you've already accomplished.

Perhaps that's why, historically speaking, trail couples break up at Castella. The task makes you reflect on your partner's flaws as if through the lens of an electron microscope. But it comforted me that Allison, by now, knew all of my weirdnesses and hadn't dumped me. She now took it for granted that I lost or broke crucial pieces of gear—the flashlight gone AWOL in a river, the shit shovel dropped in a ravine, and the thermometer I sat on until the mercury leaked. She once caught me using my dirty nether garments, which I referred to as "undie-pants," as eye pillows to block the moonlight as I slept. This did not seem to bother her. Over the past month, I'd noticed, with some distaste, that she was starting to pee standing up without taking her backpack off, and that she sometimes peed directly off the trail. This no longer struck me as bestial. Our moods were often disparate, with one of us happy and burbling, the other bored or despondent, but I accepted this. I tried very hard to pay more attention to her, not to call out military cadences when she fell behind or to cut short her well-earned breaks. I tried active listening, and to let her get in at least six consecutive sentences before making the conversation all about me. Besides, I was learning to tend to her, take care of her, elevate her knee, and feed her Excedrins, tortilla chips, and bean dip when she was in pain. I still knew how to make her laugh. For her sake, I was trying to be stoic, and complaining less. In every way, I was trying to give her more reasons not to take off into the woods by herself.

Allison's parents, wondering how we were faring, had sent us a *Far Side* cartoon showing two explorers stumbling through the hills. The man in the front is singing, "My knapsack on my back, valderi, valdera, valderi, valdera, ha, ha, ha!" The man in the back is muttering, "God, I hate him." The caption reads, "More tension on the Lewis and Clark Expedition." But by now the trail was running out of ideas to hamper our expedition. We were ruthless, skinny, stripped down, fierce. After making so much progress, we couldn't wait to celebrate with the most famous trail angel of them all. He would be the good-luck charm we needed to push us all the way into Canada.

In the heart of Castella, beneath the sharp granite crest of Castle Crags, Ammirati's Market was open, so Allison and I ducked in to inquire about Milt Kenney, but he wasn't there. I asked a store clerk where he might be found. The clerk placed a call, murmured something into the receiver, and a moment later, a navy Oldsmobile Sedan came rolling up to the market. An old man, five foot three, with a stained-felt porkpie, trousers, and a maroon cardigan got out of the car and stood in front of us. He had rheumy eyes, leathery skin, and a smile that belonged on the face of a young boy, not an eighty-four-year-old man. He'd unbuttoned his sweater to reveal a T-shirt with a Pacific Crest Trail map printed across it. The shirt listed the names of all trail supply stops along the route, including Castella, which lay an inch above the old man's sternum.

Milt Kenney gave us the litany he'd recited to hundreds of other hikers over the years. The words sounded broken in from being said so many times. "Hullo, I'm Milt Kenney and I've been greeting the hikers now for twenty years." His voice was plummy. He extended his hand, and his grip was as crushing as everybody had warned. "So what do you need? Where would you like to go? I can drive you anywhere you want. Treat you lunch? Treat you breakfast?" He said these words without slavishness, and smiled with confidence, as if his offers of generosity were a power he wielded over strangers.

Allison and I looked at each other. We were thrilled to meet a trail celebrity, but I felt sheepish about accepting favors, perhaps because I'd spent the past decade in New England small towns, where you could be curled up frozen on the pavement, turning blue, and passersby wouldn't stop to offer you so much as a small cup of lukewarm broth. It felt weird to hear someone peddling altruism, as if kindness were something to be hardsold, a zirconium bracelet on late night TV. But refusing his offers of help would have been crueler than sponging off him. So the decision was made. "Throw your stuff in the car," he said, and we obliged.

Allison and I piled into the backseat. As Milt stepped on the accelerator, and pulled out on to the highway, he admitted that his eyesight was not the greatest. He drove conservatively, but by no means timidly, as he confessed: "Don't know if I'll get to drive hikers around in the future." The speed crept up on the odometer—forty-five, fifty, fifty-five, sixty. "Depends on the cataracts. I don't know how long my eyes will hold, and that'd be a shame." Allison's hand dug into the armrest as Milt's car swept beneath the Castle Crags, swirled with mist and built like the spires of Oz. Milt laughed as he glanced up at the Crags. "Told my nephew I built those rocks up there and he believed me."

Milt drove us six miles up the road to Dunsmuir, near the Sacramento River. The whole town was peeling and sad and set close to the ground, but Milt said it was a hiker's Fantasyland, with all the food you can eat. He took us to the Burger Barn near the center of the historic railroad town and shouted out to the half-empty place, "Hey, look, I've got two more!"

We found a table and Milt ordered us a pair of "Barn Buster Burgers," enormous ground round discuses smeared with mayo. While we sat there, gulping wet meat, Milt smiled, leaned forward, and said, "It tickles me to watch you eat." In between urging us to order more food, he told us about himself. Three-quarters Swiss, one-quarter Karuk Indian, Milt was born in Clear Creek, nine miles from Happy Camp, California. As a child, he kept a bear cub as a pet and walked to school through the woods eight miles each way. He worked as a forester in northern California, felling and cutting lumber. For thirty-nine years he was married to Florence, the founder of a local school. They skied, hiked, and danced every week. "She was my buddy, my best friend. I loved her so." He bought her a heart-shaped gold nugget. In 1979 she had a heart attack and died. "It was real sudden," he said. "I did not want to live." He was so grief-stricken, his daughter, Adele, wondered if he would last the year. Winter pinochle games were the only respite from his loneliness. "I didn't know what to do with myself," he said. "But then I saw that hikers were coming through town and saw that they were good people. I decided to help them. I treat a lot of 'em dinner, treat 'em lunch, and some of 'em treat me. Some people think what I do is pretty silly, but most think it's great. Most of 'em think I'm doing all right."

When he was younger he danced with hikers. He told us stories about holding court in a nearby saloon, dancing across the floor with women a third of his age. "I'd dance 'em down!" he said. "They'd tire out after a while, and I'd still be dancing." He liked the company and the recognition. Milt showed Allison a folder of press clippings about himself, and pointed out a story in which the reporter had bungled Milt's age. In pencil, Milt had scribbled the correct number in the margin. He loved his modest legend and the "trail mayor" title, and the fact that the Forest Service had named a 0.9-mile spur trail, from the Castella campground to the Pacific Crest Trail, after him.

Outside the diner, Allison asked me to take a picture of her and Milt. I snapped a slide of Allison throwing back her hair, her long white neck exposed. She's smiling flirtatiously, open-mouthed, as she leans in and jabs Milt in the sternum, right on the place where his T-shirt says CASTELLA. Milt recoils and laughs at the same time like the Pillsbury Dough Boy.

Milt took us to a local laundry room in Dunsmuir, and waited for our loads to wash and dry. Then he took us to a drug store, where he was shocked by how much chocolate and gooey pectin treats we shoved into our grub sacks. "You two eat more candy than any hikers I've ever seen," he noted. When we were back in the Oldsmobile, or walking around Dunsmuir with Milt, an opiate calm settled on him. He smiled at all times when he was with us. But at one point that day, when Allison and I walked into a Dunsmuir bank, where we changed traveler's checks, I saw Milt's reflection backward through the bank's glass doors, when he was standing there outside the Oldsmobile and didn't know I was spying on him. He looked emptied-out, drooping like an old carnation, but when we walked out of the bank and got in the car, with us in the back, he straightened up. His face looked full again.

That night in camp, Allison and I leafed through a journal left behind for PCT hikers to sign. In it were some not-very-good poems that hikers had written for Milt Kenney. They were gooey, and if memory serves, at least one of them used the word *did* to pad out the stanzas, as in, "Milt, you did take me in, and you did treat me as though I were kin," and "Milt, you made me feel at home when into Castella as a stranger I did roam." But in spite of their thudding didness, the poems seemed sincere. In fact, the awfulness increased their power. Their uniformly low quality suggested that people adored Milt so much that they could not voice this feeling gracefully or coherently. That evening, Allison wrote a poem in Milt's honor. It was truly terrible. And yet there may have been a downside to Milt's kindness, according to another journal entry, which included a disturbing cartoon. It showed a hiker hanging in a web screaming. A spider with a porkpie hat was closing in on him. In the web were dangling treats that lured the hiker toward a slow, sticky death: cheeseburgers and fries, hung at intervals in the matrix. "Someone help me!" the cartoon hiker cries. "I'm caught in the Milt Kenney web." I understood the feeling. Why would anyone want to go back into the woods after meeting Milt Kenney? There was something about him that made you want to quit the damned trail and hang out with him forever.

The next day, Milt Kenney swung around to see us again in the campground. He handed us plum tomatoes plucked from his garden. He stood in front of us with his hands in his pockets, and this time he would not smile, even when we posed him in front of the sign for the steep, nearly mile-long spur trail. With his chin resting on the Milt Kenney Trail sign, he told us we should think about not leaving. "You don't have to go away so soon," he said. "Most hikers stay three, four days. Why, I had one hiker stay a week. You stayed a day. That's a very short amount of time compared to most hikers."

He looked downcast. I explained to him that the weather could turn on us if we did not hike northward as fast as we could, and that we had spent a lot of time and effort trying to beat the snowstorms and reach Canada before it was too late. "It could storm any second," I said.

He just looked blankly at me and said, "If it storms, come back. Treat you breakfast, treat you dinner." We walked off, and he shouted after us, "Send a Christmas card."

Allison and I stomped on to the Milt Kenney Trail, up a steep hill, and though I sensed he was looking as we faded up into the hillside, I did not look back.

We were the last hikers of the season, meaning that our leaving would condemn Milt to loneliness for the next half-year. I tried not to think about this as we pressed on, looking at the sky.

We lunched that afternoon in front of Mount Shasta, 14,161 feet above sea level. That day, a pair of semi-attached lenticular clouds hovered above the cone. The mountain is a reliable producer of these Frisbee-shaped mist formations. Smokers of exceptional marijuana and budding herbalists believe the clouds serve as a cloak for UFOs, according to a study of Shasta's "spiritual pilgrims." Indeed, one of the clouds resembled the spaceship from *The Day the Earth Stood Still*. Allison and I ate lunch, and she snapped a picture of me holding the Swiss Army knife, chopping tomatoes while my log-moss beard dangled from my chin. I looked stringy and rangy like a red coyote, my Lois and Clark Expedition Day-Glo cap tilted backward. The sky was an unapologetic blue, making Allison squint. Shasta dominates the land. Rising more than ten thousand feet above its forested base, the mountain is visible for about two hundred of the trail's zigging, zagging miles. From where I stood, I saw three of the mountain's five glaciers, hurting my eyes through polarized lenses. Native Americans believed the mountain was the palace of Skell, who dropped from the heavens to take up residency there. When I squinted at the ice fields, I made out the shape of tapering fingers down the mountainside. The glaciers near the top suggested a wrist. The overall effect was that of a giant hand reaching from the sky. I rested for a moment—woozy for no reason, no power in my legs, my chest seeming to compress. Allison did not notice that something was wrong. We had been making up crazy stories about the mountains, explaining that Shasta had a "cocaine problem," and that its glaciers were made out of "nose candy." She was caught up in this game, creating imagined histories of every mountain on the horizon, even as a mysterious nausea overtook me. I was overcome, and thought for a moment that I might pass out.

I staggered down a slope, staring at Shasta as it grabbed up the sunlight. The ominous plug of Back Butte rose from be-hind the mountain. I was lost in my thoughts, wondering about the magnetic pull of Shasta, and what it was doing to my body, when a thirty-five-ish man with wild eyes came jogging over to us on the path. The man was not right in the head. Heading toward us, he sang along with a radio station that played only in his mind. As he ran forward, he leaned toward Shasta, as if there were a receiver in his brain decoding the mountain's scrambled messages. The man wore athletic shorts, running shoes, and a metal-colored jacket. When Allison smiled at him and asked what brought him to such a place, he explained that his girl-friend had two-timed him and that he had called her a "fuck-ing liar" right to her face. His heart was broken and he was here to heal. "I want an audience with Saint Germain," he said.

The man told us that "all mountains have distinct person-alities" and that Shasta is "a place that receives God's energy, a very special place." He'd seen a photo in a local bookstore of Shasta with a bolt of purple light shooting from its rock. "I know it was real," he said. "There was no trick photography in that picture." He told us he was there to stay, and would never return to the life he'd abandoned. "Want to know what I do for work? I live. I live for a living." We refused his repeated offers to hike with him back to town and eat vegetables out of the trunk of his car, but he didn't seem offended. He told us that it was no matter, that there was all kinds of nourishment in these mountains, and that we were about to find out for ourselves that Shasta was "a very powerful place." He waved good-bye and ran south down the trail to Castella.

As he ran off, I wondered if it wasn't all in my head, if the mountain could drive a man mad. But it was hard to know for sure, especially considering that so many people who visit Shasta are crazy already. A group called the I AM Foundation uses Shasta as a staging ground for a pageant celebrating the life of Christ, sans unpleasant bits, such as the Crucifixion. About five thousand people crowded the mountain's meadows in 1987 to celebrate harmonic convergence, when the celestial bodies line up in the heavens like so many duckpins. Quite a few of them left crystals in Panther Spring in honor of Saint Germain. Park rangers accused them of despoiling meadows, building altars illegally, and causing erosion. Other Shasta pilgrims believed the mountain was a safe home for seven-foot-tall deities that are benevolent, mysterious and, like them, blindingly Caucasian. These mysterious people are known as Lemurians, modern-day descendants of a race that lived in an Atlantis-like utopia for thousands of years but fled to Shasta's subterranean chambers when their stronghold, Mu, sank in the Pacific Ocean after a volcanic cataclysm. These people fly through the sky in airborne boats, wear white vestments, and have ESP. They've got walnut-shaped sensory organs protruding from their heads, and marvelous physiques, which came in handy for their ancestors when they sculpted Easter Island's totem faces. The Lemurians were said to have porcelain complexions, in spite of the fact that they lived on a continent that served as a land bridge between India and Africa. Above all else, these people were supposed to have been very nice. As far as ethereal creatures were concerned, Lemurians were the salt of the earth. Milt Kenney, if he were two or three feet taller and had blue skin, would have fit right in.

If the spirits of kindness existed out here, so did the spirits of nastiness. Storms billowed up to cover the mountain, but Shasta revealed itself again at sunset. This time it was red and yellow, and the square snow patches looked like windows into the volcano and the fire inside it. The night was uncommonly cold, so much so that no amount of bundling and cuddling could take the edge off the chill. The water in our bottles froze. The next day, when we rose from our tents, every step felt like twenty steps. Small distances were treks in themselves. That week in the backcountry, our path crossed a deep creek. On a steep bank above the water, pitcher plants bobbed in the wind.

Dark marks branched across their throats like veins, which shone green and red with the sun behind them. Lobes in their throats give off perfume that lures flies, who climb down the tubes in search of food. When the flies turn around to leave, stiff-backed spines block their exit. The insects weaken, starve, and tumble into pools of liquid. Microorganisms melt the flies into a tonic for the plant.

As we walked among the plants, trampling a latticework of ferns, I felt woozy, cornered, dissolving. Refuges can turn into traps in an instant. The land steepens against you, and the trees rise up to seal you in. Something was going on inside my body but I didn't know what it was. I didn't feel sick just yet, but I was, as Allison said, "immunocompromised," vulnerable to infection, sapped of strength but having no idea of the cause.

"What the hell is going on?" I said to her. "You think someone served us a sneezeburger in Dunsmuir? Did we eat without washing our hands?"

She shook her head as the path pushed into the darker forests, where hemlocks grew in thickets. The path was narrow and the forest impenetrable. The trees had thrown their roots around the boulders and tethered themselves to the slopes. The Pacific Crest Trail was a spool of yarn through the boundlessness. The forest slouched. Shasta shone its firelight through gaps in the trees.

This part of the Pacific Crest Trail marked our entryway to the Klamath Mountains, which extended from the northwest corner of California into Oregon. Once attached like a conjoined twin to the northern Sierra Nevada range, the Klamath began to pull apart from its sister 130 million years ago. Scientists discovered the mountains were kin when they compared the fossils of marine creatures etched in their slopes. Long ago, the Klamaths were islands in a sea that sealed over the Cascades to the north. I walked as if I, too, were underwater. Like the Klamaths, which are squat compared to the Sierra Nevada, and receive a deluge of rainwater that makes them wear away more quickly than any other place on earth, I was ground down, eroding with every mile.

The trail wiggled all over the place as if trying to befuddle us. Such mischief is not uncommon for the PCT. If you were to draw a straight line between Canada and Mexico, it would be only 1,000 miles long, and yet the PCT takes 2,650 miles to go the same distance. Sometimes along the way, the trail seemed to derail itself and run off course. Rather than shooting north, it turned west and even went south for a while, as if giving up and hightailing it to Mexico. The path pushed us into the Trinity Alps, vast limpets and barnacles clinging to California's northern tip. The dominant feature was the snow cone form of Thompson Peak, at 9,002 feet, the tallest Alp, with glaciers fixed to its sides.

We spent one night at Siphon Lake in the Russian Wilderness, a gray expanse with a brown pipe rotting on the bottom. Mosquitoes buzzed the tent flap's mesh door. Allison watched over me, trying to squeeze the sickness out of me, pressing her body against me, sticking a thermometer into my mouth. The tent turned into a fog chamber. Allison kept asking if I was okay. Her voice echoed, her image replicated, until Allison turned into a harem of good-looking Italian women, a banquet of curves, long necks and blond hair, and yet I had no sex drive at all, and the tent was waltzing around me.

Next morning we decided to press on to the north and get out of these woods, rest up, and find an access road to civilization at the nearest opportunity—but we didn't know the lay of the land. Even now, my memories of the forest come back in a stony haze. Allison kept begging me to just turn around and backtrack to a road near Scott Mountain, where we could try to flag down a ride, but the idea of going backward on the trail still seemed unthinkable to me, no matter how sick I was. My stubbornness prevailed. But now the landscape was blurry. Waterdog Lake spun around in the sun. We passed a rutted dirt road. A motor broke the silence. Two hunters on three-wheel off-road vehicles bumped past us, toting rifles. The first was ruddy, about fifty, with a calm smile and a deep sunburn. His nose peeled, revealing a second layer of skin. His baseball cap had a cartoon showing two dancing containers of booze and the message I LIKE BIG JUGS. Mr. Big Jugs told us that Etna Summit was the most reliable access to a close-by town off the trail, but the summit was fourteen miles away, with many uphill miles. He and his friend waved as they raced down the dirt road in search of big game, and, presumably, even bigger jugs.

The feeling of walking on the bottom of the ocean intensified when we slipped on the serpentine soil. Allison pressed her hand to the cool stone and traced the coiled shapes of fossilized trilobites, underwater sow bugs stamped into the cliffs. Mr. Big Jugs had mentioned other access route options, but Allison and I didn't want to risk it; the antifreeze liquid in our latest compass had leaked out somehow, leaving the needle stranded, ruining our guidance system, and we didn't want to make a mistake. I checked the map. The names of nearby lakes were sinister: Poison Lake. Deadfall Lake. Man Eaten Lake. Toad Lake. Kleaver Lake. Every time we stopped to rest near one of these lakes, I witnessed natural acts of thuggishness and cruelty. At one pond, a fish leapt up to suck a moth down from the water's surface. Another moth fell in the drink. Somehow it managed to escape another fish, but then a water nymph rose from the bottom, grabbed the moth, beat the shit out of it, mauled it with its tail for good measure, and dragged it screaming into the murk. It was dreadful, like watching a talent show of sadistic animal behavior emceed by Annie Dillard. Some people find inspiration in nature's violence, but this display made me sick. In my diary I chided nature for "unnecessary roughness."

As I walked on, with Allison growing more worried about me, I began to pray, talking to my stomach, talking to my virus, trying to use Old Gipper encouragements to halt my illness. "I

will hold this thing back with food," I told Allison. "I can perse-
vere. I can win." But all the while, I sensed that this virus, and the
weather, had more determination and relentlessness than I could
muster. I ate and drank as much as I could but lacked the moxie
to make it all the way to the summit in one day. And yet we
could not afford to camp out here in the cold for much longer.
Though it was still hard to gauge the seriousness of what I had, if
we did not somehow drag ourselves out of the woods, this illness
was about to get a whole lot worse.

That night we were camped somewhere in the Klamath National Forest. It felt like some of my strength had somehow returned, and for a while, in camp, I was sure that the mystery bug
was finished with its business inside of me, and yet I could not be
too sure. It was a cool, clear evening in the high country. Allison
fired the stove while I traipsed across a rocky finger leading me
out into a night-black lake. I decided to filter some water from
the shallows. Just as I'd done hundreds of times before, I dropped
the intake tube—attached to a floatation device—into the water
and started pumping. Suddenly, the water near the lake shore
stirred and frothed with motion; a dozen salamanders, black, flat,
and staring, moved across the lake. In silent motion the six-inch
shadow people surrounded my filter and closed in on it, the
circle growing smaller.

The first one, with an orange belly, swam forward and kissed
the filter's intake valve in an open-mouthed, sleazy way. Then,
to my surprise, a second salamander rose up, knocked the first
salamander out of the way, and mounted my filter's intake tube,
grabbing onto the flotation sponge with all fours and thrusting
itself right into it. After a while it let go and floated back into
the pond. Salamanders kept bubbling up to take the previous
one's place. I'm not naive. I knew what was really going on
here. The salamanders were attempting intercourse with my
water filter or using it as part of a group masturbation ritual. I
was not about to sit back and let them get away with it. "*Stop*

it!" I roared at the salamanders, but they would not listen. In a savage gesture, I yanked the intake tube as hard as I could and sent the salamanders flying backward into the deep—*"Fuck off!"*—but they kept coming back for more. Soon the lake shallows squirmed in *Caligula* contortions, salamander limbs and torsos thrashing and splashing as they mounted my water filter again and again. Clearly, this was not a battle I was going to win. It was time to retreat to my campsite.

I had just enough water to get us through the night and the next day, but now it was cloudy and discolored. Perhaps it was the effect of the tiny bubbles in the water. Still, I could not help but wonder what, exactly, was floating around in our water supply. I ran back to camp, jabbering that our water filter had just been gang-raped by amphibians, but Allison did not believe me, nor did she believe it was possible for salamander jism to find its way into our water supply. But how could she know for sure?

Salamanders do produce sperm, and certain species engage in, and enjoy, sexual intercourse, although, technically, it's outercourse, because the males lack penises. As part of their mating ritual, the male straddles his salamander girlfriend, grabs hold of her pelvis, and releases a goopy pile of spermatophores, which the female stuffs into her cloacal opening, also known as a "vent." I can't say which variety of salamander released its sour payload into my filter. All I know is that the water, even when blended with Gatorade powder, was sticky and bitter that night. I drank a lot of it anyhow because I was very thirsty. Allison tried to reassure me. "It's the food itself that tastes so bad," she said. "The bitterness comes from the food, not the water." But I woke up the next day feeling sick, overcome, vomitous, staggering, barely able to move, hallucinating, out of my mind. Trees sprouted legs and surrounded me in a tight circle.

The Pain People were taking over, closing in on me, and now there was no way out.

Chapter 26

No Mercy

The steep trail showed no mercy in the Russian Wilderness. Allison, by this time, was also feeling a little ill, with some of the symptoms I'd shown a few days before; I was ahead of her on the sickness curve. In fact, I represented the future of her health, and she did not like what she saw. Still, she was stronger than me, at least for the moment. She looked scared, and for good reason. I was acting wild. My sickness made me loopy, as if I'd eaten a pan of hash-infused fudge. Sometimes I'd break into a little Morris dance of nausea, kicking up my heels, swooning through the forest.

The path cut straight and sharp beneath a boulder called the Statue, which stood forty feet above the trail; it's only a big, naturally eroded rock, but if you look at it from the south, the formation looks like a crude sculpture of a human with a jackal's head. To my tired mind, the rock was nothing less than a vengeful deity, keeping tabs on us. As I staggered behind Allison, I sensed that the Jackal God of the Pacific Crest Trail was weighing our fate. Would we push on to Canada, or would I drag down the expedition by becoming even more enfeebled? The landscape hung on this moment, now, here, where hills wobbled like warm Jell-O, where tall trees danced the hokey-pokey, and mountains warped in the sun. Standing on a crest overlooking Lipstick Lake, I stared at the slack folds of dry mountains and wondered what I had done to deserve this.

"Poor me," I thought. "Is it really too much to ask, that I get to walk a trail and reach the finish line? Is this modest ambition really such an affront to the fates of the forest? What have I done to deserve this?" And then, it occurred to me: maybe I really *had* done something to deserve this. My sickness disabled the part of my brain that suppressed the memories of nasty behavior, the small cutting things I'd said and done. I recalled, with distaste, my time in middle school when I used to pal around with Bobby Wasserman, fang-faced, pitiless, possessed of a meager intelligence. We went to Disneyland together once. There, in the no-man's zone between Fantasyland and New Orleans Square, I convinced him to spit on Donald Duck, just because I was bored and wanted to test out my theory that the walking cartoon characters at Disneyland will just keep smiling whatever you do to them. Throw Goofy into the moat around Tom Sawyer's Island and he'll still grin like he's having the time of his life. We chose Donald Duck as our victim simply because he was standing alone with his flimsy white gloves. At my urging, Bobby coughed up an enormous blob of saliva into his hand—known in middle-school parlance as a "loogie." Then he approached Donald Duck. "Mr. Duck," Bobby shouted. "I'm a big fan. I want to shake your hand."

Donald Duck wiggled his tail feather in delight. He did a little hop, threw a gleeful kick in the air, and accepted Bobby's extended hand. The two of them shook hands very hard, and you could see a tremor of shock shoot through the duck-man's body, as Bobby worked that warm and feculent saliva so deeply into Donald's glove. Bobby let go at last, and the two of us ran away, doubled over with laughter. We watched from behind a hedge as Donald Duck stomped up and down in a rage, while still somehow smiling maniacally at the sopping wet glove that he waved, in frantic motions, in front of his large orange beak.

I've performed hundreds, maybe thousands, of small cruelties like this. Were any of these things so terrible, really? No. They were all pretty small on the face of it. I'm not talking about capital offenses here. But the fact is we don't need to commit murder or grand theft to do lasting harm. These small things remain in the minds of our victims, not as individual memories but as generalized feelings of ill will or anxiety.

It was too late to apologize for all these things. The jackal gods were furious with me, and now I was going to pay.

Somehow we made our way to the Etna–Somes Bar road by following a spur trail that led from the PCT to the highway. For a while we sat to the side of the shining blacktop, resting on our packs, chins on knuckles, hearing the buzz of what we thought were car engines but always turned out to be the distant drone of planes. The sky was darkening, the steep mountains flattening into silhouettes. I wondered what would happen if no one drove past. In fact, I was sure no one would come to get us. It was all part of the Jackal God's vengeance.

Finally, a red Chevy pickup cruised around the bend and stopped. Inside was a tan, lean couple in their late thirties, Tom and Linda, who told us they were teachers who had spent the day hunting in the woods. Tom was clean-shaven, wiry. Linda had a softer appearance, with silky hair. Religious Christians, they had a stack of green, soft-bound Gideon's Bibles that could fit in your palm. They gave me one. "We stopped to help you guys 'cause that's what people do when they live out here,"

Linda said. "You help people as a way of life, but I might have thought twice about it if it was just me in the truck."

As I climbed in the cab with Allison, I wondered if Linda was just being modest. I suspect it was faith, not just the realities of country living, that made her help us out that day. Say what you will about fundamentalists. If you're stranded, and if you and your girlfriend look like Charles Manson and Squeaky Fromme, religious people are the only ones who will pick you up. If it weren't for born-agains, we hitchhikers would probably rot in patchouli-scented piles by the side of the road.

The road swept down past stables and horses in the black-green grass. Barnyards leaned in fading light. We rolled down the town of Etna's Main Street, with an old pharmacy and soda fountain, a movie theater and a corrugated building that housed the Etna microbrewery.

Tom and Linda drove through to the other side of Etna, down to the residence of a "country doctor" named Erikkson, who they hoped would cure me and Allison so we could continue our sojourn. Though he was part-retired, Erikkson still received patients in his house, which doubled as a walk-in medical clinic. Maybe the Jackal God wasn't angry after all, I thought. Maybe the born-agains and the country doctor were signs of Him smiling.

Dr. Erikkson received us at the door of his modest home. Allison waited in the living room while he escorted me to a nearby room. There was a white protective wrapper on an examination table, a cabinet with some pills, and a few pieces of equipment. Erikkson was tall and bowlegged. He looked sixty, and as if he spent more time tending and riding horses than making people well, which was true, as he admitted.

The doctor had me sit on the table, and this made me very nervous. In my youth, I hated going to doctors because they tended to bend down and squeeze my cringing and frightened testicles while making me stick out my tongue and cough, regardless of my symptoms. In fact, he went out of his way to avoid doing anything that might make me uncomfortable, such as taking my pulse, taking my blood pressure, applying a stethoscope to my chest, or bopping me on the leg with the little silver hammer that doctors often have on hand just for perversity's sake. In fact, he did so very little that, after a while, I wondered how he knew whether I even had vital signs. At last he decided to take my temperature. Only after I had the thermometer wedged very deeply into my mouth did he ask any substantive questions about my health. I answered as best I could, but it was hard to articulate speech.

"So," Dr. Erikkson said. "What do you think made you so sick?"

"I sink it was the wedder."

He harrumphed in apparent annoyance. "People are always blaming the weather. Weather, by itself, cannot make you sick. So you're hiking on a trail. You come to a town and you're exposed to all kinds of germs. Weather by itself is not a sickening agent. What are your symptoms?"

"Dauseated. No affetite. I seal like wombat vomit."

"Listen, I've got some Biaxin I can give you. It's powerful stuff. It'll knock it right out." Conveniently enough, Dr. Erikkson just so happened to have a bunch of free Biaxin samples hanging around in a drawer. He even threw in some extra Biaxin for Allison, as a preventive measure, "in case she starts feeling sicker, too."

I was happy and relieved, even though the doctor had not explained how he somehow knew what was ailing me; after all, he hadn't drawn blood. Yet I sensed that he was right, and that by some miracle, he had saved our trip. He couldn't be wrong, I thought. I'd never met a man with such Zenlike confidence in his curing powers. If all that was not enough, he wrote me up an IOU instead of giving me a formal bill, though he took down my permanent address to make sure I didn't dodge out on payment. I left his office feeling great. Dr. Erikkson was a necessary corrective to an inhumane world of PPOs and HMOs. Hooray, I thought. Our trip was saved. Our last obstacle on the way to Canada had just been swept away. Perhaps the Jackal God wasn't mad at me at all. He was merely testing me.

Chapter 27

The Jackal God
Strikes Back

When we finally left Etna five days later, we had lost the equivalent of ninety walking miles to the north—and had shelled out three hundred dollars for lodging. Allison had taken ill in Etna, and for a while, it was touch and go, as she succumbed to nausea and exhaustion. But by the time we returned to the trail, she, too, had rebounded, and now it seemed that all our symptoms had subsided. We were a bit sleepy, but the worst of our ailments seemed to be gone, and we were confident that the illness had somehow washed its way out of our bodies. Braggadocio ruled the day. I even crowed to Allison that this next section of the trail would be "as easy as knocking back a shot of watered-down vodka." Allison laughed at this, and we both broke into a gleeful song, to the tune of Sinead O'Connor's weepy 1990 hit, "The Last Day of Our Acquaintance":

This is our last part of California! Oh-ho-ho.

I'll meet you later somewhere in Oregon—Oh-ho-ho!

To our great relief, the trail was undemanding and gentle at first, as we rose up over Big Creek Canyon and dropped into creek-filled gulches choked with underbrush. Nothing was going wrong, and that was crucial, for there was no room for the smallest setback now. We were hurrying, and so, it seemed, were the creatures in the forest. Everywhere you could hear animals in the underbrush, the sounds of gathering, hoarding, and last-minute preparations. Having hiked from late summer and into the fall, I sensed the long days shrinking, the air getting colder, the sun setting faster. We rose earlier now, before sunup, sometimes when frost persisted on the grass and leaves; it shone like bits of glass. At times like that, I sensed the planet was moving toward darkness, with a shrinking wall of sunlight breaking up an eternal night. Shadows persisted. Streams got sluggish. The cold snap quickened our steps. But after a while, we couldn't will our bodies to move quickly anymore. Our weakness had returned, and then the sickness rebounded, strong as ever but different. It hit me hard close to the Kidder Lake Trail, where the trail laid siege to black-green mountains measled with red rock. As I walked up, I experienced the onset of symptoms far more striking and unique than anything that had hit me so far. The first was flatulence so devastating that the sustained whoosh of its backward thrust propelled me northward toward Canada with the strength of a pair of blazing booster rockets. But later, as the day wore on, things got even more interesting. I experienced an attack of vomiting and diarrhea so spectacular that my body transformed into an overstuffed pastry bag ruptured at both ends and squeezed from the middle.

Allison tried to make me eat, but that was challenging, considering that she was weak and nauseated, too, which distracted her from assisting me. Even the smallest bite of food, ingested for a moment, burst forth from my throat. As far as I'm concerned, the trots were the pièce de résistance; I'd never experienced anything like them in my life, not even in Mexico. Every

ten to fifteen minutes, I had to take my leave of the Pacific
Crest Trail and run into the woods, searching desperately for
a shady bower in which to void. I'd just be pulling my shorts
up when another attack would hit me—POW!—and I'd have
to look for yet another likely spot, forcing me to hop through
the underbrush, howling and yipping, my electric-blue hiking shorts fettering my ankles as I bounced like a kangaroo
from one tree to another. I was no longer hiking, per se. It was
more like a modern dance composed of physical jerks, wailing,
crumpling into trees, and writhing like Twyla Tharp. On one
such occasion, as I lay on the ground, the sun stabbing my eyes
like diamond points, and cold shivers running through me, I
wondered to myself, "What on earth could be doing this to my
body? Do I have trichinosis? E-coli? Shigella?"

I started to wonder if I had giardia, a much-feared ailment
of the backcountry. The PCT guidebook mentioned it several
times. I didn't know the particulars of this affliction then but I'd
heard horror stories about it, and spoken to hikers who'd con-
tracted it. According to a reliable medical text, those who come
down with giardia, or more specifically, giardia intestinalis, experience the "sudden onset of explosive watery foul-smelling
diarrhea with nausea and anorexia and marked abdominal dis-
tension with flatulence," perhaps accompanied by "chills and
low-grade fever, vomiting, headache and malaise." All this and
malaise, too?

It was disappointing to speculate that beaver fever had gotten the best of me. I figured that if anything caused me problems
on the trail, it would be something big and glamorous, something that would get my name in the paper, such as a savage
hairy creature or serial killer. But the truth is no Pacific Crest
Trail hiker has ever been murdered along the trail throughout
its history, and there has never been a reported serious bear attack on PCT hikers, either. Looking back, it just about kills me
to think that a protozoan parasite eight microns long, so small

that a million-population city of these tiny buggers could fit, no problem, under your fingernail, could make me so miserable. Giardia may be small but it gets around; these vicious creatures have tails that thrash like the whips of dominatrices as they dart through your intestines. Appropriately enough, when viewed through an electron microscope, they look like smirking clown faces.

Lying there on a rock, in pain, I suspected that something tiny was wreaking havoc inside me, and I wanted vengeance. I wished I could shrink myself down to the size of a microbe, just so I could punch whatever it was in the face, or at least tell it to go fuck itself, but in essence, my giardia was fucking itself already, with wild abandon. Giardia engages in asexual reproduction so quickly that just one of these pests can yield a million more in a week and a half through a process called binary fission. Even now, the creatures were proliferating and adhering to my intestines, where they were injecting chemicals into my gut; those enzymes were making it harder for me to absorb nutrition and fats, which explained the greasy, floating, stucco-colored stools. The acid in my stomach lining could do nothing to block the invasion; in fact, my body's acid actually helped the giardia by serving as a catalyst, making inert cysts hatch into swimming monsters.

In our campground, Allison was becoming sicker by the moment, but she wasn't quite as sick as I was, which forced her into the Florence Nightingale role. The view of the fog and hillocks of Seiad Valley to the north might have made for a romantic evening. Instead, she was compelled to spend the night turning green in our hermetically sealed flatulence chamber. She'd lean out from under the rain fly, take frantic gulps of night air, and then duck back into the den of misery. Watching her face turn blue from the farty excess of our nylon shelter, I no longer had any doubt that we would marry. Most marriages are travesties because of the simple fact that young marrieds set themselves up for disappointment by hiding reality from each other. They conceal their worst traits and then let it all hang out after their honeymoon—the ingrown toenails, the gnashing of teeth in their sleep, the halitosis, the habitual infidelities, the annoying folk songs in the shower. In the case of me and Allison, there was no dreadful aspect of my person that she didn't know by heart, and yet she loved me. Because of this, I felt a surge of tenderness so painful that it was hard for me to bear it. No one had ever loved me like this before, and if she ever let me go, no one would ever love me like this again. This was steely love, tested by the fires of gastrointestinal distress. And yet it made me feel strange. I wondered what I would have done if our situations had been reversed. Would I have been as loyal and patient? Feeling guilty that night, I finally reminded her that, after all, I'd saved her from drowning in Bear Creek back in Yosemite.

"Right now," she said, gasping, "I figure we're about even."

I sat there in my tent grunting like a woodland animal. I desperately needed reading material, but the only book I had was the plastic-coated Bible the Christians had given us. On the one hand, it comforted me to read about the chumps who came down with leprosy, for they were so much worse off than I. On the other hand, I found too many passages that seemed like direct references to my situation, and the fact that I had brought it upon myself: "O Lord, Your arrows pierce me deeply, and Your hand presses me down. My loins are full of inflammation. . . . My loved ones and my friends stand aloof from my plague, and my relatives stand far off. Remove your plague from me. I am consumed by the blow of your hand!"

The next day, we stumbled downhill past thimbleberry bushes, their red fruit looking like raspberries but with a dustier color and grainier flesh. Normally they were good to eat; today they tasted like old socks. Far below us, the Klamath River pitched with whitecaps. Rain came down on a muddy road that doubled as the Pacific Crest Trail. We staggered past wind-whipped horses running through a pasture; we were making our way, bending into the wind and water, when a four-wheel-drive vehicle approached. The driver leaned out and offered us a ride. Up to this moment in our journey, we had hitchhiked many times—but each time, we'd hitchhiked only from the trail to supply towns, and had always returned to the exact spot where we left the trail. We had never skipped over any part of the trail before. This stretch of dirt road was, technically, part of the trail, and we did not want to "cheat" or break the chain of our footsteps north from Agua Dulce. But this time the temptation was too strong, and the rain too hard. Anyway, we could hardly take another step. Allison and I piled into the truck without saying a word about it.

The driver dropped us off in rainy Seiad Valley, in front of the general store and Wild West Café, where there's a famous challenge to Pacific Crest Trail hikers: if you eat five of the restaurant's foot-long, two-inch-wide pancakes, the meal is on the house. But I was still nauseated. If I tried to eat even one of those goddamned flapjacks, the meal would have been on the house, literally, so Allison and I pressed on in search of immediate medical attention. With this goal in mind, we caught another hitchhike, to the town of Happy Camp, coincidentally, the birthplace of trail angel Milt Kenney, and also one of the reputed Bigfoot capitals of the world. We finagled a walk-in appointment with a local doctor, a barrel-chested fellow with pink cheeks and a faint beard. Unlike the country doctor, who, in retrospect, may not have been quite as competent as I'd supposed, this new doctor seemed to know what he was doing. He even took my pulse. He said it was all but certain that I had giardia, though he insisted that catching it from a stream was rare.

"Then how do you think we got sick?"

The doctor smiled, shrugged, and said, "As you probably know, the anus is quite close to the vagina."

This seeming accusation of accidental analingus made me choke and gasp with its cheeky rudeness. I wanted to assure the doctor that we were absolutely not having oral sex in the wilderness. As far as I'd heard, it is pretty rare for long-distance hikers to engage in this particular act in the woods, for reasons that I would rather not articulate here. But in any case, I wondered if the doctor was right that we had sickened ourselves, perhaps, by taking certain shortcuts in personal hygiene. The trouble with the trail is it reduces your hand-washing habits to third-world levels. My guess is we didn't apply enough Doctor Bronner's soap after each evening constitutional. The doctor said that we were not helping matters by staying outdoors in chilly weather with heavy backpacks. "That is, how do you say, completely meshugenah," he said. "You can always come back next year."

When I told him that I'd already attempted to get medical help, and had paid a visit to a country doctor who had prescribed Biaxin, he laughed. "Ha! Do you know that is a powerful antibiotic? And if you've got giardia, Biaxin won't do one blessed thing for you? Biaxin, aside from *not* killing the giardia, probably killed off some valuable microbes that might have helped in your defense." The Happy Camp doctor prescribed Flagyl for us—a skinny pill, bitter as hell, like chewing tinfoil—and assured us that it would churn our guts and make us feel worse for a while, but that it was the only way out of our dilemma.

The doctor's visit was fortuitous in another way. During the intake session, a young male nurse practitioner named Rob noticed that Allison and I had Connecticut driver's licenses. It turned out he went to college in the East Coast, which made him feel a certain kinship with us. Immediately he offered to let Allison and me stay in his house along the Klamath River for a week, provided that we watched after his cat, Hani, and his dog, Yeti. Rob drove us down a long driveway past blackberry bushes, past a one-eyed cat that prowled the woods. He told us where to find food in his cupboards and how to fire up the madrone log stove. Then he left us alone. I passed the days sitting under a comforter, watching movies, vomiting on my hands and knees on the redwood deck while Allison, also on her hands and knees, cleaned it up. I stepped on a scale in the bathroom one day. Before leaving on the trip, I weighed 194 pounds; now I was down to a cadaverous 163. I have a picture of Allison from that week, staring through the window at the Klamath River. She's on a rocking chair, in repose, looking beautiful in her purple Campmor fleece jacket, rain pants, and moccasins as she gazes out, hands in her lap. You can tell by looking at her face that we were not going to make it to Canada that year on the Pacific Crest Trail. Something about her expression lets you know that our northward trek was over.

We might at best make it a few miles into southern Oregon, but the Lois and Clark Expedition's planned march to Manning Park, British Columbia, was off the rails. We'd faced one too many setbacks and spells of bad luck, and now the snowstorms would soon be upon us. Already the weather was going sour, bit by bit every day, like cider turning to vinegar. In one more week, the snows would blot out the trail.

Part II

Chapter 28

Salvage

A t least we managed to finish the final section between Seiad Valley, California, and Ashland, Oregon.

Something about the impending loss of the trail made me notice what I'd blanked out before: the perfumed taste of a thimbleberry, the beads on a spider web after a rain, and the tops of the Cascades just managing to push through a gauze of mist. Allison and I crossed over the California-Oregon border in mid-October, close to a pasture containing splotchy cows and a single bull whose horns were scratched and whose huge penis drooped like a limp gastropod. The bored animal watched as we formed Os for *Oregon* with our stick-thin arms. I felt a twinge of sadness, knowing we'd never return to the trail once we left and got caught up in responsibilities, jobs, and the like. This meant that I'd never see this land again; nor would I relate to Allison in quite the same way again, with the trail and the forest framing our relationship, forcing us into simple roles: Allison manhandling maps and carving steps in snow walls, me building fires and scooping water from a brook. Suppose we needed the trail, and its shared mission, to stay together? And what of the traditions we had, all the stupid songs we sang, and our Pacific Crest tales, stories told to pass the long hours, populated with characters we brought to life in the darkest woods. What of Frankie the Were-Deer, the NRA member who turned into a stag when the moon was full? What about Taffy the Horse, the deranged pony who drank Blue Curaçao margaritas to relax, and who fought the bad guys with lethal kicks to the head? Who would sing these heroes back into being when we were gone? And what would happen to our by-laws, our private language, exclusive to the Pacific Crest Trail? When Allison talked about a "nasty-steepie," I knew she was describing a tortuous hill without end. When she warned me of "mean-greenies," I knew that horseflies were descending. In the last bit of northbound trail, I sometimes felt that the two of us had formed an independent nation, population two, that held to its traditions and had seceded, all too briefly, from the Union.

How appropriate, then, that Allison and I were walking through an area whose population had tried and failed to break off into a nation unto itself. In that push toward Ashland, Oregon, we entered the "State of Jefferson," a swath of northern California and southern Oregon that was once the target of an abortive secession uprising. In 1941, pistol-packing miners barricaded a highway and handed out copies of the Jefferson State declaration of independence, letting drivers know that they intended "to secede on Thursday until further notice." The group had a national seal—a double cross to suggest that the federal and state governments had betrayed them by letting the roads rot, hampering efforts to mine and log the area. Though there was a prankish aspect to the proceedings—they must have known that it would take an act of Congress, and approval from Oregon and California's legislatures, to create a new state—the movement reflected real animosities.

Today, antigovernment resentment remains in the State of Jefferson. These days it's all about perceived bureaucratic restrictions on land use. Locals accuse the government of trampling their economic needs by restricting development that could harm the habitat of the local Coho salmon. Personally, I tend to side with the salmon and owls, and have long held the conviction that our government, if anything, is too passive and lax toward those who would gut our natural resources. There is a populist-conservative bent to the Jefferson uprising that goes against my sensibilities as a salamander-worshipping borderline Marxist. And yet, I must admit, I shared something with the State of Jefferson: the desire to stand apart from the rest of America, the wish to be left alone, and the conviction that independence is just a state of mind. To this I could add my suspicions that the urban world, the one I had left behind, held no place for me anymore, and yet I was coming to realize that the trail was a limited refuge that shut its doors when the good weather and money ran out. The Pacific Crest Trail is a lifestyle but not a livelihood. You need to get a job eventually, and that was the problem. While the skies got wetter, my Wells Fargo account was running as dry as a Mojave creek bed in July. For these reasons, our northward voyage came to a dead stop in Ashland, Oregon.

At first, we binged and ran wild in this college town near the Rogue River. Rogue Red Ale poured from bottomless pitchers. We stayed at a hostel full of longhairs who looked like us. Besides, we visited the city at a time when America's pubescent population was going through a slob phase, involving Vans shoes, Pendleton jackets, and the worship of wildebeest-haired bands whose singers played songs about deadbeat fathers and heroin. Thanks to this trend, I received many compliments for the mixed-plaid ensemble I'd purchased from an Ashland thrift store for a buck o five. I'd conspired with Allison's father to send her a foil-wrapped devil's food birthday cake from Bill

Knapp's, a restaurant chain based in Battle Creek, Michigan. The cake was stale when it arrived in Ashland—it was like a boulder with frosting on it—but Allison seemed to enjoy it anyhow. Still, I couldn't stand the fact that our dream lay in pieces. And the more we lingered in town, the more Ashland pulled back its lips to show us its teeth. A vagrant approached on the street. With filthy hands he sketched Allison's trail-toned figure in the air. A hippie girl with star-shaped glasses leaned out of a phone booth and belched right at me as I hurried past. And I thought to myself, "I quit the trail for this?"

It's no wonder some people never quit the trail. It subsumes them. Certain nomads lose their minds when they settle in cities. Now I knew why. I would miss the constant motion, and the simple actions made meaningful in tandem. Though the trail narrows your choices—hike, sweat, piss, seek water, make love in a shady glen, eat too much rice pilaf, shit in the woods like a raccoon, repeat—it makes your existence more expansive somehow. Something about the trail rewrote our lives in boldface. I would miss skinny-dipping in moonlit lakes and being skinny, period. I would miss the lookie-loos coming up to us, marveling at our packs, and our telling them, "We walked all the way from Los Angeles to get here." Hell, I'd even miss the guidebook, accurate to a fraction of a mile. If you got lost, it was your own goddamned fault. We'd complained about the book, and laughed many times at its descriptions of geologic "noses" and "Paleozoic pits." But I'd grown accustomed to its voice. I now thought of the narrator as my life's skipper. If only the authors had written instructions for the rest of my existence.

When you've lived in the woods for a while, even though it is excruciating sometimes, and even when it makes you sick, it becomes your life and blots out thoughts of the world that exists not far from the trail—the world that created and supplied the labor and technology that built the trail. The fact is major cities and suburbs hedge the trail, and though you're socked away, isolated, you're never all that far from places like Los Angeles, Portland, and Seattle, whose buildings and freeways lie out of sight behind the mountains walling in the trail, creating the illusion that this strip of forest is all there is in the world. But I didn't like the thought of returning to any of those places, of jumping into my life again and "getting on with it"—all those details, deadlines, prescriptions, and sticky Post-it notes to plan my day. Besides, we'd spent enough time in the woods to worry all potential employers, who would notice the gaping crevasses in our résumés where jobs should have been. If we took temp work and sat around waiting for the snows to melt, devoting another year to finishing the trail, we would look undependable.

I didn't care, but Allison sure did. She wanted to make her mark, be a journalist, fight corporate polluters, and poke the patriarchy in the snoot. She wanted to confront the forces of nastiness and greed, while I merely wanted to hide from them in the trees. By now, my attitude toward careers had devolved from mere apathy to total indifference. The only job that mattered anymore was the trail. I could no longer see anything beyond it. The trail had turned into a mountain that cast a shadow on everything that lay in front of it and behind it.

I can't pinpoint when I—or we—decided to turn our shipwreck into a salvage operation. Alas, my memory is a slab of Jarlsberg cheese, rubbery and chockablock with holes. Unfortunately, my prosthetic memory—my diary from that period— has also been compromised. The same rain and snowstorms that knocked us off the trail turned many of my rantings into red and purple ink blobs. But at some point we decided not to give up, regardless of future costs. I can't say exactly what triggered the turnaround. Perhaps I convinced Allison that one more year out of our life wasn't too much to ask after all. Think of the sunk costs, of how much time and money we'd already expended. Why not expend a little more? So what if we'd be unemployable? Who needs employment? Clearly we would have to give up the dream of through-hiking the trail all in one long season. But suppose we expanded our vision a bit and made the one-year trip into a two-year journey?

The plan came together like this: For the next few months we would hole up near Monterey, California, with my sister and brother-in-law, who kindly volunteered to host us rent free. There, in the unincorporated town of Prunedale, on the foggy side of the Central Coast, we would find gainful employment as substitute teachers. Sure, it would be hard, but it would also be fun, liberating young scholars from oppression, lifting their spirits with tales of snakes and survival. Then, when the snows cleared in June, Allison and I would take a bus back up to Ashland, Oregon, and walk arm in arm across Oregon and Washington, into Manning Park, British Columbia, where we would eat thick-cut bacon, fuck like wombats, buy a metric ton of maple syrup, and drink tankards of Labatt's Blue Label until our brains went soft. I even planned to surprise Allison by breaking out a bottle of champagne when we reached Monument 78 at the finish line.

But first, before we returned to the Pacific Northwest, we had some unfinished business. You may recall that Allison and I had a great deal of difficulty getting out of the East Coast on time to start the PCT. While most hikers begin in late April, we didn't get started on the trail until mid-June. To compensate for our extreme lateness, we'd given ourselves a head start by beginning the trek in Agua Dulce, California, a dude-ranch town 454 miles north of the trail's southern terminus at the California-Mexico border. This meant that Allison and I would now have to make up that pesky section—we called it "the missing piece." We decided it made sense to do this chunk that fall. It was now late-October, and we hoped to get back down to California in two or three weeks. By the time winter arrived, we could say that we'd bagged all of the Golden State. It was all so simple, beautiful, fail-safe, and elegant. Besides, I was sure that we'd used up all our rotten luck by then.

Puffed with renewed confidence, Allison and I took our time getting back to the Southern California trail. In fact, we dawdled and stuffed our faces at various smorgasbords and checked in with countless loved ones. Time dribbled away. When at last we arrived in Agua Dulce, it was early November, and the skies were going gray. Even then, instead of racing off for the trail, we took our time, even looking up our old pal Mark the postman, who had saved our expedition from disaster half a year before.

"You're real hikers now," he said. We joked around and drank frothing mugs full of Zima, a then-popular beverage that tastes like a raunchy one-night stand involving a can of Fresca and a bottle of Everclear. Mark kept the salsa and chips flowing. "I can't believe I'm sitting here looking at you," he said. "I had no idea you guys would ever get to Ashland. I didn't think you'd even make it to the next town alive."

Allison and I looked at each other, loopy with Zima and mutual admiration. Later, I told her that the two of us just might make a career out of thwarting expectations.

"We may be dumb," I said. "But we're dumb like a couple of foxes."

We felt smart, prepared, and confident when we got back on the PCT near Vasquez Rocks, sandstone formations leaning over the juniper-speckled foothills. The path soon left the desert and plunged south toward the San Gabriel Mountains. Last time we were here, the sun sizzled. This time, clouds blocked its rays. It was so mild we barely drank water. Trail-hardened desert rats, we slept on thin rolls of foam. Our boots were soft and broken in, and our feet had calluses as thick as Doc Martens's floating soles. Though Allison still wept from the mysterious ache in her knee on the downhills, she powered up the steep slopes like her uncle's Willys Jeep in first gear. It was nice to notice the scenery for the first time, now that we weren't focused at all times on not dying of thirst. We sang our favorite Smashing Pumpkins song, the one about the "greatest day I've ever known," as we passed through the cool forests of Mount Baden Powell, named for the founder of the Boy Scouts, an organization designed to foster military discipline and love of the woods. Now we had both. I felt stripped down, ageless, and resilient. Allison was tight all over, tanned to perfection. She was straight-up blond now. Her face was creased with worry and vigilance the last time we were out here; now she wore a look of soft expectation.

We passed an afternoon in an ancient forest of limber pines, among the Earth's oldest life forms. They grew in a riot of shapes, some skinny and doubled-over, others plump in the middle and tapered off on both sides like birdfeeder gourds. Tufts of green needles puffed into the sky. Roots, clearly visible, anchored the trees to earth in thick coils. It's hard not to maintain a hushed silence in the presence of these beings. Christ was in kindergarten, and the Roman Empire dominated a quarter of the world's population, when the oldest of the pines began to grow. But the sky was a most peculiar gray up here, and thick clouds obscured the mountains to the south, toward Mexico. Out here, in mid-November, a chill settled on the landscape. Later, after a long descent on a narrow path, we found ourselves blocked by a stink beetle, two inches long with black armor, its pointy ass aimed at us like a cannon. Entomologists call this a defensive strike posture; the beetle emits dissuasive stenches from its rear to ward off predators. I smelt nothing, but its posture made me feel unwelcome. He might have been trying to warn us. Soon afterward, two burly clouds, real bruisers, filled the sky. They moved in clumsy motions, elbowing each other out of the way.

"What the hell are those?" I said to Allison, pointing heavenward.

A midwesterner, Allison knew from storm clouds, and she thought that snow was coming.

"No way," I said. "Snow clouds?" It was too weird to be true, not when there were scratchy desert plants, stink beetles scuttling, and rattlesnakes slithering. Besides, it wasn't winter yet. And after all, wasn't this Southern California? Allison got out the weather radio her father had given her. "I'm gonna fuck around with this for a while," she said, twiddling the knobs. It hissed and popped, but she couldn't catch a signal. The wind picked up. The mountains were close now, almost on top of us, but the mist blotted them out. We were camped at three thousand feet above sea level, near a few desultory stands of meager scrub, waxy succulents, and no shade cover. The landscape looked like it ought to be hot, but it was freezing. Allison and I cuddled for warmth in our sleeping bags. She pressed her face into my shoulder. From a deep sleep, I woke to hear a plop-plop-thunk-plump sound against the tent. The weight of something, like white sand, made the tent's roof sag against our heads. My watch said quarter past three, yet the night glowed bright with a false morning; I opened the tent flap, stuck my head out, and felt a cold powder on my hair, my face, my nose, and my tongue. Snow plumped up the hills, gathered on the arms of a cactus, and lit on the backs of two stink beetles. When morning broke, we pondered the seriousness of the situation. With thick snow obscuring the trail, could we make it any closer to the Mexican border? Would the trail soon be impassible? The PCT often rises up sharp ridges, close to the edge of perilous drops. We didn't want to slip off a vertical slope. Allison crawled outside and drew a big frowning face on the side of the tent. She tried to cheer me up with odd observations about nothing much: "Isn't it fascinating," she said, "that a human being can poop in all types of weather, even snow?"

She was trying hard to distract me, but we both understood the gravity of the situation. Somehow the same foul weather that had forced us off the trail in the distant north had followed us here. Now that we'd blown our chance to reach Canada that year, we'd hoped to bag the rest of California as a consolation prize. But now, even that secondary goal was in question. The trail came close to a small access road, and we could see cars skidding down the ice and powder, losing control. Allison and I attempted to walk uphill a little farther, but blowing snow made it impossible for us to see. Our boots refused to bite the ground; the snow obscured a shelf of ice, and we slipped often, sometimes falling on our asses, or sinking in white slush.

After struggling for hours, we stumbled into two hunters, one wiry and lean with a black cap and camouflage, the other with a friendly, broad face and sweaty hair. The first man, who called himself Billy, was crouched on his hands and knees while cooing and clucking in a fruitless effort to lure quail and shoot them. When he saw us, he stood up and stopped the birdcalls. He had some dispiriting news. He'd heard from radio reports that parts of the nearby mountains along the PCT were impassible now. He said that venturing out into the fast-freezing rain, now falling on top of the snow, would be treacherous at best and maybe suicidal. We took the news hard. Billy and his friend, Oscar, gave us hard-boiled eggs and cold bean burritos wrapped in tinfoil.

"Shame," Billy said. "Snow never happens out here this early. We usually don't get it til Christmas, and it's not even Thanksgiving yet. You guys sure picked a freak year."

Billy and Oscar gave us a ride in their truck to Cajon Pass, where we found a motel room. I called a few rangers in nearby stations, looking for second opinions about trail conditions. Each said that proceeding any farther south would be hazardous. We took a vote. We refused, even then, to give up the trail altogether, but we had no choice but to skip the next two hundred miles, including the San Jacinto and San Bernardino ranges. This decision was excruciating for us, but smart in retrospect. We could have gotten killed out there. In 1984, Jodi Lynn Zaitchick, twenty, and her companion, Gerald Duran, thirty-five, attempted the first winter-season through-hike of the Pacific Crest Trail. They started in Mexico and made it to the San Gabriel Mountains—the range that lay just behind us to the northwest. Zaitchick told her mother she would call her on Christmas Day, most likely from Wrightwood, a supply stop off the trail. Christmas came and went. Five days later, Zaitchick's mother called the San Bernardino County Sheriff's Department. On New Year's Eve, a search team found an empty tent under a tree, and a fresh diary entry, saying Zaitchick and Duran were hiking down to Wrightwood to buy some goodies. They never made it to town. While descending on the Acorn Trail, Zaitchick and Duran slipped on a tongue of ice hidden under a thin powder of freshly fallen snow. They fell fifteen hundred feet into a ravine below.

Instead of taking on the next piece of trail, we took buses and hitchhikes to the next accessible part of the trail, where the storms had not yet struck. But when we set out south from Warner Springs, a veldtlike expanse of soft hills and high grass, thunderheads gathered. They shadowed us as we pressed on, crossing through history. Juan Bautista De Anza drove his troops northward here through the San Felipe Valley in 1774. The Butterfield Overland Mail Line's first stagecoach trundled through this valley in 1858. It was the first cross-country mail coach, traveling 2,700 miles from Missouri and rolling triumphantly into San Francisco.

But the weather seemed determined to deprive us of our own Big Moment in history. Man-o-war clouds dragged their arms over low peaks. On went our ponchos and pack covers. "Cowboy up!" I roared to Allison. At one point, she turned to me and delivered a speech that was pure gospel truth: "Well, at least we've got some good stories to tell now. And a bad day on the trail's a lot better than kissing your boss's fat ass, isn't it?"

She had me there. The way I saw it then, a bad day on the trail was like shooting heroin with Buddha compared to most days at work. Out on the trail, even your torments are exquisite. So why, then, would anyone grouse about a trail? Sure, it's rough sometimes. It's not so great to have blood blisters explode in your socks, or to be cold at night and eat Big Bill's Beans and Rice until you blow out your colon like Mount Stromboli. But it's heaven compared to even a mildly unpleasant day at work. If people knew what the trail was really like, rain and all, they would move here by any means necessary. The U.S. economy would come to a standstill.

And so the rain thrummed our faces and necks and filled our boots while I smiled like a moron. Each drop raised welts in the mud. Each cascade brought down a river of black ooze, and yet it made me feel so clean and lightheaded. "Goody-goody!" I shouted to the skies. "Do worse! How about some lightning? How about more rain! Come on. Send in a hurricane." We pressed forward into the wind. Rain fingers plucked at the seams of our garments, searching for spots where we'd been lazy with the Seam Seal. Allison and I kept singing and smiling because the rain could not stop us. We were, after all, the Lois and Clark Expedition, who had beaten down the desert, stalked a bear, and gone head to head with giardia. Do worse, I said to the sky.

The rain stopped. Allison and I lifted our red nylon hoods and smiled at each other. The near-silence after a storm on the trail is a sound you don't forget. All you hear is the wet slosh of boots and the trees shaking their heads to dry. We'd entered the Lagunas, the fairest mountains I'd seen, impossibly green, and deserted except for us. The land was a lullaby of mist, valleys with no bottoms, and soft leaves that pressed into us as we passed by. The bushes were not scratchy like chaparral. The leaves were wet flaps that cleaned our packs and legs until they shined. A bite of chocolate restored my vitality. We paused in a clearing, under foothills, and looked at the tendrils of storm clouds retreating. I laughed. The rain had given up on us.

"Hey, Allison," I said. "I found some extra peanuts in a bag at the bottom of my pack. They're still good. Do you want some?"

"Sure," she said.

"And I found one of those cashew chews you like, if you want a piece of . . ."

Out of nowhere, I felt a warm and insistent trickle move across my back. At first I thought it was an errant droplet of sweat beneath my T-shirt. It certainly seemed like perspiration traveling in an erratic pattern, bubbling beneath the cotton fibers. But there was just one problem. The sweat droplet was flowing *up* my body, in arrogant defiance of gravity's rules. When I pressed down on the droplet, instead of dissipating against my finger, the water drop resisted my touch. In fact, the droplet was as hard as a lentil. And now I could feel that the thing had legs, and was scuttling across me.

"Oh no," I said to Allison. "It can't be. Anything but that."

"What is it?"

A thumbtack of pain shot into my right calf, then my left, and a spot close to my groin. They were all over me now—my legs, my chest, my crotch, the sides of my arms, up my back, down my back. Oh, God, no, no, no, it couldn't be. Ticks.

There were dozens of them, some flat and moving, others neck-deep in my skin, plumping on plasma. The fullest ones had a fleshy, plucked appearance, like raw Tom turkeys. A tick rolled itself into the fibers of my sweater, its thorax trapped, legs thrashing. Another caught itself in the hairs of my chest. Get the fuck off me. I went mad. I smooshed them, stepped on them, decapitated them with rocks, and bashed in their brains with pebbles. For a while I felt like Grendel laying siege to Hrothgar's mead hall, crushing the ticks to bits, pulling their little legs off, but there was just one of me and so many of them, I could barely count them all. Within the next two hours, after pressing through more bushes, I counted a total of sixty. Allison was writhing and taking her clothes off. Every leaf crawled with the little bastards. If you looked closely enough, you could see the bushes tremble with them. An army of ticks had gathered on the farthest edges of every leaf, on every plant, by the side of the trail, all of them standing at the ready, waving their forelegs like mad. I shivered. Entomologists call this the "questing position." Ticks sense your presence and wave at the air like suckling babies grasping for their mothers. They steady themselves, lean forward, and wait, positioning themselves to crawl on top of you.

Allison and I explored each other's bodies, plucking away, examining every crevice. "Get them all, Dan," she cried. "They carry Lyme disease!"

To an outside observer we might have looked like a couple of apes exhibiting "grooming behavior," lovingly plucking at every square millimeter of skin we could find. I tried very hard to leave no inch of Allison unsearched. She did the same for me. But that night in our tent, a burning sensation manifested itself in a remote and delicate feature of my lower groin.

"What the hell?" I said, sitting up in my sleeping bag.

I reached into my shorts and tried to get at the tick but couldn't grab hold; he was too damned slippery. Allison reached for the Swiss Army knife. Calm as a cat, she stuck our black, battery-powered Maglite between her teeth and extracted, from the knife, the same tweezers she'd used to pluck all those cactus spines from my lips and tongue half a year before. She leaned over me. I closed my eyes. I felt a pinch, a pull, and heard a popping sound, then a stomach-churning crunch. "I got a hold of him," she said as she clamped onto the creature's gravy-colored thorax. A tug-of-war ensued. Allison clung to the tick's tight little body while the tick seemed to bite harder into my skin. She tightened her grip. The tick tightened his.

She wiggled and jiggled. The tick did the same. She grimaced and took a deep breath. The tick, I imagine, also grimaced and took a deep breath. Allison pulled back with all her might. The pain was sharp and bright. The tick still fought her. Allison had a plan. She reached into her kit bag and removed a book of matches. She struck one, and held it straight up to the tick's body, letting the flames lick against it. The tick, at last, gave up. With one mighty tug, Allison pulled it out of me. "Thwock!" She showed me the tick stuck in the tweezers for proof.

"Give him to me," I said, hoping the victim was alive so I could torture him to death. But he was stone dead already. In fact, he was missing his head. I grabbed the Maglite, and shone the beam down to the small black hole Allison, and the tick, had left in my crotch. It occurred to me that the hole still contained the nasty little head of the tick, beady eyes, mandibles, and all.

I fell back in a swoon.

The next morning, I knew we had to leave the trail as soon as we could. The ticks and rain made the PCT feel like a haunted house, with ghosts shaking the foundations. I knew I had to get checked for Lyme disease. Besides, we were scraped up and run down. No choice. We practically ran toward the Mexican border. My Vasque Sundowner boots had cost more $175, but now they looked like someone had set off a cherry bomb inside them: the heels had rotted apart, the soles hung open, and the tongues dragged on the ground. I'd globbed the boots back together with Shoe Goo, and tied a web of black duct tape across them, but now my repair jobs were coming undone. We pressed on, jogging through eroded gullies, up and over a railroad track, and into a ravine; there, I walked right into a spool of barbed wire, which released a thread of dark blood from my right leg, just above my calf. The scar is still there. By the time we got close to the California-Mexico border, it was Thanksgiving Day.

That day we passed Morena Lake and ate our meal in the foothills overlooking the barbed wire, patrol roads, border guards, and watch towers. We chuckled ruefully as we dined on dehydrated matzo balls, instant pudding, chicken soup, and fettuccine. Allison beefed up the agony by imagining all the Thanksgiving meals we were missing. "Turkey, stuffing, biscuits, and all the trimmings," she said with a taunting smile.

And so we said good-bye, for now, to the Pacific Crest Trail, taking in our harsh food as evening fell and softened the landscape's features. Somehow the night made me forget the rains and the predatory arthropods. I leaned back and tried to drink in the night from the black bowls of the foothills. This would be our last night together on the Pacific Crest Trail, at least for the foreseeable future. I knew we'd be back on the trail together, sooner or later, but who knew what might happen between now and then?

I wanted to savor every moment of this, no matter how my tick bites scratched and my muscles throbbed. I tried to stay up as late as I could, but sleep took me in no time at all.

Chapter 29

Subhuman

We spent the winter in my sister and brother-in-law's house in Prunedale, California, overlooking a eucalyptus grove a quick drive away from a slough full of otters, seals, and egrets. Together we worked as substitute teachers at a high school that bordered a field of cows, with a swamp beyond it. Some students were the scions of middle- and upper-middle-class San Jose bedroom commuters. Others were the sons and daughters of migrant workers who labored in chemical-laden strawberry, Brussels sprouts, and artichoke fields. I was a bit frightened of the job. I feared karmic justice, considering that I had laughed so hard at dithering subs when I was in middle school. Then again, it was the best way to earn eighty dollars a day with no training or know-how whatsoever. To get an "emergency credential" for the job, we only had to pay $150 to the state and take a test that a Rhesus monkey could have passed, no problem. We needed money to get back on the trail. Allison and I signed up to sub at elementary, middle, and high schools in California's Central Coast. How terrible could it be?

My friend James, the fellow who'd suggested that we hike the trail in the first place, suggested I'd lost my mind when I told him of our latest plan. "Have you ever worked with high school kids before?" he wrote to me in a postcard. "They're bastards, astonishingly immature, even though they look like they should know better. Be firm and don't hesitate to shoot them if they act up in class. That way the rest of the kids will respect you. They'll make a movie about you . . . starring Dan and Allison as two wild people who teach California school-kids about gorp and burning turds in the wilderness."

But our love for the trail was so strong that we were willing to do just about anything. Besides, I fantasized that the kids would love me and find me cool. My own substitute teachers were old, gawky, out of touch. No wonder the kids set buckets of water over doors to douse them or give them concussions, whichever came first. I would be the "cool" sub everyone loved. In fact, I would teach them a form of radical liberation pedagogy, in which they would stand up to the forces that kept them down. I would let the students in on the fact that I had been there, too. I knew what it was like to be a teenager under the jackboot of conformity. I imagined the speeches I would give them. "Listen," I would say. "I know it hurts. I know adolescence is hard. And sometimes you've just got to go out there and represent." I would bring hipness back to the classroom. My adventures in the woods would awe the children. They would respect the fact that I liked Snoop Dogg, Green Day, and A Tribe Called Quest. Maybe I would even inspire them by standing on my desk like Robin Williams in *Dead Poets Society.*

As it turns out, I never stood on a desk, though in one instance I crouched beneath one while my lively young charges threw bolts, nails, crumpled papers, and plastic sections from an electronics kit. They took mysterious "bathroom breaks" en masse, and then showed up to class twenty minutes later, smelling like a Black Uhuru concert. They called me New Age Hippie, Miss White, Snow White, Faggot, and Poindexter. They laughed heartily at my Abercrombie and Fitch sweaters. "Never mind," I told myself. "Let kids be kids." I knew that deep down they respected me, that they honored me, and that I was getting through to them and making a difference. For example, when a strapping young lad named Elijah came up to me during track-and-field and said, "Fuck you, Mr. White, you better watch out," I took comfort in the fact that he had called me "Mister."

Nevertheless, the job began to rattle me a bit. The inane lesson plans. The use of *Casper the Friendly Ghost* and *Scooby-Doo* videotapes to drug elementary schoolers into semiconsciousness, because the teachers couldn't come up with any compelling ideas. Once, a group of students cajoled me into letting them play "clean pop music" during class. "I swear, Mr. White. There aint no bad words in this one," they said. Then I pressed the Play button on the ghetto blaster, and out came the following ditty:

> *My 12-gauge Mossberg is gonna blast*
> *All you dumb motherfuckers (who) can kiss my ass.*

Allison didn't have it much better. While her kindergarteners were cooperative and cute, she found the high schoolers harder to manage. Once, when she was forced to teach, of all things, auto body shop, the full-time teacher left a time-filler lesson plan demanding that his students draw a picture of and describe an invention that would help the human race in a profound way. One student presented to the class a hand-drawn portrait of a dildo-equipped sex machine "ribbed for her pleasure." On another occasion, Allison had to contend with a plucky girl in a home economics class. When Allison reprimanded a young lady who had flung an egg at another girl, the girl, who did not speak much English, knew enough of our mother tongue to call my beloved a "focking beech." After a few weeks of this, we started asking ourselves how badly we wanted the trail. Stress gnawed us. If the PCT had taken over our lives, did that mean the importance of getting back to the trail outweighed all other considerations? It was too big a question to answer, so we distracted ourselves by watching pelicans skim the shallows of the slough and seals lounging in pods on the shores of brackish streams.

But increasingly, Allison worried about her bum knee. Sometimes we would take day hikes far up into the Santa Cruz Mountains, to ogle the misted redwoods and pet a few banana slugs, which looked like slices of overripe mango. Even on those short walks, her knee burned with pain. After a while, she began to wonder what the hell was going on with her health. In spite of her bouts with pain, we'd been acting as if getting back on the trail was a sure thing. In fact we even had one of our inevitable knock-down logistical fights. Allison wanted to attend two weddings at the same time we were supposed to be walking to Washington. But the knee situation was a constant concern now, and the two of us could not figure out what was causing her so much agony. A fabric knee brace did little good.

At last, Allison went to see a doctor in nearby Salinas, who assured her that all was well and that she could hike the trail no problem. But the pain soon returned, worse than before. "This is getting ridiculous," she said. "I can't screw around with this anymore. I need to talk to a doctor who knows what the hell he's talking about." Fed up with the local quacks, Allison decided to book a flight back to the Midwest to see a specialist near her hometown. I didn't want her to leave, but she needed reliable answers, and she wasn't getting any in Prunedale.

One day she called me up from her parents' house, and I could tell from the tone of her voice that she'd spoken to the doctors and that this was no "bum knee," no simple injury that could be taken care of with a quick shot of cortisone. I could tell bad news was coming; I just didn't know what kind.

"So here's the deal," she said. "It looks like I won't be able to hike the rest of California. Unless things get better, I won't be able to hike the Pacific Northwest, either. I just got back from the doctor. He told me I have rheumatoid arthritis, Dan. It's a chronic disease. Basically, my body is attacking itself. Remember all those times in the woods when the pain was driving me crazy? That's why. It's attacking the cartilage in my knees."

"But . . ." I said. "Did the trail cause this?"

"We don't know for sure," she said. "But the doctors say I was born with this, that it was waiting to happen."

I had to take a breath, and focus, because one of my sister's dogs was licking my face in concern, while my brother-in-law's espresso machine was spluttering, and French horns were warbling on National Public Radio. I could not believe it. So this was it? What was going to happen to my girlfriend? Did this mean that her health was going to pieces? Was the Lois and Clark Expedition over now? No more "missing piece"? No more march to Washington State? Did this mean that Allison could never get back and finish the Pacific Crest Trail, after bagging 1,488 miles of it with me?

I had so many thoughts going on that I couldn't formulate a response.

"Dan?" she said. "Why aren't you saying anything? Look. My doctor thinks he can get it into remission, maybe, but he doesn't know if I'll ever be able to go hiking long-distance again."

As we talked, I kept wincing and swallowing hard, remembering how I'd rushed her so often on the trail, even when she was limping, and how I'd lost patience with her for taking long rest breaks and slowing down the pace, and had accused her of dragging me down. I thought of all the times I'd prayed

I could hike the trail alone. Now I felt as though the fates had stored every wrongful wish and set them into motion against me. Now the decisions I'd been avoiding—how to drum up some reliable health insurance, where to get a job, where would we live—were right around the next corner.

"Dan, are you there? I need to know that you're listening to me, Dan. Basically, there's a problem with the membrane lining my joints; it's inflamed. The cells are releasing an enzyme into my joints, and now it's chewing into my cartilage, and when it chews through the cartilage, it'll eat into the joint bone itself. I can't believe this is happening to my body, Dan. I know this is really hard for you, but whatever is going through your head, I really need you to just push it aside and be there for me." She told me that the time she'd set aside for "marching on Washington" would now be occupied with a full-time job search that she had planned to put on hold until the trip was over. "I have no choice but find work as soon as I can," she said, her voice suddenly taking on a sharper tone. "I'm gonna need the medical benefits, Dan. I don't want to sponge off my mom and dad."

I offered to fly out there and be with her, though I will admit that the offer was halfhearted. I hated to think about what was happening to Allison. At the same time, my single-minded fixation on the trail was, if anything, even stronger now that we had been off it for a while, and had worked so hard to earn money to get back on it. I swore to her that we would resume our relationship, that I would do everything I could for her, if she just let me hike that one missing piece of California. Then we'd take it from there. I told her I would try, very hard, to find a strong horse to carry her across the Pacific Northwest with me if the doctors said she couldn't hike the last piece with me. This offer was silly from the very beginning; I knew that even then. It would have been impossible to rent a horse for a thousand miles, and besides, Allison was horse-phobic; but these things didn't stop me from bringing up this possibility, and hoping she'd take comfort in my crazy idea. And so it was settled. I would hike a portion of the trail all by myself, and as soon as possible—it was mid-June now and getting hotter every day in Southern California. I had to˚ act now. "I'll do this thing as fast as I can, and then, I swear, we'll regroup," I said.

The thoughts in my head ran against one another. On the one hand, I was exhilarated at the chance to prove myself, alone, out there. At the same time, the quest would not be the same without her, and I couldn't help but wonder how I would survive without her decision-making, without our Democracy of Two. The prospect frightened me, but I was much more scared *not* to do the missing piece and nag myself about what might have been. And so I prepared to set out alone for the Southern California hinterlands, a two-hundred-mile expanse past remote deserts and parched mountains in late June, when ground temperatures would soar to 105 degrees Fahrenheit.

While buying food and getting ready in Prunedale, I ran into one of my kinder students, a bleached-blond fellow who had taken pity on me and helped where others had hindered, who had offered assistance while others had offered only spit wads. I wished him well, gave him a back slap, and told him of my big plans.

He looked at me balefully.

"Be careful out there," he said. "You could die, Mr. White."

Chapter 30

                                    Desert Rat

The trail was right back where I'd left it in Warner Springs, waiting like a king snake in the high grass. A half-eaten mouse lay dead in the dirt, a look of astonishment on its face. It was mid-June. The trail passed through an expanse of high grass over undulating terrain with rock platforms. San Gorgonio Mountain came into focus to the north, a snow sliver on top, as I pushed north, leaning into the sort of hill that could give a man heat prostration. The Pacific Crest Trail's steepness is legendary. Only 300 miles of its 2,650-mile length are anything close to level, while the rest of it has grades that can make you topple over. In fact, if you were to take all the elevation gain and loss and add it up, it would equate to fifty vertical miles straight up and fifty miles straight back down again.

As I pressed into the slope, Allison was there like a living ghost just behind me. On the trail she used to sneak up and cover my shadow with hers. It was a game; our heads and torsos connected, then split apart like an amoeba. The trail was always a shared experience, an opportunity for us to collect anecdotes so we could enthrall or bore other people with our trail tales. I liked the way we interrupted each other when sharing some memory about the outdoors, goosing and correcting each other's stories while friends listened with strained patience. "No, Allison, we saw that bear on Pickle Peak, not Warthog Meadow, and no, it was four inches of snow that fell on us that afternoon up on Asshole Mountain, not five inches. What's the matter with you?" Now that it was just me, the landscape seemed more impatient, the wind hitting me directly, as if Allison's absence had removed a buffer between me and the outdoors. The quiet was unsettling.

Small sounds, when they came at all, made me jump: a hawk's *skreek* as it dove for something hidden in the grass, and the *brrrrrr-brrrrr* of a hummingbird as it lanced a flower. That afternoon, in my twenty-three-mile push to the first water source, I missed Allison, but there was nothing I could do about that. Brainless quail bumped bellies and screeched. Instinctively I stopped and got out of the way so Allison could have a laugh at their expense. But of course, there was no one there. It comforted me to know that she wouldn't have liked the scarce signposts, the sticky-eyed lizards and dry heat pressing into her from above and below like a panini maker. But sometimes I wondered if there was a benefit to her leaving the expedition, and to my being out there alone. With Allison there all the time to keep things from careening off the tracks, it was hard to know whether I was autonomous or a dependent putz reliant on her judgment. Sometimes, hiking with her, I had wondered what it would have been like to have a "straight-up" Pacific Crest Trail experience with no one else to blame. No vetting of decisions, no debating over trail intersections and campsites. All the glory and failure would have been mine.

My first water source was an enormous white tank near a stand of ragged cottonwoods, twenty-three miles from where my dad dropped me off. It was a slog but I made it, beating

the sunset by a few minutes. The desert settled down for the
night: western fence lizards scuttled while hawks preened in
the bushes. Above them, the water tower rose like a military
pillbox. That night, I awoke and sat up in my sleeping bag,
scared to oversleep. General Patton trained his troops in the
deserts to the east of here, urging them through the box canyons and knee-cutting shrubs. That's what it was like the next
day: war games, trying to outwit the sun, hiding from it under
trees and rocks. You didn't even whisper when the sun came
looking for you like a searchlight. In a way it was glorious, the
relentless watching of the red ball as it sank, the feeling that I
had outwitted the sun, that it couldn't touch me as I took up
my pack at twilight and hiked until darkness.

Dangerous war games left no room for error, though I
made one the next day, out of exhaustion. I'd decided not to
leave the trail for a guidebook-recommended water stop at
Tunnel Spring. This is not a place where you can count on the
land when your canteen runs dry. Out here, every plant and
animal is monomaniacal when it comes to finding moisture.
The trail travels close to the Colorado Desert, where there's a
plant called the honey mesquite, which can shoot its taproots
up to 160 feet down into the ground to look for water. But
I was lazy that day. The access trail to the water looked too
steep, overgrown, and not worth the bother. The guidebook
mentioned other low-quality and unreliable water sources just
north of there. I figured it was worth the chance. Who needs
good-quality water anyhow? At this point, I wasn't picky. But
two hours later I'd found no water of any kind. Fresh out of
liquid, with bone-dry Nalgene bottles in my hands, I sat on a
flat rock and laughed at myself for a while. Another water crisis? You'd think I would have learned by now.

I backtracked a ways and scanned the maps for water sources I might have overlooked. This consumed an hour and a half,
as the sweat poured out as if from a spigot. It became hard to

concentrate, and the day turned into a daydream machine, so intense it was hard to know what was real and what was a figment. Crows descended, but they did not look or sound like any crows I'd ever seen. These were harsher when they screamed, and they wore gray armbands. I could no longer control my thoughts. I could not stop thinking about icy cold Otter Pops, frozen tubes of fruit-flavored slime popular in the 1970s, each one named for an otter who had changed history: Sir Isaac Lime. Little Orphan Orange. Poncho Punch. Alexander the Grape. Rip Van Lemon. Looey Blooey Raspberry. Strawberry Shortkook. I would have paid any price for an Otter Pop or, for that matter, a Rocket Pop or a quick lick off a Creamsicle, but out in the badlands, there was no Good Humor man, no oasis, no waterfalls, and no date palms.

I ran down a spur trail toward a water tower, but embankments and thick brush sealed it away. The tank might as well have been hiding behind a wall lined with concertina wire. At last the trail bottomed out beneath a shade tree. "Allison would be so disgusted to see me like this," I thought, "the way I'm panicking. Just making it worse." Another hour passed, and feeling there was no other recourse, I started to pray. If you've ever prayed for something, and thought perchance that God was answering back, you may have stopped yourself at some point and thought, "Well, yes, but it's probably not God speaking. Chances are, it's just me talking to myself, and I'm merely using the idea of God as a metaphysical Mortimer Snerd or Howdy Doody, a cosmic ventriloquist's dummy." But when you're incoherent and tired, the line between God as your puppet and God speaking for Himself gets blurred. In any case, when I got down on my knees on hard soil and prayed to the Lord, begged him to take pity on a wretch such as me and create some water the way He did from hard rock in the Old Testament, the booming voice took me by surprise.

"What the Hell do you want?" God said.

"Save me," I said.

"Now let me get this straight," the voice said, in a snippy tone. "You're out in the middle of a desert, in the middle of June."

"Uh . . ." I said.

"And you spent hundreds of dollars to be standing where you are right now, in the middle of this wasteland. You could be home with your girlfriend. You know what it costs for a round-trip plane ticket to Chicago? Two hundred and sixty dollars. And how much money did you spend on all that backpacking junk you bought last week? Seven hundred and eighty dollars."

"Actually, the bill came out to be six seventy," I said. "I got a rebate on the Ridgerest. They let me trade it back in for a—"

"Shut the fuck *up*," the voice said. "My point is you've chosen to be here, right now, in the middle of a fucking heat wave. That's *your* choice, my friend. You want to know what Allison is doing at this moment? Filling out job applications. Watching TV commercials. Learning all about salad shooters and fifteen-minute Abdominizers. She's putting ice on her knee right now. I bet you can't even remember which knee. And not only that, you overshot that waterhole even though the guidebook tells you, very specifically, where the water can be found. And now you're saying save me?"

"Yes. That is precisely what I'm saying."

"Save yourself."

"You must save me," I said, more harshly than I intended.

"I've got a pile of paperwork like you wouldn't believe," the voice said.

"But if you're so busy, why are you taking the time to talk to me right now? Why don't you just wave your hand and make some fucking water?"

"Don't make me put the phone down!" the voice said.

"PLEASE!"

There was silence and a dial tone, and that's when I first saw the puddle. It appeared through a clearing in the trees, a lake of muck three feet in diameter. This would be my water source. The mud was the consistency of a very runny milkshake. There was no way my filter could handle it without breaking down, so why bother? Then it struck me. Allison had told me her brother once drank standing mud from a hole in the ground during a survival training class, and though it was foul, he lived. I reached in the puddle and scooped a handful of the goo into my mouth. The taste was chalky-sour, with notes of beagle's breath, terracotta, and soiled diapers. It brought tears to my eyes. There was no way I could drink the mud, not to save my life. It was time to try the water filter.

I pulled out my new pocket filter, a different brand than the ones that let me down. It came highly recommended by the Gingerbread Man and was rumored to be unbreakable, a warhorse in the desert. Now it was my last hope. I scooped a trench in the mud hole with a piece of bark and let the water press up from the ground. I waited for some of the brackish crud to recede, and then I inserted the intake tube. "This will not work," I thought. After two powerful squirts of water, the filter seized up as I predicted. I took off my brand-new RE-SPECT MOTHER EARTH T-shirt with howling wolves and chirping eagles on it. I unscrewed the filter, took out the filth-frosted cylinder, and swabbed it clean with the T-shirt. I pumped. The Katadyn yielded a few strong squirts and clogged once more. I repeated the process. Swab. Pump. Clog. Mosquitoes feathered my arms, but now I didn't care. Two hours later, the filter was still pumping away, filling my bottles bit by bit, refusing to break down. "Saved," I said. "Thank you. Thanks for this!" to myself, the filter, and whomever else was listening.

And since no one was there to tell me otherwise, I took that mud-soaked shirt and put it on me, wearing it until the mud dried. Laden with fresh water, I hauled myself up Spitler

Mountain, and marched into a sunset over Idyllwild. I let my
water filter sit at a place of honor on the boulder where I ate
my dinner. Backlit climbers hung from the rocks. I watched
from above, and set my tent on the steep drop. Bats wheeled.
Somewhere north, through an orange haze, the end of California was waiting for me. The Devil's Slide Trail took me up
the San Jacinto Mountains to an intersection with the white
fir–lined Fuller Ride Trail, which made a staggering number of
switchbacks down to San Gorgonio Pass.

With reluctance I took the first steps down from the high
country, for the San Jacinto range had been my haven from the
heat. To the east and far below lay land so desolate that movie
companies used the landscape to duplicate the Sahara in early
silent pictures. The path plunged downhill, beneath a bridge
and past concrete pinions under Interstate 10, which crossed
California from east to west. An abandoned condo complex lay
in ruins. Eighty miles to the finish line. I crossed close to Palm
Desert and the sun-white jaw of some animal, white to match
the stones. Up I went, past an electricity farm, and fat rocks
stacked in a staircase. A dirt road bumped along a brook. The
water, when I dipped my hands in, was warm enough to brew
tea. The heat hit me hard then. I had to rest. Once I found a
shade tree near the creek, I could barely move. The hot air took
my breath away. Sometimes branches of leafless trees pulsed
red and black like retinal flashes. I worked up enough energy
to take a picture of myself right then. I snapped it right at the
time when a wave of exhaustion hit me so hard that I came
close to blacking out. I can't say why I took the picture. Maybe
I just wanted to remember exactly what it looked like at the
moment when the trees started flashing in my eyes. Puffy face.
Empty expression. Survival hat mushed into my hair. A pickup
approached on the rough road. A trailer swayed behind it. I
sank hard against a rock and propped my pack against a tree.
Two cowboys rode side by side in the cab.

"Nothing's supposed to move out here," one said. "Don't you know it's a hundred degrees out?"

I could barely respond.

"Hey," one of the men said. "I got a mad bull inside this trailer, his name is Tyler, and he's pissed off at me 'cause I've been chasing him around all day. I'm going to let Tyler out right where you're standing. I'd appreciate it if you hiked on 'cause he won't like it if he sees you."

Before I knew it, it was happening. The cowboy was out of the truck. He unlocked the trailer. Tyler trundled out, balls jangling. He was coming for me with eyes so empty they might as well have been floating in the stewpot already. He was only twenty-odd feet away from me, but I didn't get out of his way. The sun was overhead now, and it hung me up; impossible to move. The heat hung him up, too. Beyond caring, the bull wobbled past me without so much as a glance. He lowered his anvil head, walked to the warm stream, and drank. No rest for a bull. The sun dried the shade right out from under him.

It had been a week and a half now. Thirty miles to go, and I'd eaten my food down, except for the crumbs in a Planter's bag. I was running on water alone. Deep in the San Bernardinos, day-trippers camped near me. One of them hacked down a sapling with an axe right there as I watched. I asked one of them for a bit of water, seeing that he had two huge containers of Sparkletts. "No," was all he said. Keep moving.

On the last day, a long valley appeared. Two fish struggled in an isolated tributary of Deep Creek, in water the color of an untended terrarium. A third fish floated belly-up in murk. Cracks filigreed the dried mud near the tributary. Their outlet was gone. Trapped. None of those fish was going to make it out of there alive. None of my business, though. I kept on moving. The creek rushed far below me, then closer, with a few nudist guys with SlimJim phalluses and sunburned knees taking cat baths. I wanted to bathe, too, but heeded the guidebook's warnings about Deep Creek amoebic encephalitis, a condition that can crawl up your nose underwater and turn your brain into head cheese. Walk on. The creeks dripped beneath me. Lower down in the valley, I tried to ignore the spray-painted graffiti on the rocks: CARLOS LOVES LINDA. CRIPS FOUR EVER. KIL MOTHER FOKKERS. Ahead were a reservoir's sloping walls, resembling the mount of a stolen pyramid. The berm overlooked an expanse of sand so fine that it covered me when I spread my tent on it. A stream flowed past, full of reeds and dark brush. Beavers left V-shaped wakes in fading lines. They pushed offshore with paddle tails and nosed their snouts above the water. The sky grew dark. All night beavers cannonballed off the banks. Rain fell in streaks. The sky turned the color of old canvas. Clouds threw forks of light that shone on the beavers for fractions of a second. The air turned cold as the night winds picked up.

I woke to a flooded tent but did not care. I leaned my head out and let the water wash me down. At that moment, less than two miles from the end of my California trail, my home state belonged to me for the first time. Just ahead in the mist to the north lay the San Gabriel Mountains, the mountains I'd crossed already. The blue-ridge outline was as sharp and clear as a paper cutout. As I thought back on eating a cactus, the good times and rages with Allison, the tortured stories of Doctor John, the lipstick sunsets, arthropods, and all those bottles of Tylenol, I knew that every one of those memories had led straight up to this. At that moment, it all seemed well worth the effort. "Now the whole state lies trussed up and salted like a pig in a freezer," I said to my journal.

Allison was not there to see this happen. At my moment of triumph and self-realization, she was still stuck in the Midwest doing boring things, trying to find work, experiencing drudgery. In her most recent letter to me, which I carried in my backpack, she told me that she'd scraped up her car because she "spazzed out trying to get it into the garage because my dad had set up this barricade of toxic chemical containers, so now part of the bumpers came loose in the front. He knows this wastrel drunk who has a body shop in a bad part of town who's going to fix it for cheap."

Her absence was the only hole in that moment. Standing next to a barbed-wire fence, I knew there was no more California left to walk.

This she would have liked.

She should have been there to see it all.

Chapter 31

The Dark Divide

A cloud, its belly full of thunder, followed me down the Devil's Peak Trail. I had been alone on the trail in southern Oregon for two weeks, starting my push toward the Canadian border, and my mind was making figments, fooling me with visions and shapes in the underbrush and through openings in the trees. For the past few nights, something, perhaps a spirit, had been calling out of the black. I'd heard a cry in the woods, familiar but not quite human. It's strange how fast you can get onto the Pacific Crest Trail and lose yourself in its world. After finishing up California, I'd taken a long bus ride from Southern California to Ashland, Oregon, begged a hitchhike ride to the trail head, and set out north on red volcanic soil, past the up-raised fist of Pilot Rock. And here I was on the Devil's Peak in Bigfoot country, trying to outrun a cloud, the dark shape above me holding steady, letting loose. Thunder made the foothills tremble. Out in the South Cascades, rainstorms can sneak up on you. How many times did I see shapes in the periphery, and nameless things move through the woods at night?

I started to wonder if the spirits were following me here, and whether all this solitude was turning my brain into pudding. With no one to talk to, I talked to whatever was on hand. Lodgepole pines. Shelf mushrooms. Rock formations. Every once in a while I'd pass a small herd of hikers out walking for the weekend, but for the most part it was me, alone, my boots sinking in five inches of pumice ash in the Oregon Desert, fending off the Clark's nutcrackers who begged for food, and staring down at the mirror-flat expanse of Crater Lake with Wizard Island rising like a skullcap from the center of it. The lake lay in the deep hole that was once Mount Mazama, one of Oregon's tallest mountains until a volcanic explosion caused it to collapse and fold into itself. Tourists, when I saw them, frightened me. One of them, near Crater Lake, wanted to take my picture, perhaps because I looked like a common ancestor, bent over and hollow-eyed, at a loss for words. It's not that I was unhappy there or even lonely. On the contrary, most days were comfortable, the tread soft, the hills forgiving, the nights dreamless and short. The local peepers would lull me to sleep with their soft cries: "Tree-ark! Scree, scree, scree!" Sometimes these hidden beings would peep too loudly for my liking, and I'd scream for them to "shut up, please," and they would do as I told them, zipping their little mouths—or mandibles, or whatever they had. Out in the Cascades, these unseen frogs and insects were the majority, and yet they respected me. I had no real complaints. It's just that I wanted nothing to do with other humans anymore.

The scenery was so odd, I wondered if I was seeing things, making it all up. In Oregon I crossed creeks full of mineral sediments that stained the water white, making it look like lowfat milk. I climbed Mount Thielsen, "the lightning rod of the Cascades," zapped so many times that electrical charges had fused the rock crystals on its summit, forming a murky glass. I was starting to camp in places that were peculiar, even for me.

On top of bushes, for example. I'd hoist the tent atop some piece of shrubbery and lie inside it, looking down at the world six feet below me. And there was no one there to tell me this was wrong. Even my gait was protosimian now, a lurch from side to side because of my awkward load. For the past couple of weeks, I'd been plopping sticks, rocks, and other heavy things into my backpack. Feeling bereft, missing my girlfriend, I decided to pack out representative samples of each trail section, including leaves and pebbles. I did this so I could stick these sundry objects into a box at the next trail junction and send them back home to Allison, so she could assemble her own miniature version of the trail. Maybe that's not normal. In fact, Allison was starting to worry about my sanity. In her most recent missives—which I also carried around with me in my backpack—she told me to take a few deep breaths and center myself, and to fight all irrational impulses.

Dear Fishbody,

I talked to you a couple of days ago, it sounded like you were losing your marbles a bit out there. I got sort of worried. I know it must be so hard to cope with being alone with your thoughts all the time, especially when so many confusing things are going on in our lives. But Fishbody, you are strong. Here's my perspective on it. Because I can't do it, the trail has become that much more precious to me. I really caution you not to take this experience for granted. The things you are worrying about cannot be resolved until this fall when you get off the trail. Then you can start exploring your career options and your feelings about me. Set them aside until you can actually do something about them. Right now your job is just to stomp your way to Canada. That's the top priority. Along the way you can soak up funny anecdotes and details. You are well on your way to bagging Oregon!

But her warnings could not stop me from crafting dolls from yellow-green moss that hung from hemlock branches or smearing huckleberry juice all over my hair, body, and T-shirt, for reasons that did not make sense even to me. She could not stop me from inventing imaginary hiking partners, such as Snoop Doggy Dogg. Up in the Cascades, they've got a strange little mountain called Three Fingered Jack. It looks like an upright glove with some digits snipped off. The spires are so slender and delicate that climbers who've stood on the top say they shivered underfoot. That afternoon I tried to engage Three Fingered Jack in a long conversation about a friend of mine who had poor dating judgment. I don't know why this subject entered my head, but I found myself shouting into the nothingness. "Why does she have to be such a slut?" I screamed. "Why is she so stupid? Why doesn't she realize these dirtbags are just using her? Why, why, why?"

I paused for a while, giving my throat a rest, and when I turned around, some guy was just sitting there on a rock smirking and listening. He held a thick leash fastened to the neck of a fat dog. The fat dog was impatient, wanting to continue the walk, but the guy was waiting for me to say more, as if this were some Off-Off-Broadway show and the intermission was over. "Go on," he said. "This is cool."

"I didn't know anyone was listening to me!" I said.

I ran into the forest alone and embarrassed. Socialization is a series of corrective electric shocks administered for bad behavior. You learn from experience not to babble to yourself or say idiotic things that will bring cocktail parties to a standstill or make your girlfriend bar the door to her bedroom. In the woods, all corrections cease, and peculiar tendencies grow thick as kudzu. On the rare occasions when I saw people out on the trail, they hurried out of my way, as if I exuded a psychic smell they didn't like. It wasn't that I was lonely, exactly. Most of the time, the walking and the views filled me up just as much as human companionship. But the more I hiked, the more adrift I felt. Once, I was standing murmuring on a hillside affording marvelous views of Mount Jefferson and other crags while taking a lengthy and seemingly solitary piss against a rock. A backpacker came up out of nowhere and said hi very loudly. The shock of his voice made me pull up my shorts while I was in the midst of peeing, leaving an enormous wet blotch on them while he started talking to me, on and on, as if nothing amiss had taken place. That day, I ran into several other southbound hikers, who talked to me so nonchalantly, as if they didn't notice the enormous Africa-shaped stain on the crotch of my shorts, but I knew they were spreading rumors about me. I knew they were telling all passersby about the Crotch-stained Man heading north. And so I finally decided to hide from other hikers altogether. I would sit for hours by the sides of creeks watching the spasmodic motions of river otters. Sometimes I'd search the bushes for a river's tributary and find it pulsing from the ground, then imagine swimming against the current until I reached the center of the earth. I pushed north. South Sister sagged with snow. Lava rocks rose in black tunnels, looking hot and moist in the sun, like fresh horseshit. It was as if the Belknap Crater, the cinder cone to the north, had disgorged this mess last week, not three millennia ago. I saw no vegetation on the lava field, only the occasional spider, laden with eggs, rappelling down a lava knob.

And all the while, I remembered Allison's fears for my sanity, and remembered that in our phone conversations, I simply did not know what to say to her, that my mind was lost in the wilds of Oregon, that it was impossible to tell her about my experiences in a way that she could understand. And so she came to the conclusion that I was unglued, detaching myself from my life before and after the trail. On I hiked, toward Santiam Pass and its own history of detachment. It was originally named Hogg Pass, for Colonel E. T. Hogg, who tried to turn the small Oregon town of Newport into a thriving metropolis. He claimed he would do so by running a railway line over the Cascades and across North America. The trouble was Mr. Hogg couldn't stir up investor interest, so he tried to do the thing himself, hiring cheap Chinese labor to build eleven miles of track across the Cascade summit. When the task was over, Hogg told would-be investors that his railroad line had finally breached the Cascades. It was no lie—but what Hogg failed to tell them was that the line wasn't connected to anything on either side. He never built the rest of his railway. Sharp-eyed walkers can still see those eleven miles of rails to nowhere rotting in the hills.

That, sometimes, is what my own trail felt like, a phantom rail, bound to strand me. Imagine feeling the most loneliness and most rapture you have ever felt, but the feelings are inseparable. It's not that there was anything unpleasant about being in the Northwest alone. Quite the contrary. In truth, I will always remember those days as some of the happiest and most relaxing of my life. All the while I kept Allison's letters in my pocket, each one of them a reminder. Sometimes she urged me to be as present as I could be on the trail. "You must . . .consecrate yourself wholly to each day as though a fire were raging in your hair," she wrote, quoting the "Zen Master Dashimaru." But then, in the same letter, she urged me to move to a big city with her.

Pick a spot on the map where you could be happy and stay there (with me) until you make the dream job work out, even if it takes doing a few shitty, useless jobs first. What do you say? Otherwise, it's like saying my job or career is the single most important thing in my life and I'll sacrifice everything for it. That's not for me. I think Boston or near there sounds good. With Boston or New York we could both have a lot of job or school options. I know you're not supposed to think about this stuff yet but we're going to have to talk about these things.

I liked the fact that she wanted to think about location more than a dream job. And yet I could not bear the thought of a job. In the woods, it occurred to me for the first time that Allison was entering into settling-down mode, and that marriage and children were looming and inevitable. To my surprise, I realized that this thought did not appeal to me. I wasn't ready to follow her to a nesting place. In fact, the more I walked alone into the woods, the more I became curious about screwing around, literally and figuratively. As much as I loved her, I couldn't face the fact that my wild times were going to end. The closer I came to Canada, the more I longed for callow promiscuity.

My eye had started to wander a bit in the past year; during my break from the trail in central California, I'd flirted with attractive baristas and flaky female substitute teachers. I found myself drawn to women who were the anti-Allison. If Allison was forthright, curvy, and ambitious and was willing to eat any kind of food, then I longed for independently wealthy hippie girls with food allergies. If she represented stability, then I wanted someone unreliable, a woman who would get me into trouble. I loved Allison, but at the same time I sometimes wondered what it would be like to be "free," whatever that meant.

When at last I reached Mount Hood, robed in glaciers and belching sulfur, I had been walking through Oregon for almost a month. Sometimes I would walk with loose, disorganized bands of walkers, usually a group out doing a small chunk of trail. In one of these humble collectives, I walked down the Columbia River Gorge on the Eagle Creek Trail, waterfalls smashing off the side, the trail routing me through a dark tunnel behind a cataract, alongside a drop so sheer

I grabbed hold of wet rusty chains to keep from falling. I stomped to the town of Cascade Locks, the lowest point of the trail, near sea level, and marched across the Bridge of the Gods, once a land bridge, now a steel span across the Columbia River, which rushed beneath my boots at eighty-eight million gallons an hour. From there I plunged ever deeper into the Cascades of southern Washington. Though I would like to rhapsodize about them, they hid themselves in fog, except for the broken remnants of Mount St. Helens, to the west, an obscene-looking thing, like a disembodied chicken claw. For the most part when I think of the Cascades, I think of things that I didn't have to strain my eyes to see: horny toads, hemlock forests, buttes, lightning fires, sumps, ponds, fishermen on piers on backcountry lakes with gut buckets and cans of cheese bait, the watery flavor of a salmon berry, Clark's nutcrackers grabbing Doritos from my hand, the puzzle-piece bark of a ponderosa pine, and the way brown mushrooms cupped rainwater like chalices. I think of elk, big as draught horses, flattening the bear grass in their rush up a canyon wall. One early evening, I sat in the shade of a madrone, behind a rhododendron stalk, and watched a pine marten slink across the trail. Mount Rainier rose up shining. I scaled the Goat Rocks, all that remained of another wrecked mountain, once as glorious as Mount Hood. There I watched white-bearded mountain goats a hundred feet away on talus blocks above the tree line. Something startled the goats. They turned and ran up an eighty-degree wall. Even the kids charged up it. I did not know that mountain goats have suction cups for feet, or that they make use of tiny toeholds in the rock. It looked to me like they were floating up that cliff face. They slipped one by one through a crack in the mountain.

I expected to walk the rest of the trail alone. Certainly, I never expected to run into any through-hikers who had started that year down in Mexico, more than two thousand miles to the south. I'd given myself too much of a head start, in Ashland, Oregon, for that to happen. But it happened one day while I slumped over my afternoon pancakes in the Summit House Restaurant in White Pass, a don't-blink-and-you'll-still-miss-it outpost with a ski resort and highway breaching the Cascades at a low notch. I was snarfing the last flapjack when the two of them walked in. The man was all bones. The woman was hardier, with sleek muscles on her legs. Uphill Bill of Hoover, Alabama, was six foot three and weighed just 140 pounds. He had high cheekbones and a precise military politeness from seven years in the U.S. Army. One could guess he was handsome before the trail wrung the fat from his frame, but long walks make hikers look old and sickly. He was twenty-eight, but the trail had aged him. He looked twenty-eight in dog years. His companion, Jayne, from Houston, Alabama, had the kind of beauty that bug bites, wind burn, and sweat lines could not diminish. Her face was calm, with high cheekbones. Jayne was thirty-three, five foot four, with a splotchy tan. In her pack, she carried a tarp instead of a tent. Her only indulgence was a battered hound-dog plush toy, its head sticking out the back of her pack. You could tell these two were through-hikers. Veins traced their temples. They had the sort of leg muscle tone that made you shudder with vicarious pain.

I invited them to sit down beside me. They ordered endless piles of food. The way they ate was unbelievable, portions going down the hatch without a pause: spaghetti platters with fist-sized meatballs on top, French dip sandwiches dripping with au jus, two pieces of bumbleberry pie à la mode, all sloshed down with enough ice water to rinse the dirt off a Peterbilt eighteen-wheeler. When at last they were done, they told me that the next section would have striking beauty but also a dreaded "clearcut zone," forty miles of stumps from logging operations that had left hillsides bare. This ugly stuff was under the nose of Mount Rainier, king of the Cascade peaks.

Knowing this section would be hideous made me want to race through it. That's why it was hard to resist when Jayne asked me if I wanted to join up. They were going to clear a hundred miles in four days—twenty-five miles a day, compared to my sorry sixteeners.

"All you've got to do, to stay with us, is get up really early and go to sleep really late, and you've got it down," Jayne said. "Your butt is gonna hurt, but it's just pain."

This was what I'd always wanted—hiking with actual Jardi-Nazis. I'd teamed up with Wolf in the High Sierra, but back then, with my hefty pack weight, it wasn't a fair fight. Now I was in much better shape. Still, I wondered what I'd gotten myself into. "Don't you wear yourself out at that pace?" I said.

Jayne laughed. "Naw. You'll love it. We'll get you up to Canada before you know it."

We rested, and lit out the very next day. The path crossed a parking area that gave way to meadows, then ponds, mucky furrows and hills that Bill ran up. In the William O. Douglas Wilderness, we reached a plateau containing ink-dark ponds, each one of them a logical rest stop, but Bill kept going. The path vanished, at times, beneath pink and white bedspreads of mountain heather and huckleberry bushes. There was no catching Bill unless I ran.

His stamina startled me, though the PCT tends to attract this variety of athlete, who performs great feats of endurance with no audience. Another that comes to mind is the legendary Bob Holtel, who literally ran the PCT in the 1980s, throwing down the near-equivalent of a marathon every damned day for months at a time. Somehow I managed to keep pace with Bill long enough to hear some of his story. He led a tank platoon during an Operation Desert Storm ground strike in the Persian Gulf but refused to elaborate. He took part in the U.S. Army's prestigious Ranger training program, an initiation involving sleep deprivation, loneliness, and humping through

mud. Bill was holding up just fine until his knee gave out on
him one day and forced him to quit the program. It reminded
me of what had happened to Allison. Bill insisted the memory
didn't bother him all that much anymore. "Really, it's just one
of life's monkey wrenches," he said. "You can never tell who
will fail or succeed, in Ranger training or anything else, even a
trail. Sometimes the people you least expect to make it are the
ones who finish up. On the Appalachian Trail, my first day, I
was with this guy who was overweight and on his last cigarette.
We were going uphill, and he had a really hard time of it. He
said, 'God, I think I just shat myself.' He had to stop and change
his underwear. I thought, 'Oh, no, this guy's never going to do
it. It's over for him.' A few months later, I ran into him. He was
hiking southbound, I was hiking north, he was doing great,
looking great. You never know."

Still, I had never seen someone walk quite so relentlessly as
Bill. I wondered if the Ranger experience ever weighed on or
prodded him, and if he ever rubbed the memory like a charm
bracelet. After a while, he changed the subject, talking in vivid
detail about the suicides of Adolf Hitler and Eva Braun, analyzing the flaws of the Anzio beachhead battle in World War
II, and trying to convince me that amphibious assaults are a
great tactical maneuver in contemporary warfare. "After all,
you can't drop a lot of heavy equipment with parachutes," he
explained.

After a while, I had to fall back with Jayne, which was
somewhat easier than hiking with Bill. She had no trail name
that ever stuck, but as we marched toward Canada, I decided to
give her one, Wormwoman Jayne, based on a story she told me
about her early days on the trail with Bill. One day, while Bill
was watching, she drained the contents of a water bottle even
though she saw a black worm floating three inches from the
top. "Yeah, I saw the worm," she said. "But I figured I'd drunk
half the water anyhow. You should have seen Bill, all retchin' and

gaggin' when he saw me drink that water. Bill's tough but he's real sensitive. I tell him these John Steinbeck stories, the really sad ones, and he says they make him want to jump off a cliff and kill himself." She could spook him, too. She once told him, in camp, in a grove of cedars at midnight, that if you plant a cedar and it grows tall enough to shade your grave, you'll die.

The two of them met on the trail in Southern California and had been together ever since. It crossed my mind that they would have made a cute couple. But apparently they were not, in the romantic sense of the word. True, Bill sometimes called her his lovely lady, and she'd call him William in the quasiparental way people sometimes use to greet lovers. But there was no sign of that itchy codependency you get from being boyfriend/girlfriend on a trail together, mingled with that look of dopey expectation of shacking up when the day was through. They were most definitely platonic. They had separate tents. They also had a clear understanding; Bill would rush ahead, sometimes all day, but he always made sure Jayne knew just where he was, leaving her notes at intersections. Still I wondered if one-sided crushes ever sprang up on the trail. Jayne, after all, was quite pretty. If there was no Bill here, and no Allison at home, I would have been quite smitten with her. The trail itself demands the release of infatuation, if not outright lust. But for Bill and Jayne, the walk itself was the only context for togetherness. They had known only sweat and adversity. Strange to think the trail can almost pull one couple apart, and almost put another one together.

Every idyll has to end. In short order, the three of us entered Stump Land National Forest, our name for the forty miles of bald-pated hills, the dirt roads winding up them, and, in the air, the dust, the smell of fresh timber, the tinny screech of chainsaws, and the rumble of Caterpillar earthmovers. Huckleberries, a sun-loving plant, grew in sweet profusion. Most hikers despise this area, and in their diaries write tearful journal en-

tries about the pillage of Gaiea. But for me, this was a necessary display of reality. Walking through this ripped-down forest
reminded me that the PCT is a temporary refuge at best. Like
all retreats, it is not permanent. Mining claims, logging, home
building, and ski area expansion intrude on the Washington
PCT every year. Though a healthy chunk of the trail is public
land, the private parts are open to developers' whims. Besides,
this land, so painful to the eye, was hurting my body, too; all the
jarring ups and downs had left me with shin splints so savage I
had to gulp Jayne's Motrin to keep up with them.

"It's just pain," Jayne said. "Pain isn't real," but it was clear
that the shin splints, or "sheen splee-ints," as Jayne called them,
were getting worse. My pace kept dragging.

I didn't want to burden Bill and Jayne anymore. We spent
our last night together at Lizard Lake, black with silt and arguably the ugliest water body on the trail, with strewn-about
chunks of wrecked cars and dirt as fine as flour. The dust didn't
stop me from dropping my gear on the ground in exhaustion,
releasing a cloud that rose to blacken my face, blow grit into
my hair, and baste my legs in dark powder. I transformed before
Jayne's eyes into the Pigpen of the Pacific Crest Trail. She saw
me and laughed. "Look at you, you've got dirt all over you. You
look so forlorn!" she said. "In fact, you're the filthiest hiker I've
ever seen." When she said this, I got self-conscious and tried to
rub the dirt off, but that just spread it around.

She asked if I had a trail name.

"Yeah," I said. "Clark. As in 'Lois and Clark Expedition.'"

"Oh yeah?" Jayne said. "Well, it's time for a new name. From
now on, you're Dirty Dan."

I said good-bye to Uphill Bill and Jayne. I would miss them,
but it felt right to be on my own again. Still, I was grateful for
the new moniker. "Dirty Dan" sounded savage and independent, like a soap-shunning privateer. With a new attitude, and a
new identity, I headed up the trail through the North Cascades,

so covered in grainy fog that I can't begin to describe them. I emerged, unwashed, in Stevens Pass, and hitched to the town of Skykomish, where I camped Vietcong-style in a clutch of trees on a highway divider. I haunted the town for a couple of days, bought a nickel's worth of unleaded gas for my stove at the only filling station in town, and drank cold Rainier ales with the people at the bar in the old Skykomish Hotel, built in 1904. It was raining when I got back to camp. Big-rig head-lights strafed the tent, and there was nothing for supper but Cadbury White Chocolate Fingers and a sack of Spud Delites. "This here is the crazy life," I thought to myself between oily bites of fried potato. It had taken me this long to live every moment of the trail, to eliminate all distractions and just be there. In the course of 2,500 miles, I'd unlearned all the ways I'd superimposed my old fears onto a new landscape. Very soon, I'd have to unlearn the unlearning, and return to my "old self," whatever that meant. Funny how long-distance hiking, when you start, feels like an accumulation. You hoard miles like dou-bloons. Then toward the end, it becomes an act of depletion, miles draining away from you.

When the trail ran out, there would be no more Dirty Dan. All the rules were going to change. I'd find myself back in the world of showers and soap, responsibility, compromise, and Al-lison. It's not that I didn't want those things. It's just that I was happy enough right here, on this median divider on a Pacific Northwest highway, in this gritty little outpost near the Pacific Crest Trail.

The next day, back on the trail, in deep woods, I met a stranger with a familiar face. I found him at Valhalla Lake, a reflecting pool beneath the pines and rock debris under Lich-tenburg Mountain. The man was on his back, sticking his big feet in the lake. He was hanging with two hiking friends in their mid-thirties, both tan and stocky with slender packs and walking sticks. With a twinge of surprise, I realized the man looked like Todd the Sasquatch, the hiker Allison and I had met back in Agua Dulce at Mark the postman's house. Back then he'd shaken my hand so painfully hard I thought my arm would pop right off. Back in Agua Dulce, he'd asked us how far we thought we'd make it on the trail, and had given us a hard time for carrying so much gear. He was boastful, loud, braying like Tarzan on the vine. But this couldn't be the same Todd. For one thing, this man seemed quiet and gentle and unassuming. Besides, the man's pack looked enormous and bulging, far heavier than anything I'd lugged. The Todd I'd known carried a svelte pack with hardly anything in it. And yet it was the same man.

"Todd?" I said.

He looked up, startled. He smiled and leapt to his feet. I was surprised at how good it felt to see him, this man I'd cursed behind his back.

"Dan," he said, taking my hand with a much softer squeeze than I'd remembered. "Look at you!" he said. "You're a real hiker now."

It was good to see him. But why on earth was he still here now, when I'd first met him on the PCT a year before? At the rate he was traveling then, he should have finished up last September at the latest. I was about to ask him about this but he cut me off.

"Hey, Dan," he said. "I heard some rumor that you've been spreading this nickname about me, Sasquatch, all around the PCT, and it wasn't necessarily complimentary."

He smiled. I blushed, and to my relief he let the matter drop. We were ready to accept each other as different people now and let old grudges lie. The two of us got to talking about our past year. I told him what had happened with Allison and her knee. I told him she wasn't doing the trail with me anymore. He looked concerned. Perhaps to make me feel better, he shared his own story.

"Last year everything changed for me," he said. "It hit me all at once. I'd been speedwalking through California. I hit Oregon and was headed for Washington. And suddenly, two realizations hit me. First of all, I was not having a good time, and second, I was hiking so fast I couldn't absorb anything. I knew I'd finish the trail that fall, my friends would throw me a big party, then what? The trip seemed so empty to me. I couldn't go on after a while."

From how he described it, it was more of a reconfiguration than a nervous breakdown. He quit the trail for the year and ended his relationship with Sweet Elaine. Todd would not elaborate on why they broke up, and I did not press him. He rented a Forest Service hut near Mount Adams, just off the trail in southern Washington. There he holed up with cans of food and skis while the snowdrifts walled him in. While stuck in that cabin, he changed his mind-set, transforming himself from mile-bagging Jardi-Nazi to Zenlike slack-packer, slowing the pace, exploring glaciers en route, refusing to do the big miles that were once his trademark. He urged me to hang back with him for a couple of days, and hike at an eight- or ten-mile-a-day pace for a while. "What's the big rush?" he said. "When will you ever be back on the PCT again?" It pained me; by then I was accustomed to going as fast as Todd did in his mile-bagging days. Besides, I'd sacrificed so much time to come this far. Suppose unseasonable snowstorms swooped down on me, and my margin of error was the amount of time it took to "catch up" with Todd for two or three days? But it seemed churlish to say no, so I agreed.

"Fine," I said. "I'll take it easy with you for a little bit."

The next morning, Todd and I and his two buddies were walking away from the misted lake, through Union Gap. "It's pure insanity to run through a place like this," Todd said. "Don't you think so? I mean, what the hell's the point? What would that prove? To rush through a place like this, and then it's all gone. Who knows what the future will bring? Who knows if you'll even be in this place again?" I agreed—it was really very nice here, but it struck me that Todd hadn't changed. It seemed he'd merely shifted, refocusing that same old fervor 180 degrees. As we walked on, at an inchworm's pace, Todd stared at a distant summit and his eyes started watering. "Holy shit," he said, his cheeks turning red. "That's just unbelievable. Goddamn it, holy shit, it is almost . . . it's almost fucking unbearable." I remember thinking, why yes, it is a very pretty place, but I wouldn't go so far as to call it "unbearable."

But Todd wasn't talking mountains. He was talking about his crotch. "I've got this weird pain," he said, bending down, clutching his groin. He folded his hands on his belly. "I'll tell you what this is, Dan. It's a fucking hernia. It's been acting up for a while, but never this badly. I'd laugh if it didn't hurt so much, because it's so goddamned funny, the fact that this has to happen now, after all this time, when I'm almost done with the trail."

One of his friends stopped him then. "I hate to say it," the man said, "but I think it's time to get real. I don't think you're gonna finish the trail this year."

Todd looked stricken at the thought of going home. But he seemed to know it was inevitable. "Yeah, you're probably right," he said. He was in no state to walk that day so we pitched an emergency camp in a clearing. In the evening Todd saw me struggle with a large food bag packed with candy treats. I had been splurging on sugar, with several pounds of Hershey's Cookies and Mint, Snicker's bars, and Mounds. Todd looked at my grub bag, with strewn-about junk-food wrappers, and grimaced. "Why did you want to bring all that junk on the trail, Dan?" he said. "Haven't you learned anything?"

For just a second, the old boastful Todd had returned, and so had the old peevish Dan, the envious one who spread unkind nicknames around. His eyes flashed at me, my eyes flashed on his, and for just a moment, the meanness came back, and with it, a gleeful sense of schadenfreude. But then he softened, and I softened, and we both backed off, and we smiled at each other. He pulled himself back into his tent. I wished him farewell, and the best of luck, and I really meant it.

But I was gone, heading north at first light, before they were even awake.

Chapter 32

Monument 78

My 2,650-mile Pacific Crest Trail hike began in a desert and ended with a flood. A downpour came, and rarely let up for four days. Even the garter snakes and slugs dove for cover. Rain clouds sealed the mountains. I spent the night in a car camp, and watched the campers dig canals in the mud around their tents to channel the falling water into a lake below us. The muddy dikes burst, and the water spread out, washing over tents and people. A man tried to cook a meal in his tent that night to stay dry, but the flames seared a hole through the roof. The tent went up, and the man scrambled out of his miniature Hindenburg. The next morning I hiked on, and in rare moments when the rain stopped, I ran through the fields in search of large rocks in patches of sun. When I found one, I flung my tent and clothes across the boulders to dry.

One afternoon, the fog spilled from the mountains in a slow gravy, so thick you couldn't see the treetops. Frogs flumped from puddle to puddle. Cold dampness sank into my shirt. The guidebook raved about Glacier Peak, known to Native Americans as Da Kobad, the Great White Mother Mountain. The mountain was just above the trail, according to the book, but there was nothing to see. The mist was so thick the trail could have led me straight through the streets of Elizabeth, New Jersey, and I'd have been none the wiser. In a clearing with the clouds close on, I'd had enough. I had no more dry clothes to wear, and every inch of me was mud-spattered. Such a waste, I thought, to pass through God's country and find myself stuck in a cloud bank. I started bellowing to God, or whoever was listening. "Come on. This is a waste of my time. I've been through a lot to be here, and I've come all this way. I could have quit a thousand times but I didn't, and the least you could do is give me one little lousy glimpse of the North Cascades. I don't see why that's so much to ask. Why don't you do me a favor and make these fucking clouds lift, just for one second, so I can see something."

I sighed at the futility of my tantrum, and regretted my use of the F bomb in a petition to God. I sat down on a boulder to rest my thoughts. And suddenly, the sky changed. The sun came out, and it looked as if someone had pulled the plug on the fog chamber. The rainstorm stopped, not incrementally, but dead. Clouds broke like smoke around Glacier Peak until the mountain lifted its head up high and assembled itself in patches of brightness, starting with the base, then rising to the middle, and tapering, until the whole mountain flashed like fire. Glacier Peak made a burning crown with the sun behind it. A pine forest spread across its base. As the sun came down on the trees below the mountain, the forest looked as if it were burning. As I stared at the peak, I could barely move or even breathe. After several minutes, when I'd regained my senses, I managed to reach in my pack and remove the lens of my monstrous Pentax K1000 camera, but an even coat of mist had pressed itself into the glass like a ghostly thumbprint. This moment wasn't meant to be photographed.

I didn't hike the rest of the day. I just staggered, and could not get the vision out of my mind, even when I sank in the fizz of Kennedy Hot Springs, which smelled like the Devil cooking breakfast, but I felt safe, in spite of the scent of eggs and rot around me. I was warm enough, though the rain was coming down hard again. Glacier Peak's thermal vents heated the springs around me. The waters fizzed, and lulled me into semiconsciousness. My face was cold, and so were my shoulders, but the rest of me sank in warm murk. I slept in the water for hours.

My old life waited over the next horizon. I could not—would not—think about it. It would just happen, and I would deal with it then. For now, all I could think about was Dirty Dan, and the fact that his habitat was damned-near gone. Up ahead of me, the 2,650 miles of Pacific Crest Trail suddenly turned into fifteen miles, then ten, then nine, and before I knew it, it was the last day ever on the trail, in a meadow with the rain fly lying limp across my tent. Two mule deer stood in a clearing before me, ignoring the rain, ignoring me, chewing devil's club thorns.

On the last day of the trail, I don't remember the landscape, the trees, or even the quality of the trail tread. All I can remember was flying across that trail, unable to stop myself from running to the end, my backpack bashing against me as if trying to slow me down as I pushed myself faster. I wanted to be mindful of all this, savor the moment, and think about what it meant, but for some reason I could do none of those things, so I sprinted down the rows of final switchbacks, never slowing no matter how much my knees ached. And when I'd used up the last hairpin curve, the trail shot me out toward a clearcut gap in the trees, marking the border between America and Canada. I found myself in a clearing, and there in the clearing was Monument 78, scraped-up, battleship gray, only four and a half feet tall and shaped like the Washington Monument.

Though I tried to restrain myself, I ran screaming toward

the monument, while wondering who might try to stop me now, and why this was easy after everything before it had been so hard. I half-expected a self-repatriated grizzly from British Columbia to sideswipe me at the last second. I accelerated, even faster, until I was only twenty feet from the monument, then fifteen feet, than five feet, then no feet at all. I reached out and touched that monument—in fact, I whapped it with my fist so it made a hollow *plong!* And then, for reasons that weren't clear to me then, I burst into a loud Hebrew prayer, the Shma.

Shma Yisrael Adonai Elocheynu Adonai Echad
Baruch Shem kevod Malchuto Le O'lam Vaed.
Hear, O Israel, the Lord is our God, the Lord is One.
Blessed be the Name of His glorious kingdom for ever and ever.

I must have sung the Shma fifty times before my voice quit. I threw down my pack and began to dance around Monument 78, shaking my shoulders, doing a rough jig. Think of the jitter-bugging apes circling the black obelisk in the first scene of *2001: A Space Odyssey*. Beyond reason, I unscrewed my Nalgene bottle and dumped my last container of filtered spring water all over the monument, as if to consecrate it. I had no witnesses, no one to snap my picture. Instead of bemoaning this fact, I lifted off the obelisk's detachable top to glance at the notes in the hollow base. Such was my exhaustion that I could barely lift the top. It nearly gave me groin-pull. Finally I set the top on the ground, and there in a hollow were hundreds of notes from hikers who had made it this far. Some were fresh. Others bore the smudges of a hundred thumbings.

Far up in the pile I found a note from Uphill Bill, the speed demon who'd traveled with me and Jayne through the clear-cuts south of Snoqualmie Pass.

"I finished the trail today as I started it: alone and uncertain," Uphill Bill had written, in a note dated September 9.

"I learned much along the way about stamina, about mental toughness required for 20-plus mile days, about the beauty of the forest and the kindness of strangers. The most important and terrible lesson I learned too late. When one shows weakness before one's inner demons, one pays a terrible price, as do those one professes to love. Happy trails and inner peace."

Inner demons? I swallowed heavily. Why on earth had he finished the trail alone? Why wasn't Jayne with him? I would find out, much later, secondhand, that Jayne and Bill were seen finishing the trail separately, and that Jayne was spotted all alone, crying, near Manning Park lodge. I also heard that the two of them boarded a bus together out of town. That's all I ever got. I never found out what had caused the falling-out. A dozen other notes had similar existential anguish. "I've tried this wilderness lifestyle," one read, "and I knew that in a perfect world it is all that would be asked of me, but the world is not perfect, so now I will be thrust back to a world that doesn't know, doesn't understand, and doesn't care."

"Wow," I thought. "That was one sorry-ass hiker." I looked around to see if he'd strung himself up in sight of Monument 78. Thank God, then, for the Gingerbread Man, who had left an open letter to all the hikers who came after him:

"I don't get all this 'hate to leave the trail' mail," he said. "People's lives must really suck in the cities but if it wasn't for civilization churning out dry food, light equipment, money, and the trail itself, we couldn't even be here." He ended his note with a poem.

> I've been a through hiker for many a day
> Living on berries and pine nuts, oy vay.
> They don't have many calories, they make you go fast.
> But unfortunately, many poor hikers got gassed.
> Oh, PCT. Oh, PCT. How I love thee.
> You killed most of the Donner Party, but ah, yeah, try me.

I reread his note and snickered, while still waiting against hope for someone to come along and take my picture. Nothing doing. At last I sat down and left a little note of my own.

> Hello!
>
> *Oy vay I made it, and no one thought I'd even make it to Tehachapi alive. It's September 20 at 9 a.m. and I've just finished my two-season walk from Mexico to Canada. I made it here only to get a near-hernia lifting up Monument 78. This is the adventure of a lifetime. I arrive in good health. The PCT brochure says, "find yourself on the PCT." Not exactly true. I think the biggest change comes when we first decide to do something this strange and ambitious. I dedicate my hike to Allison, who could not finish because of a severe knee problem. The lesson I learned is, don't postpone adventure because you never know what will happen. As Erma Bombeck said, think of the fat ladies who waved away the dessert cart on the Titanic. Thanks. God bless.*

In retrospect, the note strikes me as glib. The truth is I had *no idea* what the moment meant then. When you cross a finish line, there is supposed to be that "Zap!" feeling, when the significance whams into you, knocking you over with its profundity. That did not happen at Monument 78. It would take months, years even, before I began to digest the moment. It was too big to see. I felt something there but couldn't put a name to it. Nevertheless, I stuffed the note in the hollows of Monument 78, as if I'd figured it out already, as if I'd said all there was to say about it.

And I was just about to walk back in the woods when I remembered to lift the detachable top and put it back on the monument. Perhaps my hands were too sweaty from excitement, or maybe my arm strength failed me, but when I tried to raise it back up, the top of the monument slipped from my hands and fell to earth with a great *bonk*. "Dammit!" I said. I seemed to have left quite a scrape and a dent, though it's possible they were there already. Dropping a part of Monument 78 felt like a minor act of unintentional sacrilege. I vowed to make penance, perhaps by donating my time to the Pacific Crest Trail Association. But first I had to put the goddamned top back on the obelisk. This time, with every last strength in my legs and back, I hoisted the top in place. I circled the monument another time, partially to savor the moment, partially to search for additional damage.

Then my business with the Pacific Crest Trail was over. I pulled my pack onto my shoulders, drank the last drop from my almost-empty Nalgene bottle, and headed for civilization.

Chapter 33

Reunion

Allison had wanted to meet me at Monument 78, but her knee now hurt so much she didn't want to hike the eight miles into the forest to greet me. Instead we decided to meet at the Manning Park Lodge, where we'd booked a room for two nights. I'd arrived there well before she did, talking up the female clerks about my hike and converting some traveler's checks to funny money with Queen Elizabeth's pinched-nostril face on the bills. I loved the way the young ladies at the lodge gathered around me. It seemed to me that "Dirty Dan" exuded an irresistible psychic musk. When Allison pulled up to the lodge in her rented car, I practically mauled her, lifting her off the ground, kissing her, almost smothering her. Having her there beside me in the hotel room threw a light switch in my head. It seemed I hadn't killed the Lois and Clark Expedition after all. Perhaps we were just on hold. When she pulled out a cool bottle of Korbel, I felt like a man who wanted for nothing.

When we filled the glasses and were getting ready to guzzle, she turned to me and said, "Just one glass for me. That's all I get today."

"Say what?" I said, for we'd laid waste to armies of bottles in our time, lining up empties like toy soldiers.

"I'm on medication, remember?" she said. "I've got to choose my drinks carefully from now on."

"Oh yeah," I said. "I forgot all about it."

Allison sat on the bed, still smiling but arching her eyebrows at me. She turned away from me. Took a deep breath. "I've got something for you," she said. She reached into her suitcase and pulled out construction paper flags of all three countries spanned by the Pacific Crest Trail: Mexico, America, and Canada. The eagle on the Mexican flag was bent over and slouching, like a vulture. I teased her about this. "Eagle?" I said. "That's nothing but a buzzard."

I expected her to bust up at this. This was innocent teasing, Lois and Clark style. She smiled but didn't laugh. "I did the best I could," she said. "At least it's a raptor."

This was minor stuff, I knew. A paper flag was nothing worth fighting over. But my words sounded funny to me that afternoon. Every sentence came out sharper, snarkier than I'd intended. I wasn't Clark anymore. I wasn't Dirty Dan, either. Now I was turning into an unnamed third party who existed outside the trail, and I had no idea what the hell this man was supposed to say or do or how he was supposed to behave when other people were around. Allison unrolled a T-shirt she'd had custom-made for me, showing the Pacific Crest Trail map in the front, and DIRTY DAN in bold letters on the back. I loved it, though it was a size too small, even for my trail-attenuated frame. I wore it anyhow, as not to hurt her feelings, but it squeezed me so tight it shrank my shoulders and pushed out the breasts I never knew I had. I forced myself to keep the shirt on me while we drove all around Manning Park in the rental car, blasting Green Day, Jimmy Buffett, and Sheryl Crow. We headed out to the PCT trailhead one last time. Allison took a picture of me standing next to the turnoff sign. Limping badly, she even managed to lope a short way onto the access path leading to the trail that she would probably never finish in her lifetime. She managed a stiff smile. I clicked the shutter.

Back at the lodge I drowned in burgers, and though we clinked glasses of skunky Moosehead, and licked the foam from the top, and ordered shovelfuls of fries, incorrect thoughts flickered between each bite. I was thinking about Allison, and how she couldn't be my drinking buddy anymore. Or my hiking buddy, either. What the hell would we do all day long, then? And what about all these damned calories? No miles to burn off the calories anymore. *And everything cost money all of a sudden. Every goddamned thing cost money now.* Allison filled up the rental car with princely priced gasoline. So expensive. Did they start rationing gas while I was out in the woods? I found myself feeling crowded out, even in that small, practically deserted settlement of Manning Park, longing for the emptiness of the forests. Back at the lodge, Allison sat on the bed. She threw a passel of multicolored leaflets on the bedspread. At first I wondered if it was another construction-paper flag she'd made to celebrate my walk. But when I looked closely, I saw that they were FAQ lists with information about her rheumatoid arthritis. "Could you please just take a quick scan at these when you get a chance?" she said. "They won't take long to read. I just wanted to give you the basics."

I picked them up and, absently, without thinking very much about what I was doing, began to fan my face with the pile. I stopped myself, set them back on the bed, and stared at the leaflets but not at the words printed on them.

"Could you please just read one of them?" she said.

"Now? I want to give these things my full attention, but I can't now. I'm just not in that place right now. I guess it's what they call a trail high."

"Just take a look, for one moment."

"No slack at all?" I said. "No slack time at all for a guy who just got off a national scenic trail?"

We left Manning Park and drove on out to Vancouver, walking around the rainy towns with one-way streets and salt air blowing thick off the Pacific. We were out near Gas Town one night, heading toward a restaurant. Allison was trying to talk to me. She said something about going fishing with her dad, about how they walked into cold rivers that wrapped around them to their waists and how the two of them had played Dolly Parton's hits on a ghetto blaster. I listened in a glaze, enough for the words to register in my memory but not enough to react while she was saying them. The trail had stopped dead but I couldn't see that then. I was still searching for the rest of it. You'd think the trail, after all those miles, could find some way to keep going north out of sheer will, if not inertia. I wondered what it would be like if I could find some northward spur of the trail and just keep going. And I thought of all those Civil War veterans who lost their context after the final battle, and sat around in their underwear all day, doing nothing, until they finally decided to recreate what they'd barely survived, dressing up in period uniforms with brass buttons cured in their own urine, then going out into a field and recreating Pickett's Charge. Was that my future? Was my life's sole event really over?

And what about *us* after the trail? I used to think of our wilderness march as a proving ground before we stood at the altar, in the synagogue or church, before a group of well-wishers. It still amazed me that we'd walked for five months without turning on each other. But now I wondered if the Lois and Clark Expedition could survive a life of normalcy, after what we'd done and seen. After all, it was extraordinary to walk a national scenic trail, but any old schmuck could get married. Between two hundred and three hundred people attempt a through-hike of the PCT on any given year. Only a fraction of them succeed. In comparison, 2.3 million couples get hitched in the United States every year. If you break this down, it means that six thousand couples get married every day, a statistic that brings to mind H. L. Mencken's observation that "no man [is] so repulsive that he can't find a wife. Midgets, cripples, dirty men, hideous men, idiots—they are all dragged to the altar."

We drove on to Seattle. Allison was hungry. She found an impressive bakery with a glass case over Napoleons, cream horns, and French-style doughnuts baked with real eggs. Allison bought a fat éclair and took a sharky bite from it before we were out the door. Without thinking, I blurted, "We're not on the trail anymore. Do you know how many calories they put in one éclair?" I felt like an outside observer, listening to what I'd just said, and feeling put off, because I didn't know who was talking anymore. Words were spoken, but not by me. Allison looked up at me, and then she looked down at the grease-flecked little doily that had held the éclair and now held only traces of its crème and the bitten-down chunk still remaining.

"Thanks for that," she said. "Thank you very much." She stuffed the remaining piece of éclair into the nearest garbage can.

Every would-be celebration felt like conspicuous consumption now, and Allison had to drag me everywhere. She took me to a "splurge" celebration meal in the kind of sushi restaurant where raw fish rides little boats in a miniature canal, like the passengers on the "It's a Small World" ride. Every time you unburden the boat of a passenger—an ebi, a California roll, a slab of maguro—the bill goes up, up, up. She tried to talk to me in the hotel that night, her back to the door as if I might make a break for it. "Okay," she said. "We need to go over a few things. We need to stop putting off these conversations just because every stressful subject makes you uncomfortable. I just need to figure out what we're going to do, Dan. I can't just sit here in limbo and hope everything works out all by itself."

But we didn't have The Talk that night, at my insistence.

I convinced her to go dancing instead.

Allison figured that a change of venue might do us some good. Get out of the city. Camp for a while. That way we could be closer together, and have a nice experience, and still save money, like I wanted. She drove the rental car along a fog-bound freeway and out to the coast, straight up the on-ramp of a ferry that sailed us out to sea, past a pod of seals. Seagulls wheeled in our wake. When the boat reached Orcas Island, we drove off the ferry and onto a blacktop road past a break-water and up to a wooded campsite in the hills. But when we crawled into the tent, I remembered all the downsizing I'd done on the trail. I'd replaced our spacious two-man Bullfrog nylon shelter with a single-man Northface survival tent. It was so cramped in there we barely slept, waking each other up, our faces smooshed against the mesh siding. The next morning, ex-hausted, we shoved our things into the trunk of the rental car. Allison still wanted to talk. We sat in the front seat of the rental. She was staring at me.

"I know what you want," I said. "I know. And I'm still not ready to decide what we should do. I just have no idea. I don't even know where the hell I want to *live* right now. My head is in too many places right now. I mean, I just got off a national-al scenic trail. I feel completely overwhelmed, like my brain's back on the PCT somehow. Don't you remember how it was when we got off the trail down near Mexico? Hanging out in San Diego? Starbucks everywhere, and all that concrete?"

"We can't just keep putting off the conversation forever."

"But we don't *have* to talk about it *here,* where it's beautiful. Why don't we wait until we're *off* the island to have the big old knock-down-drag-out, 'where the hell are we going in our future' conversation?"

"You know what, Dan? I've been sitting around for two years waiting for you to just get your shit together. I need you to step up. This isn't funny anymore. I'm sick of you just blanking out every time we talk about an unpleasant subject. You think it's a 'difficult' situation, you think I'm being a 'difficult' girlfriend, now? Well, I can't help it. Things are difficult. I need the best of you right now. You're a pretty funny guy. So why don't you cheer me up right now? Why can't you be strong for me? Be funny for me."

"I'm sick of things always being hard."

"And you've been off the trail for all of one week."

"I don't want to move on just yet."

"There's no more trail."

"But I don't know what I want to do."

"You're gonna have to start figuring that out."

"But I'm really scared."

"You're a coward," she said.

We drove the car back on the ferry and wound up in Seattle, where Allison had booked a flight to take her home. I didn't book a flight, though. I still did not know where I wanted to live, even for the next few weeks. I said I'd tell her very soon, when I was less confused, when I wasn't "in transition" anymore. I couldn't think properly, couldn't will my mouth to say one thing to comfort her. That week, in Seattle, Allison was sitting in the next room, reading a freebie magazine we'd picked from a display case near a supermarket. I picked up the phone and made plans to have lunch with an ex-girlfriend in Seattle, hardly even realizing what I was doing or why. I flirted on the phone. Talked loudly. Couldn't control the volume. My larynx was set on "speakerphone." Allison heard the whole thing. "How could you?" she said. "When I'm sitting right there, bored, in the next room? Have you lost your mind, Dan? This isn't even mean anymore. It's just crazy. It feels like you're doing everything you can think of to drive me away."

"It's just lunch," I said. "It's nothing."

The next night, we booked ourselves into yet another

cheapskate motel, this one just outside the Seattle airport, on the free-shuttle route. This was the time for me to "step up" and say all the right things, but I couldn't do it. The sheets were overstarched. They felt like concrete. I hate it when maids overstarch the sheets. You'd think they would give them a good rinse or something, soften them up a bit so a man could get some decent sleep. Allison left on a shuttle to her terminal the next morning, when the sun was barely up.

It didn't seem right just to get on a plane after all that walking, so I hung around town awhile. I had lunch with my smart and pretty ex-girlfriend, who was finding herself, working in a bookstore. Same light blond hair, thick glasses, high cheekbones. She still favored natural cotton fabrics. We ate cheap pad Thai, mine with shrimp, hers with tumescent clots of tofu, because she was still a vegetarian. I thought I'd try to flirt with her a little. See how far I might get. Who knows? I'd never really gotten over her. Our relationship had always felt unfinished to me. I talked to her in some detail about the Pacific Crest Trail. Told her all the good anecdotes, but with Allison clipped out of every scene. It occurred to me that all my best stories were on the damned trail, and that Allison figured in a great many of them, and yet I didn't say one word about her. My ex-girlfriend smiled at me in a familiar way.

"What's funny?" I said.

"Oh, nothing," she said. "It's just that I never would have known that you got through with finishing this national trail unless you'd told me. There's nothing about your face, or anything about you, that looks different. You look like the same Dan I knew from before. Only older."

Chapter 34

Striking Pyrex

I decided to head back down to California for a while, just to clear the mental fog. It didn't seem right to jump on a plane after walking the trail, so I got on Green Tortoise, the counter-culture's bus line. These buses have mattresses, so you can watch the woods and cities slip past while you're on your back with your feet in some ponytailed Earth Firster's face. The bus line's motto: "Arrive inspired, not dog-tired."

We made our way down south, stopping for a naked sweat-lodge ceremony and a vegetable barbecue, then on through the violet dark beneath the streetlights of nameless towns, and finally to the Safeway supermarket in Santa Cruz, California. A teenage girl in a rainbow batik dress peered into the bus. "Love the bus, killer scene," she said. "Anyone have a pipe?" The driver scolded her. "Believe it or not," he said, "we're sub-stance-free." As the girl wiggled back toward the grocery store, the driver turned to us, smiled, and said, "A lot of heads live in Santa Cruz. If you're confused, move there. I guarantee it'll fuck you up even worse."

I moved to Santa Cruz shortly thereafter.

I immediately got my job back as a substitute teacher. "We're desperate," the human resources woman at the school said.

I missed Allison in Santa Cruz. I didn't miss Allison in Santa Cruz. I wanted Allison in my life, and yet I wanted freedom. Santa Cruz is the kind of place where you can have it both ways, or at least think that you can. It all seemed so easy there. They've got banjo pluckers and skateboarders sitting around on city benches in the middle of a Monday afternoon. They've got a farmers market every Wednesday, with people selling nectarines and fennel and doling out free copies of the *Socialist Worker*. I would miss Allison every few days, check in with her, and she was cordial, even flirty, on the phone, and then I'd hang up and dream up strategies to entice the ladies of Santa Cruz onto my jet-black futon, where they would recline against my natural-fiber pillow covers. I could not commit to flying out and moving in with Allison, nor could I abide the thought of our breaking up, and so I kept her in an in-between state, tied to the hemp lanyard of uncertainty, never knowing where she stood.

About a month had passed since I finished the trail and hung out with Allison in Canada. I thought nothing was amiss, that we were in a pleasant state of stasis, when I called her up on her twenty-seventh birthday.

"I've been sleeping all day," she said when she answered the phone. The abrupt tone surprised me, and so did the way she bit off the ends off of every word she spoke.

"But that's silly, sweetie. You should be out enjoying your big day."

Silence followed.

"What's the matter?" I said.

"I don't think we should be together anymore."

"What? It's not . . . I mean, it hasn't come to that yet. I don't see why you'd jump to something so extreme without . . ."

"I'm not going through this again. If you want to talk about this later on, we can, I guess, but I really don't think there's anything to talk about."

The conversation limped along for a while, and then we hung up. This talk did not bother me because I sensed, even then, that it wasn't real. She was merely confused. No problem. I was confused, too. I'd already decided that the only way to gain some clarity was to play the field for a while, weigh the situation and see if we could work our shit out. Allison *had* to understand that the trail had made me cool. How could I sort out what I needed out of life when there were so many beautiful women waiting for me? How could I act like nothing had changed when the trail had turned me into a viable person for the first time in my life? In a word, I was lost. On the trail, I'd convinced myself that The Goal was all that stood between me and the rest of life. But the trail was over, and the rest of life was more nebulous than ever. I missed Allison, always, yet the thought of flying out there and being with her paralyzed me.

I couldn't figure out what I wanted, and so I got into yoga for a while, ostensibly to center myself, but really just to meet hot hippie women. There was a swishy-rumped girl in my class, in her early twenties. Her Danskins could hardly contain her vegan, carb-enforced curves. "Okay," the yoga instructor said. "Time to pair up with someone else. Don't be a stranger! We're all friends here. What I want you to do is pick a partner, and help them with the first stretch. Grab your partner's thigh, and we'll see just how far they can bend." Score, I thought. I loved yoga classes. The women in yoga classes will assume poses you really couldn't pay them to do in any other context. So I took a couple of giant steps toward the holistic nubile, perched like an egret on her cerulean yoga mat. But when she saw me, she froze. If you've watched the Discovery Channel's footage about wildebeest mothers protecting their young, you have a good idea of this girl's facial expression. She saw me coming, and she retreated, straight through the wall of vertical beads marking the entrance to the women's changing room. I was waiting her out, waiting, waiting, when it became clear that she was just not coming back. And then, at that moment, I heard a male voice, a plummy German accent, and turned to see a thin man with mousy hair and huge glasses standing behind me. "I'll be your partner, if you like," he said. "In fact, you can stretch first. It's no problem at all." Before I could say one word, he'd already grabbed my thigh and lifted up the end of my right leg and started to grind my bare and horrified foot straight into the bulge in the groin of his leotard. For three minutes I stood there on one foot, flash-frozen in repulsion, my toes being dragged repeatedly against my yoga partner's seemingly stiffening knob. "You're all doing great," the yoga teacher said in a chirpy voice, as my partner softly moaned.

I tried not to let this minor act of yogic molestation get me down. I persevered. I even got set up on a hot blind date with an attractive young Bay Area journalista. We flirted like mad on the phone. "You're funny," she told me. She came to my house; we'd plotted out a day on the beach. When I answered the door, she was even more gorgeous and perky than I expected, and when she saw me, and after she'd looked me up and down, she said, "Is Dan White here?"

Allison had been out there waiting for me, so I assumed that all these other women were waiting for me, too. Now it occurred to me: perhaps I was wrong. Maybe all these women were just signposts directing me back toward the only woman in the world who had ever put up with me for more than seven months running. Maybe "Dirty Dan" was never real, except in my mind. Perhaps I wanted my old identity back, my old shape, my being, my erstwhile purpose. And maybe Allison was the only woman in the world who could give me back my shape. Allison and I did quite a lot of baking together—brownies, turnovers, pies, you name it—so you will forgive me if I indulge in an extended baking metaphor. Perhaps Allison was the ramekin, while I was the pudding. I occupied her center, and weighed her down in a way that gave her comfort and happiness, at least for a while. You might even say I *filled* her ramekin, while she shaped me and baked me as best she could. But when we broke up, perhaps I was not fully baked. The oven setting was too low, and the timing was wrong. When the ramekin dumped me out, I splattered out like a blob of cheesy, eggy custard goo.

After the Pacific Crest Trail, I settled into the sort of ego-flattening funk you can only have in Santa Cruz, that funky little beach town, that gentrified catch basin of the unhinged. It's not that people were mean to me for acting crazy. Quite the contrary. In Santa Cruz, people are serious when it comes to letting you follow your bliss, even if your bliss is really a form of depression. I began to walk aimlessly around the town, wearing hemp vests with purple paramecium, vests with puffy elephants, vests with dreadful spangles on the shoulders, reversible vests that were black on one side, red on the other, so people could dig my mood. I became a lounge lizard with no lounge, and it was becoming clear that I must have Allison back, that without her there would be no girl, no adventure, no purpose, no mojo, just existential horniness and confusion. We still talked on the phone, as friends. It seems to me that we were close. She confessed she was still "fond" of me, that she liked the sound of my voice. I held out hope. I would look through our boxes of shared things and take comfort in the fact that I still had so much of her Pacific Crest Trail gear, and all those lovers' coupons she'd given me for Valentine's Day long ago, good for a free yoghurt, good for a dozen doughnuts. I had tangible things, in boxes under my bed, and these things meant I still had a connection to her. But the link was still tenuous, so I had to make a plan. I began to write an irresistible letter to get her back. I was in the later, revision, stage, contemplating when I might actually finish the thing and put it in the mail. There was no hurry. Drafting takes time. But one day, about four months after I last saw her, I opened up the mailbox just after New Year's Day and found a letter from her. I tore it open.

The intention of the letter was clear.

She wanted all her gear back.

So anyway, I made a list of all the stuff I could find of yours, including the infamous kite. I was wondering if you could look for a few things that were missing from my pack: one of the compasses, a Maglite, my knife, an orange whistle, the snakebite kit and First Aid stuff, a couple of Nalgene [bottles] and a pair of leather mittens with white fleece inside. It seems unfair for me to pay for half the Katadyn filter when I never got to use it. I think you should buy out my share of it and I should buy my share of the tent. Let's say Dan pays Allison $125 and keeps the water filter. Allison pays Dan $150 and keeps the tent. Does that work out right in your opinion? Do you think we need a trial lawyer? You let me know what you think. Say hi to everyone out there for me!

It was over then. Undeniably over.

A year passed, and in that time I gained and lost a job, gained and did not lose thirty pounds, went on unemployment, and moved into an attic in downtown Santa Cruz. When the checks ran out, I entered my third tour of duty as a substitute teacher.

In every relationship, attraction is the lure, but maybe it's only the entry point to an intimacy that counteracts silliness, superstition, awkwardness, and loony behavior. Allison and the trail were no longer there to hold these things back like a dam, and soon they ruled over me. My long walk provided me with the time and the space to develop strange thinking patterns.

The forest had given rise to a dog's breakfast of superstitions, animism, and pantheistic piffle that dominated me now. In Santa Cruz, a year and a half after returning home from the trail, I still hadn't adjusted. In fact, I had become irrational, or at least more irrational than usual. Santa Cruz's cultist and New Age emporiums were the ready recipients of the dollar bills I doled out in exchange for the restorative voodoo candles, amulets, plastic knockoffs of Zuni bear fetishes, poorly carved Ganesh figurines, herbal snake-oil ointments, and fakir-blessed trinkets that crowded my apartment and turned my bedroom into a stinking, incense-choked ashram. But none of these elephant brooches or herbal rescue remedies could fill me up like Allison and the trail had. No amount of sorcerer-blessed gewgaws could put my noggin to rights or make me sleep at night. And so I spouted inanities and wore hideous pants made of sustainable materials. I wrote zany affirmations on bits of paper that I rolled into scrolls and stuffed in my pockets to carry around all day when I was subbing for some kindergarten class, in the vain hope that the the affirmations' enthusiasms would leach into me. "Free the body!" they said. "Cave in to pleasure! Inner space, flow, one, one, one! There is peace in every day, perfect moments, the cool of morning, and moments of stillness. Man, in his natural state, is calm and centered." These affirmations were desperate and untrue. After walking the trail, I knew full well that calm centeredness was *not* mankind's natural state. Mankind had evolved over millions of years on the African plains. They had hyenas out there the size of school buses. "Peace out," and you will be ripped in half.

I began to suffer nervous attacks that went on for days at a time. After a while, I started showing up late to my teaching assignments. Then I stopped showing up altogether. The phone would ring and I'd let it go. Friends became alarmed.

One day, when things were feeling especially chaotic, and I hadn't held a job for months, I tried to do a self-intervention.

On that day I paused and declared that this was the absolute bottom, and that there was no lower level of muck in which to mire myself. In Santa Cruz, it's never a good idea to make such a proclamation. In this town, where marginalia can become more marginal, you should never tell yourself you've hit bottom, because the bottom will move to a lower elevation. There is always some other substrata of bottomness you have not considered. In Santa Cruz, you can wind up in a tape loop of backsliding and recovery that folds back on itself like an Escher staircase. Your life can turn into a bottomless Stouffer's lasagna; no matter how far down you reach with your plastic fork, there's another layer of nasty noodles and cheese before you hit Pyrex.

I became an insomniac, thoughts circling my head until they screwed me right into the ground. Thoughts twisted so fast I could not control them, slow them, or even separate them after a while. I was up for eight days straight, rarely nodding off for five to ten minutes at a time, even when I gulped a bottle of melatonin or took an herbal sleep aid or, on one memorable occasion, whole bottles of sleep aids. My eyes bugged out as I hid from friends and daylight, peering Boo Radley fashion from the blinds of my attic hideaway. And then, on the eighth day, I tore my room apart, in between guzzling organic Chenin Blanc and an unholy mixture of other substances, bouncing all about that place, ripping posters off the walls.

I suppose I would have gone on spiraling forever, if not for the fact that I ran out of energy, and spirals, and places to spiral to. And when there was no more spiral, I collapsed. Perhaps it would be overstating matters to call this a Pacific Crest breakdown. All I know is that my rational mind went on an extended backpacking trip somewhere in the North Cascades while my body remained in Santa Cruz. I did not realize this at the time, but my little spinout was, quite possibly, an example of post-trail withdrawal. I have heard about other hikers who returned too abruptly from the wilderness and experienced the psychic equivalent of the bends, the condition deep-sea divers face when yanked too abruptly out of the ocean. I have heard about fresh-off-the-trail hikers breaking down and sobbing on city streets.

It took a considerable amount of debt, boredom, and un-employment to bring me back from my long daze. My re-covery was far from smooth. In the months after my Pacific Crest Meltdown, I found ungainful employment at temp agen-cies, which tried to slot me into corporate offices. I tried hard, but my behavior got in the way. I filled out time cards with a large black crayon, pilfered office supplies, and hit on a sleepy-eyed, bosomy coworker named Genevieve. I tried to woo her by giving her Bigfoot sculptures I'd fashioned out of faux fur, Coke bottles, doll's eyes, and oversize paper clips. They fired me quickly; the supervisor asked me to stay away from the office.

"But what about the mess on the desk?" I said.

"We'll take care of it," she assured me.

Adapting to my old life was a struggle for Dirty Dan. The disassociations, and social blunders, kept creeping up. One of my friends took me to a sushi bar on Pacific Avenue, where I placed a large glop of wasabi into my mouth, forgetting that it wasn't pistachio sorbet. I sprinted for the washroom, with magma-hot horseradish drooling from my mouth. Afterward, we took a wild ride in my car, driving around downtown Santa Cruz. When she asked me what the hell I was doing, I told her that I was "looking for my car."

"You're *in* it," she said.

As soon as I was feeling more reasonable, I launched a bid to get my sanity back. I started by laying siege to the ridicu-lous gewgaws and tinctures I'd amassed since washing up in Santa Cruz. I uncorked every accursed tincture of St. John's Wort, milk thistle, and melatonin and dumped it down the toi-let where it belonged. I loaded my voodoo candles and smiling

Buddha onyxes into the nearest Dumpster. I filled out a job application, this time without a crayon in my hand. I cleaned up the room I'd trashed and apologized to the friends I'd freaked out. And one summer day, I even worked up the nerve to call Allison, not to get her back, plead for sympathy, or even apologize, but just to let her know how I was doing.

"It's nice to hear your voice," she said, and I unloaded on her, giving her the unexpurgated version of my post-trail spinout. It was an easy talk, no motive or quest.

"All I can say is, I'm not surprised," she said, in reference to my confession about my 192-hour sleeplessness. "You always had so much energy." We talked about everything and nothing, her freelancing, her reporting gig out in the Midwest, what it was like to be off the trail. And then, very casually, around the halfway point of our talk, she dropped in the name of a man she'd met. Somewhere between the beginning and ending of my temporary lunacy, she'd fallen in love. "We get along really well," she said. "You and I had some good times, but it just wasn't worth it." We hung up after a while. The conversation had dribbled away. It didn't even feel like two exes talking. It felt like easy friends who had parted company and were probably not going to speak again, not out of rancor but from circumstance, distance, and sheer inertia. When I hung up the phone, our conversation left no residue. It was all done now.

I moved on, at least from Allison. The trail never really left my head—it's still there—and that's not necessarily a bad thing. The trail did not bring about all of the behaviors that some people clump together when they think of "Dan White": my loud monologues when I think no one is around, or my occasional bouts of vigilance, as if every street corner might conceal a cactus waiting to stick it to me. But the trail at least reinforced these behaviors. For six years after the trail, I even toted a gallon bottle of water for fear of dehydration, even in cities. Sometimes I still do.

But the trail didn't just turn me into an occasional head case. The trail also gave me my first story, and exposed me to something larger than myself. I now have a certain kind of "hardship" as a frame of reference, along with a willingness to admit that most of the hardships I encountered on and off the trail were self-inflicted. It had been *my* decision to be there. I could have quit any time. The fact that I did *not* quit means something to me. I'm not suggesting that I'm brave. After all, a lot of people have hiked the same trail without significant problems. You might even say that I went with much trepidation where hundreds had gone before. I'm not suggesting that I'm a competent outdoorsman, either. A couple of years ago, after I wrote an article about hiking through a remote section of Maine without a map, a woman wrote me a letter assuring me that I was a "disgrace to the national backpacking community." She had a point, but perhaps getting lost is the final frontier. If I had known what the hell I was doing upon embarking on the PCT, my finishing the trail would not have been significant. The fact that I winged it but did not die still moves me. I'll never be as fast or as light as a Jardi-Nazi, but I'm tenacious as the ticks that bit me in the Laguna Mountains. More than ten years have passed since I set foot out of Agua Dulce with Allison and Big Motherfucker. Since then, I fell in love again. My wife and I have been married for three years now. Big Motherfucker is with me still. I've resisted the impulse to send him out to Gregory Backpacks to have him fixed up. He retains all the scars, mouse bites, and duct-tape patch jobs he sustained on the trail. Though I've washed him twice since then, Big Motherfucker still bears the rank aroma of the PCT.

The odor reminds me of what I learned. The trail was a harsh teacher, and most of the lessons had nothing to do with backpacking. Now I have a yardstick to measure beauty, all ugliness, slack times, good times, and privation. When a snowdrift buries my car on the streets of Manhattan, or my wife and I are squawking about a bill or a misunderstanding, or my writing students are panicking about their essays, or my upstairs neighbor wakes me up at 4:15 A.M., pounding away at his girlfriend on the hardwood floor while emitting nasal quacking noises, I think to myself, "Well, yeah, but I drank mud. I ate a fuckin' *cactus*." Most people, upon meeting me, would never suspect I come from an ultrawealthy suburb. I don't expect black-truffle shavings on my chocolate sundaes. In fact, I expect all worthwhile things to be a slog, whether we're talking about marriage, trying to get published, moving my car back and forth across the street to stay ahead of the sweeper, looking for jobs in academia, searching for aircon units on Craigslist, or doing battle with Manhattan's parking police.

While the PCT provided me with a framework for my life, the trail did not improve my hiking style. I still get lost constantly, even at the mall. I visit the woods almost every week. But every walk I take is the un-trail. I no longer freight each walk with grand expectations. I would never hike a national scenic trail again—nor do I have any desire to make up the piece I missed, near Seiad Valley, when I accepted a hitchhike just south of town. If I tried to walk another long trail, I would most likely die. My backcountry luck ran out a long time ago. These days, I'm less likely to moon over the PCT or try to sneak it into every conversation. And yet the PCT left me with nostalgia I've never felt for, say, college or high school. When I look out the window at a set of low-lying mountains twenty miles off, I remember what it was like to stand in a valley and stare off at some distant escarpment and know I'd be walking around up there, looking for a campsite, by the time the sun went down. Sometimes I find myself falling backward until I'm on it again. For a long while after the trail, I had a dream with variations, sometimes twice a week. The setup was always the same. I'm out on a trail that passes through a cleft in a granite ridge, so high up only dwarf trees and krummholz grow there. There's a young couple out on the trail just north of me, hiking slowly. There are scattered clouds, but now they're bunching together, making a storm, and so I walk faster, even though experience tells me I can't outrun a storm. I catch up to the couple without even trying. For some reason, they can't see me. They look right through me as if I were made out of Saran Wrap. The man and woman make their way to a rocky bowl containing a lake. The lake has no name, so they name it after themselves, for a laugh. Now the couple has stopped for the night. They sit down cross-legged and cook supper: protein chunks bobbing around in a slippery liquid. Their meal smells nasty, and yet they slurp it up. My eyes settle on the woman. She's pretty, with blond hair and burnished skin. The man grunts as he tends the stove. His beard is full of dirt and gunk, but the woman doesn't seem to care. She's looking at him as if he's handsome. It's getting cold out here. She leads him into the tent. After a while I hear muttering and murmurs, and I watch the motions and silhouettes of their sleeping bags clumped together. After a while, the tent goes still, the sky turns black, and when it becomes too cold for me to stay out here any longer, I leave them be, and retreat down the ridge alone.

No moon is out, but the trail announces itself in a ribbon of light that takes me down the valley.

Author's Note

This is a work of narrative nonfiction. I have tried to re-capture my mind-set and Pacific Crest Trail experiences as accurately as I could, with the help from my often comprehensive, sometimes less than comprehensive, and sometimes threadbare diary entries. I have had to contend with the fact that some of the diary entries are exhaustive and chronological (such as the cactus-biting scene), while others are scattered pieces, written in a hurry and out of sequence. I consulted my boxes of slides, post-trail interviews, and an early "Vomit Draft," in which I attempted (perhaps unwisely) to fill in the blanks in the diaries and "narrativize" an otherwise random-seeming bunch of strange events. The early draft has been helpful in the sense that it caulked a few cracks in my diary—it's strange how one can remember items that aren't in any journal, and how a journal can "remember" forgotten anecdotes—and frustrating in the sense that I wrote the rough version so quickly after coming home from the trail that it suffered from tunnel-vision, instant-replay contextualization attempts, and storytelling bluster. In the past few years I've had to triangulate between memory, images, the PCT guidebooks, and various (and sometimes conflicting) versions of the written record, including diaries, the "rough-cut" version, and a peculiar comic book/graphic novel version of the trek, which I crafted in order to frame events in time and space. This "final" version is an attempt to square this draft with other versions. In many instances the dialogue is close to verbatim—for example, the disturbing exchange with Oedipus Rex in the High Sierra section, the back-and-forth with Milt Kenney (reinforced by subsequent interviews), and my Tehachapi crossing with the Gingerbread Man. In other instances I am relying only on the power (such as it is) of memory while consulting correspondence and memories of habitual conversation topics, conversational tics, speech patterns, mannerisms, and so on. Where possible, I've tried to square my memories of various lakes and cloud formations and volcanic protuberances with slides, pictures, and YouTube images while filling in a few gaps of ignorance (e.g., biography, natural history) with book reading and databases. If I've misdescribed any of the personages here, or if any shrub, arthropod, woodland mammal, or lizard feels misrepresented here, or if I've transported any creatures to the wrong ecosystem or life zone, the fault lies with the author, not the sources. In some cases I have identified trail "characters" only by their trail names. In some instances I have changed names for reasons of privacy. Above all else, this is my vision of the trail. If you hike it, you will most likely not eat a cactus or watch in horror as your water filter is violated by a bunch of amphibians. Consider yourself lucky.

Acknowledgments

With love and gratitude to my wife, Amy. My *Cactus* diaries and rough drafts would be sprouting poisonous mushrooms under my desk without your unflagging support. Thank you for encouraging me to follow my dreams and crisscrossing this country with me twice. (Not on foot!)

With love and appreciation to Mom and Dad.

With love and gratitude to Doug and Edie Achterman: You were our cheering section throughout the Manhattan Project and beyond.

I would like to extend an enormous "thank you" to Patricia O'Toole for her invaluable friendship, insight, and wisdom, and for convincing me to take a worthwhile risk. I am extremely lucky to have such a mentor. (Also, thanks for the helmet!)

Many thanks to my agent, Kris Dahl, at ICM for her work on *Cactus*, and to Michael Signorelli at HarperCollins for his attention and care (and to John Williams for believing in this project). Thanks to all of my talented fellow workshoppers (and while they are too numerous to mention by name), I want to give a shout-out to Bronwen Dickey for being the first to read through the completed version and offering "instant feedback" suggestions. Thanks to Paul Douglass, coordinator of the Martha Heasley Cox Center for Steinbeck Studies at San Jose State University, and to Martha Heasley Cox for her generous endow-ment of the Steinbeck Fellowship, which helped me finish this book and nail down the P.S. materials. I'm grateful for the shaping hand of Richard Locke, for the first-rate workshops of Michael Scammell and Leslie Sharpe, and to Phillip Lopate for his unvarnished feedback. (An additional thanks to professors Locke and O'Toole for cheering on our class at the School of the Arts thesis readings; both of your enthusiastic presences made a huge difference for all of us. It was much appreciated!) Thanks to Dave Howard for brotherhood, friendship, and guidance, to James Shiffer for coming up with this crazy plan in the first place (and for saving the correspondence that I used in several sections of the text), to Peggy Townsend and Shmuel Thaler, who took a gander at the "rough cut," to Didi Dayton, Will Zilliacus, Shawn Parker, and Whitney Grummon for their friendship and encouragement, and to Scott Williamson, uber-hiker, for his sound advice. I am grateful to Phil Sexton for information pertaining to the unfortunate Elisha Stephens (see the P.S. for additional readings and information sources on Stephens), and to all of the hard-working, boundlessly creative students in my Fall 2006 undergraduate writing class at Columbia. That class turned into a kind of "laboratory of ideas" that helped inspire this book's deep ecology and man-in-relation-to-nature themes. Many thanks to the staff at the California history room at the Martin Luther King Library at SJSU, and to all the real-life heroes who helped with my expedition—in particular, the tireless Wolf and the endlessly inventive Gingerbread Man. While writing this, I found inspiration in the writings of Ray Jardine (I hope some day to live up to his lightpacking example). Many thanks to Angela Ballard and the Pacific Crest Trail Association, and all the Trail Angels—in particular, the late Mily Kenney of Castella, California, the "mayor" of the Pacific Crest Trail.

About the author

About the book

Read on

Insights,
Interviews
& More . . .

Meet Dan White

© Amy Ettinger

DAN WHITE is a journalist and author from Palos Verdes, California. White has written for the *New York Times*, the *Los Angeles Times*, *Backpacker* magazine, and the *Santa Cruz Sentinel*. He holds a bachelor of arts degree from Wesleyan University and an MFA in creative writing from Columbia University. Before embarking on his writing career, he was a substitute kindergarten teacher, part-time janitor, grocery store bag boy, seaside amusement park burger flipper, and manual forklift operator. White lives in the San Francisco Bay Area with his wife, the writer Amy Ettinger. He can be found online at www.cactuseaters.blogspot.com.

The Pacific Crest Trail Association and the Future of the PCT

IF YOU WALK the Pacific Crest National Scenic Trail, you may wonder if we walked on the same footpath. Milt Kenney has passed away. The Gingerbread Man has moved on to other adventures. Many of the other Trail Angels and personages have moved away, and the trail itself keeps changing. Erosion, right-of-way issues, forest fires, and construction change the look and the feel of this path from Mexico to Canada. I spoke with Angela Ballard, Pacific Crest Trail Association (PCTA) editor and publications manager, about the PCT's future.

Ballard is also the coauthor of "A Blistered Kind of Love: One Couple's Trial by Trail."

CactusEaters: First of all, what exactly is the Pacific Crest Trail Association, and how can through-hikers get involved?

Angela Ballard: The PCTA is recognized as the government's major partner in the operation of the Pacific Crest National Scenic Trail, and we are the PCT's steward and advocate. Our mission is to protect, preserve, and promote the PCT as an internationally significant resource for the enjoyment of hikers and equestrians and for the value that wild and scenic lands provide to all people. We are a membership-based organization and we're very vocal. We have about six thousand members that bring in donations and an astounding number of volunteer hours—in fact, tens of thousands of volunteer hours and donations each ▶

> 66 Milt Kenney has passed away. The Gingerbread Man has moved on to other adventures. Many of the other Trail Angels and personages have moved away, and the trail itself keeps changing. 99

year: 55,400 volunteer hours and $536,000 in individual contributions in 2006 alone. During those volunteer hours, PCTA members clear and repair the trail and generally do the maintenance that's needed to keep it open from border to border for 2,650 miles. As you can imagine, that's a mammoth job. In part because our volunteers give so much of themselves to the trail and PCTA, we have a strong voice, and the more members we have, the more clout we have when we lobby Congress to provide funding and resources necessary to protect and manage the trail.

CE: What challenges does the PCTA face when trying to preserve the trail?

AB: Approximately three hundred miles of trail are still on private land, with the trail crossing those private parcels thanks to right-of-way easements. But the language on those easements varies greatly, and compliance with the language and spirit of the easements also varies. You can have easements that protect hikers' rights to walk through the property, but they must stay within a narrow four-to-eight-foot-wide corridor, and often the land around the trail is not protected in any way. Wherever the trail is on private land, we worry about its future and the future of trail users' experiences there. We've had some crazy situations. People have built fences across the trail and even put "For Sale" signs next to the trail. Solidifying and protecting the trail's route and environs in perpetuity is one of our top priorities right now.

CE: How can the PCTA prevent private interests, development, and timber-harvesting from damaging the land around the trail?

AB: Well, we are very vocal whenever we hear about something that could harm the character of the trail and detract from the experience that people expect to have on a national scenic trail. Often, plans may be proposed without the developer or timber company in question really even considering the impacts on the PCT. It's our job to question such plans and to remind the parties involved that Congress set aside the PCT and designated it a national scenic trail because it is a unique and special part of our country and, as such, it deserves unique and special consideration. Given that the trail runs the length of the nation through three states, you can imagine the number of threats that arise.

Here's just one example of a project we're working on. In Washington State and in Northern California the trail passes through timber lands with histories that date back to when the first cross-country railroads were built. In order to encourage the rail companies to build the railroads in the nineteenth century, the U.S. government gave those companies every other square mile of land along the railroads routes, up to twenty miles back from the tracks, on either side. The sections not granted to the railroad were retained by the government. Later, many of those checkerboard parcels of land, as they are now called, were sold to timber companies. In Washington, as you hike the PCT in certain areas, you may find yourself in a square mile of old-growth forest one minute, and then in a square mile of forest that has been logged or clear-cut the next. Perhaps the logging occurred long ago and the forest floor is now in a stage of regrowth, or perhaps there was recent logging and the earth may be churned up and crisscrossed by logging roads. To protect that land into the future, and to make its maintenance and management significantly easier, it makes sense for those checkerboard parcels to be in public rather than private ownership. And once logged, the checkerboard lands can—and do sometimes—come up for sale. The PCTA is working hard with the Forest Service and other organizations like the Trust for Public Land to find parcels of land near or along the PCT that are for sale. Then we track down the money that the Forest Service needs to buy the land and put it in a public holding as part of a national forest.

CE: What are the single biggest threats to the PCT right now?

AB: Here are just a couple of examples: A major power company in Southern California is talking about a huge power line across the PCT towards San Diego and the original plan had the power line paralleling the trail for a number of miles. If the power line is inevitable, which I don't believe is the case, why not just cross the trail once to limit its impact? Many new and expanded wind farms are going to be built close to the trail in Tehachapi, California, because of the call for more alternative energy sources. That's a good thing, but we do not necessarily need our national scenic trail winding through more wind farms. Perhaps the trail needs to be moved to a different location, or perhaps the plans for the wind farms can be tweaked? We're working on that. The Forest Service is in the midst of a nationwide plan to designate ▶

The Pacific Crest Trail Association and the Future of the PCT
(continued)

areas where off-highway vehicles (OHVs) are allowed to "play." This is good because under previous policy OHVs were allowed anywhere except where they were expressly prohibited, but we must pay attention because we don't want an OHV zone too close to the PCT for fear of illegal use of the trail by vehicles, damage to the environment, and noise pollution, among other things. As I mentioned earlier, we are very vocal. When these sorts of things come up, we make phone calls, we campaign with letters and e-mails, we attend planning commission meetings as well as private meetings with developers and other involved parties. Usually, our concerns are taken under consideration and are well received, and we work hard to find a compromise that's good for everyone.

CE: Are there use conflicts between different users of the PCT?

AB: The PCT is designed and mandated for equestrians and pedestrians only, but it's very tempting for all-terrain vehicle (ATV) and OHV users to hop on it—either knowingly or unknowingly, and I can see why: it's beautiful. But vehicles and bicycles can severely damage the trail and its drainage, making the work we do to keep the trail open each year that much harder. Vehicles and bicycles also don't mix well with backpackers and equestrians. Safety issues can arise, especially if bikes or OHVs are moving down a narrow curvy trail and switchbacks at high speeds. But most importantly, there is a spirit and aura about the PCT that is paramount. I know that if I want to slow down, reconnect with nature and myself and my loved ones, and be filled with the peace that only a wild space seems to provide—I head to the PCT. It is important for us all to know that such spaces for solitude, quiet, and reflection exist, and so it's our job to limit conflicts between users and remember why the PCT is special and keep it that way. ∽

For more information about the PCTA, go to www.pcta.org. Membership in the organization costs thirty-five dollars, which includes a subscription to the bimonthly PCT Communicator *magazine, along with the chance to join trail crews and the right to obtain a PCTA hiking permit to hike 500 or more continuous miles of the trail.*

Living the Pacific Crest Trail
A Profile of Scott Williamson

by Dan White

IF NOT FOR THE MAN who gunned him
down, Scott Williamson might have chosen
a different path. He might be working in
an office now, stuffing forms into a bleeping
fax machine. Instead, he became the world's
most prolific Pacific Crest Trail through-
hiker.

Williamson, thirty-five, has walked
the PCT from end to end ten times. That
amounts to 26,500 miles, or 2,000 miles
longer than the earth's circumference.

To pull off these walking feats, Williamson
carries a seven-pound pack, not including
water, and eats gruesome low-weight food,
including dehydrated beans: just add
water, and you will get a block of sludge.
He consumes this with tortilla chips, and
gleans extra calories from the wheatgrass
milk shake he makes himself.

These foods taste as good as they sound,
but, to borrow a line from Skippy peanut
butter, they "fuel the fun." Williamson can
throw down forty miles a day, though he
prefers not to because it forces him to take
too many recovery breaks. He would rather
take it easy and walk thirty-three miles a day.

This hard-core trail philosophy helped
him make hiking history. In 2004, Williamson
became the first person to "yo-yo" the trail—
or hike the entire PCT end to end twice in
one sustained effort, a feat he pulled off a
second time in 2006. This long walk gave ▶

> 66 Williamson,
> thirty-five, has
> walked the PCT
> from end to end
> ten times. That
> amounts to
> 26,500 miles, or
> 2,000 miles longer
> than the earth's
> circumference. 99

Williamson a place among the nation's elite backpackers—a group that includes Brian Robinson, the first person to hike the Pacific Crest Trail, the Continental Divide Trail, and the Appalachian Trail in a single year, covering a distance of 7,000 miles.

Williamson doubts he'd be so consumed with this hike if he hadn't been working that extra shift at a neighborhood liquor store in Richmond, California, on a winter afternoon in 1996.

It was a sleepy Saturday in this crime-ridden city of a hundred thousand people. Williamson wasn't even supposed to be there; the boss had called him in to work an extra shift. Williamson was reading a magazine when a fidgeting man in a hoodie sweatshirt walked in and asked what time it was. The stranger fumbled in his pockets and pulled out a pistol, which he pointed at Williamson.

"I am going to kill you," he mumbled.

The bullet passed through Williamson's face, tearing into his salivary gland and coming to rest against the first vertebra at the base of his skull. If that bullet had landed just a quarter-inch lower, it would have center-punched Williamson's spinal cord, killing him instantly or making him a quadriplegic.

Somehow, Williamson found the strength to flee the gunman, who gave chase and took five potshots at him.

The police never caught the man. Williamson still walks around with the bullet inside him. His doctors told him that scar tissue wrapped around the slug, encasing it, turning it into a "benign object." He can't feel the bullet inside him. He never has.

Four days after getting shot, Williamson left the hospital. Now he was set to change his life. He'd almost lost movement in his legs and arms—now he wanted to put his limbs to use every day, while following the path and living the life he wanted to live.

The PCT was the obvious choice. Even before getting shot down, he was well aware of it: in 1992, he walked the California section of the trail.

"I had no idea what the hell I was doing," he said.

On that first trek, Williamson carried a seventy-pound pack, including two stainless steel pots and a half gallon of white gas—before learning that a ten-ounce bottle would suffice. He had multiple changes of clothes, including Levis, and a $400 Swiss altimeter, "although I had no functional use for it."

But now he wanted to hike the entire thing. The PCT became his focus. In fact, it became the *only* thing. He became determined to lose himself in the simplicity of the trail, and be far away from the dangerous city where he grew up. He dreamed of getting on the trail and never getting off again.

"The trail is a place to seek solitude," he explained. "You would think, 'Well, this guy has hiked the trail ten times,' but it's never the same. I see new things every time. To me, it's more meaningful than the average life that most of Western society is living right now. Some people speculate that I am searching for something out there, or escaping. (But) I just think of it as natural and right to be out there. Geez, you know, normal life is a thousand times more complicated."

Sometimes he hiked alone, but he also formed enduring friendships. His favorite trail companion was Kenny Gould, who became his best friend and initiated the idea of trying to "yo-yo" the trail in the first place.

They logged countless miles together, and went on peak-bagging adventures. Gould even gave Williamson one of his earliest trail names— "Duckface." But they never quite pulled off a "yo-yo" hike together.

Gould was irrepressible, and immune to fear. Williamson remembers getting the fright of his life while climbing snowbound Forester Pass, on the John Muir Trail, and worrying that he would toboggan down the icy slopes. All the while, Gould stayed calm and focused.

But Gould's life off the trail was nothing like his trail adventures. He was emotionally fragile—and Williamson was not entirely surprised when Gould told him that he suffered from mental illness.

But Williamson did not know just how bad things would get. In 2002, Kenny Gould leapt to his death from a rocky bluff in the Sierra Nevada. Williamson was devastated, but he decided to press on without his hiking partner, and try to "yo-yo" the pathway in Gould's memory.

"The way he lived became a template for me," he said. "Kenny was one of those people who never had anything bad to say about anyone. Not ever. He just accepted people for who they were."

The more he walked, the more Williamson freighted his hike with new meanings. After losing Gould, he only redoubled his focus on the long walk. But as the hikes themselves became "heavier," the load he carried shrunk down to the bare essentials.

Part of his "real simple" trail philosophy is carrying the absolute minimum he needs to get by in the woods.

In those times, carrying less than twenty-five pounds was considered "ultralight." But on subsequent hikes, Williamson—after following the ▶

Living the Pacific Crest Trail *(continued)*

advice of ultralight-pack guru Ray Jardine—figured out how to get by with only ten pounds, not including water weight. In later years, he managed to whittle this paltry load down by another three pounds.

Carrying little makes his walks more comfortable, though he admits to drawbacks.

"When the weather does turn inclement, you have to be a lot more careful," he said. "You have much less latitude in terms of being wet and cold. You really have to guard yourself much more carefully against hypothermia."

Williamson has had some chilly days and nights because of his light-pack philosophy—and he's encountered a few other hazards. To avoid excess weight, Williamson never carries a water filter, and he doesn't treat water with iodine or chlorine.

Usually, he avoids catching beaver fever, but sometimes his luck runs out. In 2007, Williamson, already feeling a bit queasy from gastrointestinal distress, drank some unfiltered water just south of Kennedy Meadows, California.

After swallowing a large mouthful straight out of the river, he glanced up at the stream and was in for a shock.

"There was a dead cow right in the middle of the river, and it had actually kind of blown open, rotting or whatever. I don't know if that made me sicker—I already had something in my intestinal tract that had been bothering me for a while—but there was a definite psychological effect."

This is one of many close calls. In past years, Williamson, who has also through-hiked the Appalachian and Continental Divide trails—has been sniffed by a bear, crossed swollen rivers, and inhaled smoke during the devastating 2007 fires in Southern California.

Because of his devotion to the trail, his off-trail life can be equally hazardous. To get by, he does seasonal work as a self-employed tree trimmer, a risky profession that requires him to stand 150 feet off the ground.

"My off-trail life is a continuous financial struggle because of the hiking," he said. " I am usually living job to job in terms of finances and at this point I have no retirement, no financial future . . . That is a terrible thing sometimes, but on the flip side it is an incredible amount of freedom. I don't have any debt, which is a good thing, but because of that, I don't own a home, I drive beat-up vehicles. In some regards I have a very unconventional life because of that, but the frugality and willingness to sacrifice have allowed me to be on the trail."

Williamson's achievements have earned him cult status within the hiking community, and international publicity, though he is hardly a household name. Perhaps, if he lived in a different era, he would be more of a celebrity, and earn his living from his walking feats. Take, for example, the mid-nineteenth century, when Edward Payson Weston was an international superstar. Among other things, this extreme pedestrian from Providence, Rhode Island, stomped 3,600 miles across the U.S. at age seventy-one. In his many walks, he never failed to get an avalanche of press attention.

And Weston was not alone. By the 1860s, so many people had taken to roads and trails, and were covering so much territory, that the *Times* preached caution against the "pedestrian mania (that) seems to afflict this country now. We hear of erratic pedestrians rushing across the country in every direction. . . . Side by side with telegrams announcing the progress of events in Italy, we find, day after day, telegrams announcing that of a pedestrian walking so many miles a day for so many thousands of dollars. Mayors greet him, roughs assail him, children are kissed by him, and every detail is telegraphed with pre-Raphaelite minuteness."

Needless to say, things have changed. If Williamson had taken up a bicycle, or a shot put or javelin, who knows what his life would look like today?

After all, these things are visible. Provable. Observable. Extreme bipedalism is not a spectator sport.

Considering the risks he takes, and the money he expends on his adventures, it's impressive to think that Williamson somehow manages to get back on the trail every year, almost without fail.

In fact, his constant presence on the trail gives him an unusual perspective about the ways the trail has changed and stayed the same. Female through-hikers—once a rare sight on the trail—are now out in force. The trail, once obscure, is enjoying a newfound popularity. About two dozen people tried to through-hike it when Williamson started out. In his last go-round on the trail, about four hundred people tried to through-hike it.

Even the light-packing world has changed. Today's "extreme" ultralight-packers now carry even less than he does. "Now there are people who are hiking the trail with five pounds or less," he said. ▶

Living the Pacific Crest Trail *(continued)*

On top of all this, the telecommunications boom has changed the rules. In the 1990s, when you hiked the trail, you were all on your own and far out of range. Cell phones were bulky monstrosities that looked like bludgeons. GPS units were for ships and planes, not walkers. These days, Williamson will often see through-hikers making cell phone calls home from remote PCT campsites, and passing the time with their iPods.

Even some of those legendary waterless stretches are becoming anachronisms; far more people have been placing caches of bottled water along the trail (a practice that might have prevented this author from getting sun stricken and fellating a prickly pear all those years ago).

As for the trail itself, Williamson says it is much more "open" and easy to follow than it used to be, thanks in large part to the army of brush-clearing Pacific Crest Trail Association volunteers.

On the downside, he's watched the glaciers recede—and he attributes his "yo-yo" success in part to global warming. He tried to yo-yo in 1996, 1997, and 2000, but High Sierra snowfall stopped him every time. "Winter used to come early, but for the last few years, snowfall has been coming really late." Williamson knows a hiker who followed his example and managed to yo-yo the trail in 2007. "His breaking success was due to the fact that this was one of the lowest snow years in the Sierra Nevada in the past fifty years. The Tahoe region was thirty-one percent of normal this year."

Williamson has seen some dramatic changes in his own life because of the trail.

He recently married his longtime girlfriend, Michelle Turley, an acupuncturist with her own practice. They are hoping to settle down in Truckee, California, near Donner Pass.

But he has no plans to stop long-distance walking.

And he still can't think about the lifestyle he chose without reflecting back on the man who almost killed him that winter day in Richmond, California.

"Had that not happened, I probably would not be focused on (the Pacific Crest) adventure," he said. "I probably would be leading a much more conventional life. In some ways, being shot in the head was one of the best things that ever happened to me, as strange as it may sound." ༄

The Cactus Eaters
Songbook
The Ultimate PCT
Soundtrack

THE TRAIL IS ALL ABOUT SINGING your
lungs out, to pass the time, amuse yourself,
and, most of all, to antagonize your hiking
partner. Music was a constant part of my
walk. I sang singles, novelty tunes, and whole
albums, including Joe Jackson's *Look Sharp!*.
I am not the only one. The year I walked the
trail, I heard about a Springsteen freak who
sang the Boss's entire output, song by song,
in order, starting with "Does This Bus Stop
at 82nd Street?' and ending with "Human
Touch,' then starting up again.

Here are a few of the songs that rattled
through the skulls of the Lois and Clark
Expedition—and, later, "Dirty Dan," during
my solo trail sojourn.

"My Name is Norman Bates" by Landscape
This is a dumb song—it was one of Allison's,
and it's just some guy mumbling "My name
is Norman Bates, I'm just a normal guy" over
and over in a disturbing voice. Allison sang it
just to freak me out.

"Fire and Rain" by James Taylor
If you're hiking with a group of strangers,
and one of them starts singing this one over
and over, really loudly, there isn't a whole lot
you can do but sit back and take it. Either
that, or you could wake up really early and
try to ditch him in the North Cascades.
That's what I did! ▶

The Cactus Eaters Songbook *(continued)*

"Bring tha Noize" by Public Enemy
(I'm talking about the loud version, with Anthrax, from Apocalypse
91 . . . The Enemy Strikes Black.*)*
    The pre-trail Lois and Clark Expedition saw them live once in New
Haven. I even shook Flavor Flav's hand and convinced Chuck D to sign
his name on a beer-smeared cocktail napkin, right in the middle of
"By the Time I Get to Arizona." I have that napkin to this day.

"Buck Naked" by Hank Williams, Jr.
This was one of Allison's. I never quite got the hang of it.

"Bring Your Daughter . . . To the Slaughter" by Iron Maiden
An irresistible song in camp, or anywhere else on the Pacific Crest Trail.
Who wouldn't love the chorus, and the way Bruce Dickinson's voice
goes from a growl to a screech in the middle of *"slaugh-terrrrrrrrrrrrr"*?
It frightens the bears away, that's for sure.

"Connected" by Stereo MCs
For some reason, this damned song entered my head in the western
Mojave and it would not leave. It just stuck in there like a foxtail. By
the time I reached Tehachapi, that "wonk-wonka-wonk" saxophone
riff was driving me out of my mind.

"Insane in the Brain" by Cypress Hill
Allison thought that this song was about meningitis.

"The Humpty Dance" by Digital Underground
Allison and I sang this one constantly. Round the clock. All the time. In
fact, in a mountain town in Southern California, we once spent the night
in a host-home that included this very nice but thugged-out white kid
who started rapping out this song to shock me. He was the one who was
shocked when he saw that I knew the words by heart. Best line: "I once
got busy in a Burger King bathroom."

"Gangsta Gangsta" by NWA
I've sung many parodies of this song, changing the lyrics to reflect the
hiking subculture. This one sounds great when you're screaming it off
some mountaintop.

"You've Never Been This Far Before" by Conway Twitty
I saw this guy once just before he passed away. He was one of those
sexed-up country crooners from the old school. He breathed heavily.
He practically humped the microphone. I sang this one several times
while walking through the hideous Tejon Ranch section of the PCT.

"He Stopped Loving Her Today" by George Jones
The octave leap is brutal on this one. You could tear your lungs out.
It's best to be hiking alone when the urge comes on to sing it.

Recommended Further Readings

Karen Berger and Daniel R. Smith, *The Pacific Crest Trail: A Hiker's Companion*, Woodstock, Vt.: The Countryman Press, 2000.

William Cronon, *Uncommon Ground: Rethinking the Human Place in Nature*, New York: W. W. Norton & Co., 1996. (In particular the first chapter, "The Trouble with Wilderness, or, Getting Back to the Wrong Nature." This chapter influenced my "take" on the forest surrounding the PCT.)

Francis P. Farquhar, *History of the Sierra Nevada*, Berkeley: University of California Press, 1965.

Tim Flannery (responsible for my current obsession with megafauna), *The Eternal Frontier: An Ecological History of North America and Its Peoples*, New York: Grove Press, 2001.

Philip L. Fradkin, *The Seven States of California: A Natural and Human History*, New York: Henry Holt and Company, 1995. (An indispensable resource for anyone interested in California cultural and natural history.)

Barbara Hurd, "Refugium," featured in *The Best American Essays*, New York: Mariner Books, 2001 (editors, Robert Atwan and Kathleen Norris).

Frank McLynn, *Wagons West*, New York: Random House, 2002.

Henry Miller, *The Colossus of Maroussi*, Toronto: Penguin Books (Canada), 1941.

Frank Mullen, *The Donner Party Chronicles: A Day-by-Day Account of a Doomed Wagon Train,1846–47*, Reno: Nevada Humanities Committee, 1997.

Roderick Nash, *Wilderness and the American Mind*, New Haven: Yale University Press, 2001.

Marc Reisner, *Cadillac Desert: The American West and Its Disappearing Water*, New York: Viking, 1986. (My chapter on William Mulholland owes a debt to the late Mr. Reisner's research and observations; on top of this, I spoke with the author at some length about Mulholland while he was visiting the Pajaro Valley Water District in the mid-1990s.)

Allan A. Schoenherr, *A Natural History of California*, Berkeley: University of California Press, 1992.

Jeffrey P. Schaffer, Ben Schifrin, Thomas Winnett, and Ruby Johnson Jenkins, *The Pacific Crest Trail, Volume I: California*, Berkeley: Wilderness Press, 1995.

Susan Snyder, editor, *Bear in Mind: The California Grizzly*, Berkeley: Heyday Books, 2003.

Kevin Starr, *Americans and the California Dream: 1850–1915*, Oxford: Oxford University Press, 1973.

David Wicinas, *Sagebrush and Cappuccino: Confessions of an LA Naturalist*, San ▶

Recommended Further Readings *(continued)*

Francisco: Sierra Club Books, 1995.
(This is a terrific book about urban
ecology; I recommend it highly.)

Also, if you would like more information
on the adventures of Elisha Stephens,
I recommend the following sources:

James Rose, *Sierra Trailblazers: First Pioneer
Wagons Over the Sierra Nevada*
(pamphlet), Lake Tahoe Historical
Society, 1995.

Irving Stone, *Men to Match My Mountains*,
New York: Doubleday, 1956.

George Stewart, *The California Trail*, Lincoln,
Neb.: Bison Books, 1993.

Phil Sexton tells me that there are "several
other volumes about the CA trail that
mention Stephens (misspelled Stevens),
mostly as an afterthought." However, I'm
happy to report that Mr. Stephens now has
a mountain named after him in the northern
Sierra Nevada range! Congratulations,
Mr. Stephens; you deserve it.

Don't miss the next
book by your favorite
author. Sign up now for
AuthorTracker by visiting
www.AuthorTracker.com.